D0151430

Literary Criticism and Cultural Theory

Edited by
William E. Cain
Professor of English
Wellesley College

A Routledge Series

Literary Criticism and Cultural Theory

William E. Cain, *General Editor*

Negotiating the Modern
Orientalism and Indianness in the Anglophone World
Amit Ray

Novels, Maps, Modernity
The Spatial Imagination, 1850–2000
Eric Bulson

Novel Notions
Medical Discourse and the Mapping of the Imagination in Eighteenth-Century English Fiction
Katherine E. Kickel

Masculinity and the English Working Class
Studies in Victorian Autobiography and Fiction
Ying S. Lee

Aesthetic Hysteria
The Great Neurosis in Victorian Melodrama and Contemporary Fiction
Ankhi Mukherjee

The Rise of Corporate Publishing and Its Effects on Authorship in Early Twentieth-Century America
Kim Becnel

Conspiracy, Revolution, and Terrorism from Victorian Fiction to the Modern Novel
Adrian S. Wisnicki

City/Stage/Globe
Performance and Space in Shakespeare's London
D.J. Hopkins

Transatlantic Engagements with the British Eighteenth Century
Pamela J. Albert

Race, Immigration, and American Identity in the Fiction of Salman Rushdie, Ralph Ellison, and William Faulkner
Randy Boyagoda

Cosmopolitan Culture and Consumerism in Chick Lit
Caroline J. Smith

Asian Diaspora Poetry in North America
Benzi Zhang

William Morris and the Society for the Protection of Ancient Buildings
Andrea Elizabeth Donovan

Zionism and Revolution in European-Jewish Literature
Laurel Plapp

Shakespeare and the Cultural Colonization of Ireland
Robin E. Bates

Spaces of the Sacred and Profane
Dickens, Trollope, and the Victorian Cathedral Town
Elizabeth A. Bridgham

The Contemporary Anglophone Travel Novel
The Aesthetics of Self-Fashioning in the Era of Globalization
Stephen M. Levin

Literature and Development in North Africa
The Modernizing Mission
Perri Giovannucci

Literature and Development in North Africa

The Modernizing Mission

Perri Giovannucci

New York London

First published 2008
by Routledge
270 Madison Ave, New York, NY 10016

Simultaneously published in the UK
by Routledge
2 Park Square, Milton Park, Abingdon, Oxon OX14 4RN

Routledge is an imprint of the Taylor & Francis Group, an informa business

Typeset in Adobe Garamond by IBT Global
Printed and bound in the United States of America on acid-free paper by IBT Global

Library of Congress Cataloging-in-Publication Data

Giovannucci, Perri.
Literature and development in North Africa : the modernizing mission / by Perri Giovannucci.
p. cm. — (Literary criticism and cultural theory)
Includes bibliographical references and index.
ISBN 978-0-415-95818-9
1. Arabic literature—Africa, North—History and criticism. 2. Arabic literature—20th century—History and criticism. 3. North African literature (French)—20th century—History and criticism 4. Literature and globalization—Africa, North. I. Title.

PJ8390.A355G56 2008
892.7'09961—dc22 2007043393

ISBN10: 0-415-95818-0 (hbk)
ISBN10: 0-203-92808-3 (ebk)

ISBN13: 978-0-415-95818-9 (hbk)
ISBN13: 978-0-203-92808-0 (ebk)

Contents

Acknowledgments

I wish to acknowledge a number of people whose insight, guidance, experience, and friendship accompanied me throughout the project of this book. Foremost, I would like to thank John Paul Russo, Ranen Omer Sherman, Lindsay Tucker, and John Ready at the University of Miami in Coral Gables. This work would not have been completed without them; however, any mistakes are entirely my own. To Leslie Bow, I am grateful for an excellent suggestion. To Justine Buisson, Margaret McPeake Maraviglia, and Linda Weissman, I offer my affection and gratitude. I thank also Lolita Hernandez of the University of Michigan, Michele Beer of Florida International University, and Jessica Harvey of the American University in Dubai. Finally, I thank Rayfield Allen Waller for a thousand points of light.

Introduction

Postcolonial critics such as Edward Said and Abdul JanMohamed have argued that Western conceptions about the global "East" derive from Orientalist or colonial discourse. However, with the break-up of the old colonial empires—e.g., the British and the French—in the latter half of the twentieth century, the Western conception of the East began to reflect another influence, that of "modernization." "Modernization" refers to the Western "development" of poor nations said to be "underdeveloped," or lacking in the attributes of Western capitalist society, i.e., innovation technology, privatized economy, etc. A broad program of cultural, economic and political agenda, "modernization" encompasses both an ideology and a "praxis." Ultimately, it subsumed the "civilizing mission" as the ideological mandate of Western intervention in the East. One may say that since the fall of the old empires, the West has assumed the mantle of a "modernizing" mission in the "developing" worlds of the East.

The influence of "modernization" corresponds with the rise of U.S. domination in Western global politics after the Second World War. The "modernizing" view is characteristically "American," as distinct from "European," in that it lacks historical depth and is based upon the fetishization of technology and American notions about the "free market" economy. With the collapse of the Soviet Union at the end of the Cold War and the emergence of the U.S. as the sole global superpower, "modernization" has garnered nearly universal acceptance as a theory and as a discourse throughout the West and internationally, though it has undergone various refinements. Thus, pluralistically, it is now seen that there are many ways in which modern development may occur, not merely the "standardized" American style. Lately, the "modernizing" world view is called, "globalization." In short, "modernization," "globalization," and relatedly, "development," are more or less interchangeable discursive terms which issue from an international agenda generally driven and led by U.S. interests. The apparent primacy of U.S. interests, the broad "official" acceptance of the agenda, and the widespread promulgation of the ideology necessitates that "modernization" be analyzed and challenged.

The uncritical acceptance and promulgation of "modernization" by local and international institutions of governance, the media and universities, and of course, by private multinational corporations, appears to have established a dominant world view comprised of modern, "universal truths." But modernization theory is based upon several logical fallacies. Indeed the very premise, which identifies two opposing spheres, the "modern," and the "traditional," is an erroneous perception. The modernizing view envisions a "First World" associated with "the West," and a "Third World" associated with the former colonial nations, the latter construct subsuming the Orientalist notion of the "East." Onto each sphere is projected the image, respectively, of the modern world and the traditional world. In a view marked by ahistoricity, each "world" is essentially characterized by the possession or lack of capital, technologies, secularism, etc., according to "modernizers." Samuel P. Huntington's influential *Clash of Civilizations,* for example, in which the author asserts that on "a [global] level, the dominant division is between 'the West and the rest,'" (183) follows this paradigm.

The modernizing view is fallacious, however, because it disregards the colonial relationship which has obtained between "First" and "Third Worlds," East and West. The criteria upon which each sphere has come to be identified as either "modern" or "traditional" is seen as an essential quality, rather than as material conditions stemming from the legacy of colonialism. But in fact both worlds, the "Third" as well as the "First," are thoroughly modern as the conditions of each were largely determined through colonial industrial production. Two central fallacies of modernization discourse therefore regard the elision of history and the misreading of material conditions as "traditional culture" in the so-called underdeveloped nations of the East or "Third World." "Modernization" posits that poor nations are "underdeveloped" because of static, oppressive and otherwise retrograde and/or recalcitrant cultural traditions. "Traditionalism" is associated with certain phenomena such as: allegedly "inefficient" agricultural modes; rigid gender codes and the oppression of women; religious conservativism or so-called fundamentalism; provincialism or tribalism; and, so-called folk practices. These phenomena are often said to be the target of, and the justification for, "modern reforms," or "development." Yet many so-called traditions are actually developed or created by modernization practices (such as by private foreign investment, for example) or else are local responses to Western intervention.

Chapter One, "Modernization and Its Discontents," examines the fallacies of modernization discourse and its relationship to the rise of American influence in global politics after World War Two. Daniel Lerner's *Modernizing the Middle East* (1958) marks the conceptual shift to the "Americanization" of Western development and exemplifies some typical problems with the terminology and perspective of modernization theory. Since Lerner, several observers have seen the shift to "Americanization" in the light of old colonialism. Gilbert Rist, Wolfgang Sachs and David Korten, among others, see the material practices of modern development arise from nineteenth and twentieth century colonial production. Recently, Rashid Khalidi, Mahmood Mamdani and Tariq Ali analyze how the American "empire" has developed the existing conditions of life and strife in the Middle East today. Their views have resonance in the current moment as, since the events of September 11, 2001, the U.S. has embarked upon both a "war on terror" and a "great reform" initiative in the Muslim East.

Proponents of modernization often claim that multinational development is a progressive social force in "developing" nations. Development is said to encourage not only local prosperity but also secularism and equality for women in "traditional" societies. Jagdish Bhagwati and C.K. Prahalad argue this premise, respectively, in their recent works, *In Defense of Globalization,* and *The Fortune at the Bottom of the Pyramid.* But this premise is culturally essentialist; it disregards the exploitation and repression of former colonial nations under generations of Western imperialism and posits instead that "traditions" are the bane of society in the East or Third World. Some interlocution is needed, therefore, to challenge the views of modernization, especially as erroneous conceptions are the basis for Western "development" practices, e.g., "structural reforms," privatization, etc.

An alternative perspective upon global "development" is provided by the center-periphery model of the modern world system, a critical theory associated with Immanuel Wallerstein, Fernand Braudel and Samir Amin. The center-periphery model recognizes the historical-material relationship of the First and Third Worlds. The model theorizes the role of colonial production in creating, on the one hand, the wealth and development of the West and, on the other hand, the poverty and underdevelopment of the former colonial nations. By applying the perspective of the center-periphery model to some of the claims of modernization discourse and by examining a little of the colonial history of the East, one may get a clearer sense of the problems with so-called global development. Foremost, one sees the issues of sovereignty and social justice which are at stake—not only in the "developing" nations of the East, but also in the "developed" nations of the West.

The anti-colonial writers of the postwar generation such as Frantz Fanon, Albert Memmi and Jean-Paul Sartre recognized that Western imperialism was the root cause of the poverty and abjection which characterize the material conditions of the so-called "developing" nations. They also saw that the violence inherent in Western imperialism created also the conditions for militant resistance. Chapter Two, "North Africa and the Anti-Colonial Critics," looks at some fundamental observations by Sartre, Fanon and Memmi, who wrote toward the end of colonialism and, consequently, at the rise of "modernization." They analyze the role of violence in colonial society. Fanon, Sartre and Memmi have argued that because colonial society is repressed through violence (i.e., military occupation, police repression, etc.), revolutionary violence, or armed struggle, is rendered as the basic means of native resistance. These writers regarded native armed struggle as a progressive force which would recreate local society—ultimately by achieving liberation and independence. But they did not so much embrace revolutionary violence *per se* as see it necessary to depose colonial rule. The concretized, structural nature of peripheral society facilitated and maintained colonial oppression; this structure could not be negotiated, they believed.

In Fanon's *Wretched of the Earth* and Memmi's *Colonizer and the Colonized,* one sees a local society composed of two spheres which are structurally opposed to each other, that of privileged French *colons* and that of North African natives who are relegated to second-class status. The notion of "dualism" in French North Africa is also discussed by Abdallah Laroui in his *History of the Maghrib.* Contemporary liberals proposed that "assimilation" into the French nation would better the abject conditions of North African natives through "development." Like "development," however, "assimilation" was a fallacious term. In practice, "assimilation" referred to the economic appropriation of North African resources (Haddour). Anti-colonial writers such as those whose views are discussed here saw that the "second-class citizenry" of natives was endemic to French colonial rule. It was an end to colonial rule rather than "assimilation" which would better the conditions of natives, these critics maintained.

The violence inherent in French Algerian society was the struggle of the colonizer and the colonized, as Memmi observed. It was also a struggle for legitimacy and authority within local society; and at a very basic level, it was a struggle over land. This struggle is apparent in what can be called the predicament of the *pieds noirs* in Algeria, the settlers or *colons* of French or European ancestry. *Les pieds noirs* sought to establish legitimacy in Algeria through symbolic representation as well as through the more material means of French administration. Symbolic native identity was invoked through autochthonous representations which associated *pied noir* society with the Algerian landscape. Even the name, *pieds noirs,* which refers to the booted or soiled feet of the settlers, signifies a connection to the land.

Albert Camus' novel, *The Stranger,* exemplifies the *pied noir* predicament and the violence inherent in the "nativism" claimed by the settlers through the displacement, both discursive and literal, of actual Algerian natives. My interpretation of *The Stranger* differs from many American readings of the novel which tend to emphasize a universal-humanist or existentialist interpretation. In this case however, a more specific reading of the work emphasizes its importance as a critique of *pied noir* society, a society from which, of course, Camus himself derived. Thus *The Stranger* can be read in light of the perspective offered by the anti-colonial writings of Sartre, Fanon and Memmi, even as Camus himself disagreed with their views. Foremost, he denounced the use of violent methods by all parties in the Algerian conflict. Camus felt that the "dualism" of French Algeria could be dissolved through the assimilation of native society into that of metropolitan France.

Much of Camus' thought about Algerian reform replicates the fallacies of modernization discourse. In this regard, he represents the liberal tendency to see "modern development" as a panacea for Third World ills. Chapter Three, "The Non-Color of Nonviolence," examines Camus' logic and that of Assia Djebar, who tends to concur with his views about nonviolence and peaceful reform. Camus' vision for postcolonial Algeria is portrayed in the short story, "The Silent Men" (*Exile and the Kingdom*). The story can be read as an illustration of the center-periphery relationship and as an invocation of assimilation. But again, one may find the fallacious logic of a "development narrative" within the short story.

More recently, Djebar's *Algerian White* looks at the role of violence in Algerian society from the guerrilla war of independence through the recent era of militancy. However like Camus, her perspective replicates some of the central fallacies of modernization discourse. She does not really differentiate the motives or material conditions which create conflict. The decontextualized or fetishized portrayal of "violence" in her book, significantly, is a notion already appropriated and mobilized by "modernization." Decontextualized terms such as "violence," "history" and "poverty," etc., are central to, and distorted by, the logic of modernization. More important than semantics however, material violence is often exacerbated by the lack of analysis given to understanding the root causes of conflicts. Lack of analysis is something which is fostered by "modernization." If nothing else, the lack or failure of understanding implies that the conditions which produce violent conflicts, and therefore the very acts of violence itself, will simply persist.

The center-periphery model views the classic methods of colonialism, i.e., foreign occupation and military violence, in tandem with an "economic imperialism." Economic "violence" may take its toll as much as, if not more than, colonial militarism. Colonized nations, to great disadvantage, were bound to a peripheral role in colonial production. The peripheral economic role impacted the "shape" of local society or, in the terms used by Amin, Wallerstein and others, impacted the "social formation." Two local features which characterize the "peripheral social formation" are: 1) the hegemony of an elite class maintained by, or beholden to, the West; and, 2) the disenfranchisement of the impoverished majority, regarded as the locus of "backward" traditions said to conflict with "modernity." "Modernizers" claim that the benefits of "development" will eventually "trickle down" from the elites to the impoverished masses. However, the disparity between the "haves" and "have-nots" may be seen as an entrenched condition of local society, sustained through the peripheral role in global production. "Development" concretizes local class disparity and drives the local majority deeper into poverty and disenfranchisement. Although "Eastern" societies are clearly not inherently "classless," Western development exacerbates pre-existing social forms and often creates entirely new hegemonies within local societies. Thus, even in the absence of an occupying colonial army, modern economic development may create or sustain neo-colonial conditions in the periphery.

One may look to the colonial past in the East for insights about global development there today, even as we understand that the examples we examine are not intended to be seen as identical to, but as indicators for, the direction of contemporary "modernization." One sees that similar practices and rhetoric as were invoked under colonialism are today invoked under "globalization." The emphasis which "modernizers" place upon loans, privatization, and market reforms which privilege foreign investors, is very similar to colonial development practices. The practices of development then as now have led not so much to economic prosperity and cultural progressivism in local society as to instability, poverty, debt and repression. In this regard, the example of Egypt during the modern age is a case in point. Chapter Four, "Paris on the Nile, Egypt on the Plantation," reviews some of the modern productive history of Egypt which is typically elided by modernization theory.

Chapter Four also considers how colonial "underdevelopment" may be achieved through methods other than, primarily, military force. Egypt had entered the nineteenth century poised to develop itself into a modern nation state through undertakings which were basically autonomous. Muhammad Ali pursued local reforms to develop civil society, secularism, industry and sovereignty. But these modern reforms were hindered by the series of capitulations to the West made by Ali's successors. Subsequently, Western-oriented programs drove the country deeper into feudal-like conditions. These programs were financed by Europe and entailed excessive loans, dependency upon foreign capital and technologies; inhibited native enterprise; and, patronized *comprador* elites and their imitative attempts at cultural "Europeanization." The Egyptian economy meanwhile became bonded to the monocultural production of cotton in order to serve the needs of the British textile industry, a situation which one observer likens to Egypt "having . . . been made into a cotton plantation for Lancashire" (*Unequal Development* 303.) While a cosmopolitan elite class enjoyed the trappings of Western "modernity," accorded in large part through their roles in managing agrarian production or supporting the British administration, conversely, the majority of native, "traditional" society lived disenfranchised lives as peasant laborers or itinerant workers. It is apparent that Egyptian society was hindered by Western productive development in many ways, the very ways it seems, which modernizers claim are the keys to "progress" and prosperity.

In modern Egypt, the local elite played a significant role in colonial, or "peripheral" production beginning in the nineteenth century when a small industrial class, ancillatory to the plantation economy was formed. These "Westernized" elites eventually came to be known as Egypt's "cosmopolitan" community, about whom Lawrence Durrell wrote so voluptuously in his series of novels, *The Alexandria Quartet.* They were a small class comprised mainly of foreign nationals, ethnic and religious minorities who identified culturally with Europe and Turkey and politically with the goals of empire. They were engaged in peripheral production at all levels of class society, as agents and as colonial subjects, actors as well as acted upon by both external and internal forces. It is important to recognize the complexity, as well as the complicity, of the roles which Egyptian elites played in colonial society. One does not intend to "villainize" local elites; their roles may be understood as structural features of colonialism, rather than as self determined. Nor should one see elite society as a "monolith." The individual conditions of those who may be called "elites," in comparison with the masses, varied greatly. By centering a materialist view upon the function of ethnic elites, however, one may get a sense of how "modernization" has established the self-perpetuating institutions of peripheral underdevelopment. Perhaps with the materialist view, one may also avoid the bourgeois "racialism" which often flattens or elides class disparities in the academic approach of postcolonial studies.

Chapter Five, "Letters of a Lost Generation," considers how religious, national, ethnic and cultural signifiers all figured materially within Egyptian society. These signifiers ostensibly marked the possession, or the lack, of class power; in effect, Egyptian "identity politics" were quite visibly "real politick." The conditions of the minority elites in Egypt may be observed in the memoirs of the contemporary authors, Gini Alhadeff, Nawal El Saadawi, Andre Aciman, and the late Edward Said. All provide significant historical, material, social and cultural detail about upper class, "cosmopolitan" Egyptian life. Their accounts allow a reader to observe how cultural identities and class status figured within Egyptian peripheral society before 1952. Ethnic group identification and the inclination toward nativism, nationalism and transnationalism were some of the defining cultural trends of the period. These trends were not simply "cultural" expressions but arose from the material conditions established through peripheral production.

The system of colonial hegemony favored a "Westernized" elite comprised of Eurocentric or Turcocentric ethnic minorities. But it also inculcated among them a dependency upon external agency and a tenuousness of position locally. The status of Egyptian minorities depended upon local laws, established by the foreign powers, regarding citizenship, religious affiliation, nationality and commerce. The legal criteria which favored minorities were shifting and unstable, impacted by local and international factors. As well, the maintenance of ethnic minorities as *compradors* by the West engendered their own problematic legitimacy as elites. It was the common view in Egypt that the class interests of elites coincided with colonial power. Local elites were typically seen in nativist terms as the emissaries of foreign rule. Thus, the hegemony of Egyptian elites was belied by chronic insecurity regarding their social status and cultural legitimacy within the broader Egyptian society.

Not surprisingly then, one finds that elites engaged in various strategies aimed at securing legitimacy for their status through cultural means. The "cosmopolitanism" of Egyptian elites can be analyzed and defined as an associative strategy engaged among a diverse and heterogenous element to consolidate class power. However in spite of the cosmopolitan veneer, mutual sectarianism and prejudices were well extant among the Egyptian elite and were often heightened by various political and material phenomena. The tolerance attributed by observers to the Egyptian cosmopolitan community appears to have had a "plasticity" or arbitrary tendency. Or much like elite status itself, cosmopolitan tolerance was dependent upon local and international influences. Other strategies which elites engaged to shore up their status were "Europeanization;" associations with imperial power and with "modernity;" and the invocation of certain religious and nativist "signs." Ultimately these attempts at legitimacy failed as they did not, and indeed could not, address the fundamental crisis of mass native disenfranchisement and abjection upon which elite hegemony was based.

All four memoirists, though individuals of different background and strata, were eventually displaced or dispossessed after Egyptian independence. The fall of the cosmopolitan community has often been attributed to Gamal Abdel Nasser, who led the military coup in 1952 known as the Free Officers' Revolt and who later became the Egyptian President. Nasser's policies of land reform, nationalization and the expulsion of foreigners disrupted the lives, property and livelihoods of the commercial and landowning elites. In effect and by design, the Nasserist reforms dispossessed and dispersed the ethnic elite. State appropriations and mandatory expulsions, or arbitrarily, the refusal of visas, were largely aimed at foreign and ethnic minorities. However it may also be observed that the commercial and legal status of minority elites was eroded along with the colonial relationship sustained by Britain and Europe. The hegemony of elites had been quite ostensibly underwritten by the West. This observation does not dismiss nor make light of the fate of Egyptian minorities under the Nasser government. But rather, one acknowledges that the situation could hardly have been otherwise, given the polarized conditions of Egyptian society, conditions established through Western "development."

The "modernization" of Egypt established a class polemic marked by cultural association or identification as well as by unequal material conditions. This pertained even to the vehicle of Egyptian independence, the *Wafd* Party, which had been born through conflict with the Western powers in 1919. By the late 1940s however, the *Wafd,* always a party comprised of big landowners and rich "notables," was generally out-of-touch with the broader society. As Naguib Mahfouz portrays in *Autumn Quail,* his novel of the Egyptian Revolution, the *Wafd* was largely seen by native society to have "sold out." Thus one sees the rise of Egyptian nativism, or rather, the nativist tenor of the Egyptian independence movement after World War Two. Chapter Four and, subsequently, Chapter Five discuss the implications of Egyptian nativism as a movement apart from the Egyptian nationalist movement which preceded the Free Officer's *coup d'etat.* The discussion draws upon the novels of Mahfouz and Nawal El Saadawi, respectively, *Autumn Quail* and *God Dies by the Nile.* One may note that Saadawi's novel is as critical of the independent government after Nasser as much as Mahfouz' work criticizes the *Wafd*-dominated parliamentary government which had preceded it.

Well before Egyptian independence, the concept of "native" identity was contraposed to "Westernization." However the very fluidity of the concepts, "native" and "Western," took in various, often overlapping, and even counter-intuitive criteria. The criteria for what was presumed native or Western, native or foreign, etc., depended upon how these terms were mobilized by discourse, by agenda and by material "praxis." Although the criteria for what may be considered "native" is fundamentally abstract, the political and material agenda of nativism is typically quite concrete. Egyptian nativism, both as popular sentiment and as, more or less, public policy, accounted for the expatriation of the Egyptian memoirists considered here—including Nawal El Saadawi who though a native Egyptian has experienced the political backlash of both "progressive" and "conservative" forces respectively claiming the "native" interest. The mobilization and revision of Egyptian nativism over the first few generations after independence in 1952 afforded Saadawi varied and conflicting experiences. Chapter Six, "Radical Surgery," considers the various incarnations and understandings of "native" identity, Egyptian identity, and Arab nationalism, which obtained during Saadawi's generation. One can observe that these concepts emerged because of the contesting claims to authority and legitimacy which characterize colonial society.

Many strategies of identification, "native" or otherwise, aim at "authority" or "legitimacy" by making reference to the body. Such references conceptualize identity as located in the body. Chapter Six looks at ways in which "physical evidence" has figured to "legitimate" or "authorize" one's identity. The association of identity with the body is variously portrayed in the memoirs of Saadawi, Gini Alhadeff (*The Sun at Midday*), Andre Aciman (*Out of Egypt* and *False Papers*), and Edward Said (*Out of Place*). Notably, "the body" figures as a central metaphor for Egyptian native independence in both of Saadawi's memoirs, *A Daughter of Isis* and *Walking Through Fire.* However, one does not seek to privilege "nativist" claims or nativist conceptualizations of Egyptian or "Eastern" identity. Rather, the point is to observe how contesting claims to the "East" have taken shape and how and why they have arisen.

The material conditions of "peripheral" society, which were developed through "modernization," may be seen as the catalyst of anti-Western sentiment and anti-Western reaction. This was the case with Algeria and Egypt, where generations of unequal development by the West had created mass disenfranchisement and alienation. These conditions necessarily invoked the terms of their own reaction. Yet "modernization" pundits hold that anti-Western reaction, especially that of the impoverished masses, is born of "jealousy," "envy," "ignorance," or indeed, blind "hatred." Such contentions are routinely made, for example, by Western commentators about the Islamist movement which is in reaction to the West today. But one may clearly see—if indeed one wishes to see—that materialism belies the "cultural logic" of such Western fallacies about the "East." To recognize that many colonial practices are simply reified as "global development" is key to understanding much of the current so-called "war on terror." For however much cloaked as a charitable mission to "install democracy," the American intervention in the

Middle East can be seen as an imperialist aggression which begets resistance. The discourse of "modernization" is the cloak of that aggression.

Throughout the book, I have made reference to foreign language texts in English translation, such as those of Fanon, Memmi, Sartre, Camus, Djebar, Saadawi, Amin, Laroui, Berque, etc. Some of these, for example, *Wretched of the Earth* and *Colonizer and the Colonized,* are considered seminal texts of postcolonial studies. One may wonder about the relevance of a study which refers to works like those of Fanon and Memmi as primary texts. After all, these seminal works of postcolonialism have undoubtedly been covered and recovered in the field. What new insights about colonialism could such retrospection yield? My perspective sees these works as yielding valuable insights about contemporary globalization. Perhaps the most important insight they offer obtains through analogy. The conditions and conflicts analyzed by Memmi and Fanon were specific for their time and generation. Yet one sees essentially the same conditions and conflicts at large now in the "globalized" world as in the colonial one. It appears that the same kinds of struggles as were waged under colonialism—struggles over power, resources, sovereignty, and the means of production—are those which rage today. Indeed the term "postcolonialism" appears to be a misnomer.

The critique of modernization as neocolonial suggests not so much any kind of uniformity or universality, but rather, variations on a theme. A critical analysis of "development" is necessary to trace the motifs of that old theme. I have also tried throughout the book to relate literature, movements and trends which are not American to texts and phenomena which are. This consideration is necessary, in my opinion, to understand the "Americanization" of global development which Lerner so adroitly recognized. In the case of the Francophone or Arabic texts which I have used here, the work of language translation has already been done to make these texts accessible to Americans. The next step of the process, in my view, pursues an understanding of how things "postcolonial" are critically relevant to Americans today. We need to understand just how far the "globalization" project may go in the footsteps of development's would-be crusaders.

Chapter One

Modernization and its Discontents

1.1 THE CULTURAL LOGIC OF MODERNIZATION

Modernization is not a transparent concept. Even given, or perhaps in spite of, the self-reflection of postcolonial academic debate in the West, the power relations inherent in the concept have tended to remain largely unexamined. "Modernization" regards the relationship between the so-called "developing" nations of Asia, Africa, Latin America and the Middle East, with the so-called "developed" nations of North America, Europe, and to a lesser extent, Australia and Japan. It typically entails the "developmental" aid of one nation or group of nations to another. The relationship is signified in the related terms, "East and West," "North and South," and "First and Third Worlds." These regional terms arose from the international institutions which took shape after the Second World War, when the old empires of Europe began to break up. Much of what is imagined as the North and South, East and West, the First and Third Worlds, corresponds with the regions defined through colonial history. These regions cast a historical shadow; they are the former colonial powers and their former possessions, the colonies and protectorates. The colonial past figures into their relations, however, in ways which are concrete and material as well as discursive and conceptual.

The very terms, "modernization" and "development," are vague and their meanings are variously understood or intended, depending upon the context or speaker. Harry Truman is thought to have first referred to "development" at his presidential inauguration in 1949: "That Truman coined a new term was not a matter of accident but the precise expression of a world-view: for him all the peoples of the world were moving along the same track—some faster, some slower, but all in the same direction."[1] International institutions, the media, commercial organizations and others generally portray modern development as a "technocratic" process. For a country to "modernize" usually implies that it transforms from the "underdeveloped" conditions associated with the so-called "East," "South," or "Third World," to the "developed" conditions associated with the "West," "North," or "First World." Those nations which are considered to be "making progress" in this regard are called "developing;" the means of transformation is called, "development." Sometimes "developing" nations are distinguished from "underdeveloped" ones according to various criteria such as their international credit rating or their levels of per-capita income. This criteria emphasizes the features most strongly associated with the so-called developing world: poverty and debt.[2] Generally "developing" and "underdeveloped" nations share similar features and conditions and the two terms are often used interchangeably. P.T. Bauer, writing in 1971, rightly observed the arbitrary nature of the definition, "underdeveloped," and the complexity and multifluidity of the "world" it presumes to classify:

> [T]he underdeveloped world is a vast aggregate of different peoples, societies and countries with widely different faculties, attitudes, modes and conditions of living, as well as widely different densities of population, levels of income and rates of growth of population and income. It includes areas in which progress has been relatively slow, such as parts of Central America, Africa, India and Pakistan; and countries which have advanced very rapidly, such as Colombia, Venezuela, Malaya and Hong Kong; very densely populated regions such as Java and much of India and Pakistan; and the sparsely populated areas of Sumatra, Borneo, and most of Africa and Latin America. It includes traditional and highly stratified societies such as those of India and Pakistan and the Moslem middle east, and the much more fluid societies of south-east Asia and Latin America. It includes the semi-deserts of the middle east and the tropical jungles of Africa, Asia and Latin America; the thriving modern cities of south-east Asia, the tribal communities of Africa, and the millions of aborigines in Asia, Africa and Latin America. (46–47)

Yet despite his interrogation of the term, "underdeveloped," Bauer is unable to skirt the related terms, "progress" and "advancement" and the world view they imply, i.e., the view shared by Truman that the peoples of the world are all on the "same track" towards "modernity" or a state of modern "development." The discourse of modernization often seems to collapse an alternative language of dissent, even among dissenters. Nevertheless, the tendency of modernization toward monolithic precepts is something which Bauer addresses, as have many other critics.

Technology and production are considered key aspects of modern development. To say that a nation is "underdeveloped" implies the lack of an industrial base; the general lack of the kinds of technologies currently used in the West; the lag in state-of-the-art innovations in the public and private sectors of society; and the predominance of a "traditional" agricultural base. The economic features of "underdevelopment" typically regard a "centralized" or state-run economy; chronic, widespread impoverishment and the related social ills and health problems which are associated with poverty. "Developed" nations, conversely, are viewed as being at the forefront of technological, productive and commercial advances; economically strong and diverse; broadly privatized; and are seen to possess the high standard of living associated with societal stability. "Modernization" is presumed to remedy the lack and lag of Western-style production and technology in "underdeveloped" nations and to redress the insolvency of their loan-riddled, centralized economies. Indeed the latter presumption is inherent to an economic understanding of what it means to modernize; "developing" nations are typically exhorted to "reform" their state-run enterprises through economic "restructuring" to allow foreign investment, i.e., multinational privatization. This much may be clear to any observer of "modernization." However the terms, assumptions, policies, goals, means, agendas, benefits and disadvantages of "modern development" are far from clear or objective phenomena.

Modernization entails a subjectivity and ideological premise which must be analyzed, if for no other reason than the very pervasiveness of the concept. It is widely embraced and promulgated as a panacea for all the world's ills. "The misunderstanding would not be so troublesome," writes Gilbert Rist, "if 'development' discourse was not built into relationships of power. For when the pretence is made that everyone now believes in that discourse, the reason is doubtless that no one has the choice of doing otherwise and distancing themselves from the shared belief. Paradoxically, 'development' is becoming universal, but not transcultural" (44). In *The History Of Development,* Rist likens the acceptance of the modernization concept to that of Christianity in the West. He criticizes "development" as the unquestioned "faith" of self-described "modern," ostensibly secular, society. Indeed like religion or any other ideology, modernization may be recognized as a discourse, based upon a set of assumptions which are taken by the "faithful" as universal "truths."

As a discourse, modernization may be examined for its rhetorical logic. There are some fundamental precepts upon which the discourse is built. First, "modernization" poses a conceptual polarity between the "East and West," "North and South," "First and Third," "developing and developed."

The "West," etc., is portrayed as the author and source of "modernity," which is conceived as synonymous with capitalist wealth, progress, industry and other associations. The "East," etc., is portrayed as the site of "lack," which is conceived as synonymous with poverty, stasis or retrogression. Modernization discourse envisions the "West," etc., as the necessary patron or bestower of "modernity" upon the "Third World":

> [T]he development/underdevelopment couplet maintain[s] a gap between different parts of the world, but justifie[s] the possibility—or the necessity—of intervention on the grounds that one cannot remain passive when one is confronted with extreme need. On the one hand, "underdevelopment" appears to exist without a cause, as a state of "poverty" that is a "handicap" and produces "victims" oppressed by "hunger, disease and despair." On the other, "development" is a state characterized by affluence, by wealth "that keeps growing and is never exhausted," by resources that have only to be mobilized and brought into play. (Rist 77)

The necessity of "Western" intervention into the political economies of poor nations is a fundamental principal of modernization discourse. The intervention is conceived in regard to a greater whole, the global or world system, and, ostensibly, for the greater good. But it builds upon a past which is substantially less than benign. The conceptual polarity posed by modernization discourse obscures the material relationship between the developed and the developing nations. That relationship was principally engendered through colonial "development." Western capitalism since the nineteenth century has largely resulted from the exploitation of resources in the former colonial world. One recognizes that, far from being "underdeveloped," the East has always been engaged in modern production, if principally as an unequal partner.

The history of Western development in the so-called underdeveloped world is, in large part, the history of colonialism. While colonialism embodied a broad range of phenomena, it may be noted that the "development" of local resources in the colonies and protectorates were central to the so-called "world market" dominated by the Western colonial powers. Local resources in the colonized world—e.g., sugar, coffee, tobacco, produce, spices, opium, minerals, rubber and eventually, oil and gas—were the point of the colonial system, all rationalizing ideologies—e.g., "manifest destiny," "civilizing mission"—aside. Colonial "development" entailed the intervention of the West into the political and economic autonomy of the colonized and "protected" nations and communities. The concrete practices of colonial "development" were military occupation, metropolitan administration, the privatization of local resources, and foreign capital investment. With only slight modification—or perhaps with little or no modifications at all—one may observe that the practices of colonial development are those of post-colonial "modernization." Wolfgang Sachs, writing in *The Case Against The Global Economy,* finds that the two systems share a common goal:

> If development and colonialism (at least, in its last phase from the 1870s onward) are the same process under a different name, it is largely because they share the same goal. This goal was explicitly stated by its main promoters. For instance, the infamous English businessman and colonialist Cecil Rhodes (who named Rhodesia, now Zimbabwe, after himself) once frankly declared that "we must find new lands from which we can easily obtain raw materials and at the same time exploit the cheap slave labor that is available from the natives of the colonies. The colonies would also provide a dumping ground for the surplus goods produced in our factories. (254)

Indeed, many critics see the same practices extant under contemporary globalization.[3] The discourse of modernization regards many of the kinds of production practices and implicit objectives—if not the terms of foreign intervention—which carry over from colonialism. Cecil Rhodes, as Sachs notes, may have been a bit more frank about the project than other colonialists. Yet the colonial system had its own discourses of apology which claimed the benign mission to enlighten and to "save." If "development" is perhaps the "faith" of modern society, it may also claim its "mission" and its "burden" among the "underdeveloped."

The polarity between the "First and Third Worlds," etc., envisioned by "modernization," is a fundamental precept of the discourse. But it does not account for the material conditions engendered by global production. "Modernization" gives way instead to a cultural essentialism which displaces the history of development. In the absence of history, cultural essentialism arises to explain away the features of a chronically exploitative relationship between the "developed" and the "developing" nations. Often material conditions in poor nations are simply attributed to "poverty" or perhaps even to vague "history," just as conditions in rich nations are attributed to "progress" or "prosperity," or related notions, all of which are easily made abstract. Rather, modernization posits the opposition of terms as reason enough for their existence. One is portrayed as "modern,"—i.e., the "developed" world—and the other as "traditional"—i.e., the "developing" world. The "West," and all good things associated with it, is taken as essentially "modern." So-called "free market" economies, new technologies and commodities are held as the signs of modern society. As the simulated "signs" of modernity, detached from their referents, the "free market," technology and commodities are taken as wholly cultural forms. "Modernization" reifies these "signs" as the mark of progress, liberalism, liberation, democracy, etc. The West is, above all, considered to be secular and liberal. These qualities are conceived as essentially "Western." Conversely, the "East," "South" or "Third World," etc., are portrayed as the locus of things "backward," reactionary, provincial, inefficient, static, unenlightened and repressive. Because those qualities are seen as the antithesis of "modernity," they are presumed to be the essence of "traditional society." The American sociologist Edward Banfield once summed up the essential traditionalism of the "East," and its polarity to the modern "West," in his 1958 study entitled, *The Moral Basis Of A Backward Society:* "There is some reason to doubt that the non-Western cultures of the world will prove capable of creating and maintaining the high degree of organization without which a modern economy and a democratic political order are possible" (8). The view that "Eastern" cultures may be incapable of "modernizing" implies the need or the mandate that the West "help" them to develop their economies and political institutions. (It may even be claimed, as was done recently with Iraq and Afghanistan, that "democracy" can be imposed from without.) Of course, the kinds of economic and political institutions which so-called developing societies are encouraged or pressured to develop, with Western aid, tend either to resemble those in the West or else seem palatable to Western developers. Such developments are considered by proponents of modernization to be progressive and liberal. They are thought to bring modernity to traditional societies. So-called traditional norms are typically associated with such phenomena as rigid gender codes, religious conservatism, paternalism, provincialism, social castes, etc. These so-called traditions are taken as the signs of the East, South, or Third World. They are conceived as essentially "Eastern," or characteristic of the "Third World." That is, the West is perceived as being free of rigid gender roles, religious orthodoxy, paternalism, provincialism, social castes, etc. Indeed where these things may be observed in the West, they are portrayed in the modernizing discourse as anomalies or aberrations, "throwbacks" or "exceptions to the rule." Banfield, for example, found postwar Italian village life more suggestive of Oriental feudalism than of Western modernity and "closely similar to that of the Mediterranean and Levantine Worlds" (2). He did not question the material precedents of the conditions he observed but rather attributed them to moral torpidity on the part of the villagers. His view exemplifies, among other things, the *apriori* acceptance of cultural essentialisms in place of the material history of development in the East and West.

Modernization discourse mobilizes the alleged "essences" of East and West precisely because it elides the history of colonial relations among nations. "Essence" is supposed to explain the material conditions of the developed and the developing nations. This is illustrated by how "developing" societies are conceived to "modernize." They are envisioned to relinquish "traditional"—i.e., "backward"—cultural forms and to acquire "modern"—i.e., "progressive" or "liberal"—forms. To relinquish "traditions" is presumably to enter "modernity." Thus the essentialism propagated by "modernization" precludes the material analysis of Western development. Instead, the discourse offers a tautological and fallacious reasoning which may be called its own "cultural logic." I do not refer to Fredric Jameson's well known work about postmodernism, in which he popularized the term "cultural logic" in reference to various styles and motifs of contemporary aesthetics.[4] Rather, I refer to modernization's discursive practices; its elisions, conflations and substitutions. Because the discourse returns again and again to the putative notion of "culture," it obscures or subverts recognition of the material practices of development. This does not suggest that cultural approaches to a subject, any subject, are necessarily flawed. But the modernizing notion of "culture" effectively displaces material factors which are inherent in the political and economic history of nations and communities. The discursive displacement of material factors by presumptive, usually essentialist, notions about culture attests to the ideological nature of modernization discourse.

The rise of "modernization" appears as a new articulation of Western intervention into the so-called developing world after the more or less collective fall of the European empires after World War Two. The discourse may be correlated to the expanding role then assumed by the United States in international affairs. The shift in power was reflected in the discourse of the period, as noted by Daniel Lerner in his 1958 study of several "developing" countries in the Middle East:

> The term [modernization] is imposed by recent history. Earlier one spoke of Europeanization, to denote the common elements underlying French influence in Syria-Lebanon and British influence in Egypt and Jordan. More recently, following a century of educational and missionary activity, Americanization became a specific force and the common stimuli of the Atlantic civilization came to be called Westernization. Since World War Two, the continuing search for new ways has been coupled with repudiation of the Western aegis. Soviet and other modernizing models, as illustrated by India and Turkey, have become visible in the area. Any label that today localizes the process is bound to

> be parochial. For Middle Easterners more than ever want the modern package but reject the label, 'made in U.S.A.' (or for that matter, 'made in USSR'). We speak, nowadays, of modernization. (45)

Lerner's work, *The Passing Of Traditional Society: Modernizing The Middle East,* has been described by Fouad Ajami as a "once influential" study.[5] Significantly, it sets out some of the tenets of the modernization concept as it was then understood. For Lerner, modernization is a technocratic process. Foremost, he sees so-called urbanization and the "mass communications" media as the catalysts of modernity in the Middle East. His emphasis upon these features, or signs, of "modernity" seems consistent with the times and with an intellectual atmosphere then reflective of Marshall McLuhan's ideas about communication and modern society. While urban life and the mass media are still considered as features of modernization, today they are overshadowed by multinationalism and high technology. Whereas Lerner refers to a mass communications characterized by television and radio broadcasts and off-set printing, today the concept regards the internet, fiber optics and satellite networks of contemporary globalism. Yet the latter features constitute only a small semantic modification. It is basically the same concept which identifies technology as the essential sign of modernity. The measure of "progress" is defined by the presence of Western-style gadgets and systems. Whether "high tech" is conceived as Magnavox color TVs or as global positioning networks is a relative matter. The West is yet perceived as the source of "state-of-the-art" modernity through association with its technological "signs."

The primacy of technology, as the sign of modernity, is central to the modernizing view. Generally it regards the West both as the source of new technologies and as that which defines "modernity" for the "developing" world. These assumptions obscure a number of issues, such as how societies develop certain characteristics, how technologies are to be used, and by whom and to what purpose technologies are applied. "The naïve beliefs of Marshall McLuhan notwithstanding," observes Samir Amin, "history does not unfold in a manner directly governed by technological progress. History, rather, is a matter of struggle for control over the way in which these technologies are to be used, and this, at bottom, is an aspect of struggles within society, including class struggles and national struggles" (*Spectres of Capitalism* 129–130). One sees that modernization discourse fetishizes technology as a thing apart from how it is "developed" and implemented. The idea that "history" is a teleological process, characterized by "progress" in the ways and means of production, obscures consideration about the relations of economy, politics, society, environment, etc., which are inherent in production.

Lerner's conceptualization is predicated upon Western bias and replicates some of the central fallacies of modernization discourse. He notes that "recent history" has imposed the term, "modernization," where "Westernization" had once sufficed. Yet the supposed imposition of "history" is an abstraction which does not really regard the imposition of Western will. The disregard is suggested in his discussion of semantics. Lerner notes the connotative shift from "Europeanization" to "Americanization." But he erroneously attributes the shift to cultural influences. In doing so, he fails to recognize the material objectives of Western interventions in the Middle East. The portrayal of Western imperialism as a predominantly cultural phenomena is an error which would make history moot. Indeed, Lerner's view elides material history in favor of the allegedly benign, if ill-defined, "cultural influence" of the West. Rashid Khalidi refers to some of this history, noting that encounters with the West did have positive influence upon Middle Eastern societies in several regards. But he observes that the broader context of the encounters, and the more pervasive influences, were debilitating to local societies and communities which found themselves no less subjugated to the West:

> Long before the United States became a power in the Middle East during World War I, only to virtually disappear and then return during World War II, the peoples of that region had lengthy experiences with the West. These experiences had both positive and negative aspects, and the resulting associations would later on attach to the American newcomers to the region. The positive aspects were associated with Western scientific, technical, educational, and cultural advances, military and governmental efficiency, and liberal values, all of which came to be appreciated by increasing numbers of people in the Middle East, particularly intellectuals, the educated, and the growing middle and urban working classes. The desire to emulate and to reproduce these values gradually spread in these sectors of Middle Eastern society. On the other hand, the negative aspects affected nearly the entirety of society. They related primarily to the gradual domination and subjugation of the region, and ultimately the occupation of most of the countries of the Middle East, by the European powers. This lengthy and painful process left deep and lasting scars, and naturally affected the reception of Western values among Arabs, Turks, Iranians, and other Middle Easterners. (10)

A more balanced look at history sees Western "cultural influences" in perspective to the much larger phenomenon of the colonial project. While there were aspects of Western life which were acculturated or admired by Middle

Easterners, these aspects were not "power-neutral" or apolitical. Again one asks, for whom and to what purposes was "Westernization" put? Western religious and educational programs seem a ready case in point. The foreign schools and missions which were established throughout the Middle East helped to develop the "cultural" infrastructure of occupation, if not always by design. Typically such schools and missions served a small elite which functioned, more or less, or were expected to function, as a local managerial class under colonial administration. The same may be said generally of other aspects of Western influence, such as liberal values or technical methods. Khalidi touches upon the role of elites in the adoption or adaptation of Western forms and emphasizes that the benefits which accrued to them were disproportionate relative to the broader society. Indeed in several Middle Eastern societies, "Westernization" in one form or another came to be associated with the local hegemony of elites at the expense of the native community. It might be observed that the "development" of an attenuated class disparity in the Middle East was one legacy of Western influence.

The "Americanization" of the Middle East came about, Lerner asserts, through U.S. educational and missionary activities in the regions formerly administered by Britain and France. The claim seems like a willfully naïve gloss, especially for the time it was written. Contemporary events and controversies bore the recognition that U.S. foreign policy was invested in the Middle East. This foreign policy had engineered a coup in Iran,[6] produced the Baghdad Pact, and resolved Egypt's Suez War. The U.S. was also by then notably committed to Israel, having steadily increased its support for the young state in the decade prior to Lerner's study. Yet while Lerner might have recognized these events, his "cultural logic" supplants U.S. foreign policy in the Middle East with the influence of American aid workers, missionaries and teachers. There was indeed a program of American missionary and educational activities in the Middle East; however, the overall objectives of the U.S. interventions there were not spiritual and pedagogical but material and strategic.

Further, mere cultural influence would not have accounted for the predominance of the U.S. among the European allies, what Lerner refers to as the Americanization of the "common stimuli" of the West. The Second World War had allowed for American commercial, political and military strength to take hold both in Europe and in the European colonies and protectorates. There were attempts to displace French power in North Africa beginning with the Allied landing at Casablanca in Morocco. One attempt was to intervene in the nativist movements there for independence. A compelling example, recorded by Jamaa Baida, regards two separate nativist factions which received the support of two American companies whose rivalry is somewhat legendary in American popular culture: Coke and Pepsi, reciprocally, favored the Reformist Party and the Moroccan *Istiqlal* (Independence) Party:

> The American attitude toward the Franco-Moroccan conflict was shaped in part by global considerations. The State Department followed a policy which aimed at orienting Moroccan nationalism in a pro-Western direction. The Americans wanted, above all, to prevent the nationalists from swinging to the communist side . . . American companies operating in Morocco shared the same convictions and therefore showed several signs of goodwill toward the nationalists. [O]n February 10, 1952, Abdelkhalek Torres, leader of the Reformist Party organized a reception in his Tetouan residence after his return from exile at which soft drinks were served thanks to a gracious donation by the Coca-Cola Company in Tangier. [I]n February 1953, the *Istiqlal* Party published a booklet on the occasion of the *Fete du Trone* with the financial assistance of the Pepsi Cola Company.[7]

If the rivalry of colas replicated the binary mentality of the Cold War, it was because there was more than mere "market share" at stake. Indeed as much as Coke and Pepsi serve as icons of American culture and commerce, they also signify American imperialism to much of the world. It may be recognized that the commercial and military initiatives of the U.S. were often coextensive. Allied Operation Torch appears to have established in North Africa both the U.S. military presence as well as the local desire for American consumer goods. One finds the recurring images of American G.I.s, Yankee consumables and U.S. dollars in the memoirs of contemporary North Africans such as Fatima Mernissi, Mohamed Choukri and Albert Memmi. Conversely, one also sees images of North Africa in the American films of the period. *Casablanca,* Huston's *Journey Into Fear,* and Hitchcock's *The Man Who Knew Too Much,* portrayed to American viewers the familiar faces of Humphrey Bogart, Ingrid Bergman, Orson Welles, Sidney Greenstreet, Doris Day and James Stewart against an exotic landscape otherwise largely unconceived in the popular imagination. Even the *Maltese Falcon*—which is not set on Malta but simply conjures its putative sense of intrigue and mystery—served to familiarize Americans with an unfamiliar arena of U.S. postwar interest. The North African terrain, of course, had been traversed by other Americans who told of it, such as the authors Edith Wharton and Paul Bowles, the American expatriate who lived most of his life in Tangier. While Bowles' work did not garner a wide readership in the U.S. upon publication after the war, he was "rediscovered" in the 1960s and '70s, when a new era of American tourism opened in Morocco. (Bowles has actually been "rediscovered" twice; Bernardo Bertolucci's English-language film, *The Sheltering Sky,* is based upon Bowles' 1945 novel and follows in the wake of the author's second "rediscovery" in the 1990s.) American tourism to Morocco seems to have increased at a time when U.S. military and diplomatic relations with Rabat had developed in a new direction, toward postwar objectives.[8] The "cultural" phenomena of books, movies and tourism were therefore likely the result of more material encounters between the U.S. and North Africa. This is an important distinction because one locates the materialism which engenders cultural effects. One does not simply regard the "cultural" effects *per se* as that which defines the encounter between nations.

Thus after World War Two, a period of "Americanization," or "modern development" opened in the *Maghrib* as well as in the *Mashriq,* respectively the "West" and "East" of the Arab world.[9] Many native North Africans had believed that the Allied victory in Europe would bring also their liberation from French colonialism. Indeed, in return for native support, they had been encouraged to believe so, if not told as much, by the Allied leaders.[10] Native support may be seen to account partly for the success of Operation Torch. But if the U.S. had ever intended to truly liberate French North Africa, that is, liberate the *Maghrib* from foreign control, then it betrayed that alleged aim. Instead the U.S. appears to have pursued a different aim. With the Allied victory, the Americans remained in North Africa and established U.S. military bases, despite having reinstated the French after all. According to the *Bulletin Of Atomic Scientists,* a belatedly declassified Pentagon document reveals that the first U.S. nuclear weapons deployed abroad were in Morocco.[11] (They were later removed.) The nuclear deployment may not have been commonly known at the time. However, the American presence did not go unobserved by the other relevant parties; Moroccans protested it and the French demanded compensation.[12] Morocco's position both in the Mediterranean and as a gateway to the Middle East was likely viewed as strategic by the U.S. during the Cold War. One sees that there was more than American "cultural influences" at work in the region.

U.S. intervention in North Africa can be observed, actually, well before World War Two. The U.S. had long sought after commercial rights there, and had even sued for them at the Hague.[13] Thus a contemporary observer might have considered how the Middle East pertained to the U.S. postwar agenda. This insight is lost, however, upon a perspective which regards "modern development" as an inherently technocratic and cultural process, and at that, as a relatively recent one. The material conditions of the "East" and "West" developed through their historical relations with each other. Those relations were political, economic, strategic, and militarist. Certainly, "cultural influences" have played an important role among nations, but arguably a significantly lesser role. Cultural encounters do typically follow in the path of soldiers, merchants and proconsuls. Yet "cultural influences" do not define those encounters nor characterize the interventions of the West in the so-called developing world. It is a fundamental fallacy which portrays the development of the "East" in isolation from the historical and material relationship with the "West."

While Lerner reflects the conventional ideas of the early postwar, his view is not really all that dated or defunct. Later observers follow in the vein of the accepted "wisdom" about the cultural encounters of the East and West. For example, the work of Samuel P. Huntington, *The Clash Of Civilizations,* reasserts the notion that "culture" defines the polarity, or rather in his view the polemic, of so-called modern and traditional societies. Huntington accepts the idea that the "West" embodies liberal and progressive values while the "rest," i.e., the non-Western cultures, embody the opposite values. His ideas about the "capabilities" of the non-Western cultures of the world to manifest modernity concur with Banfield's assessment of the same. The difference is that, for Huntington, "culture" is signified mainly by religion. The reduction of "civilization" to a monolithic perception of "religion" seems already overdetermined. But the paradigm represents the relations of nations and communities in a way which makes them immaterial and apolitical. The idea of "religious fundamentalism" as the bane of modernity might therefore be seen as another colonial narrative, similar to the pretense of the "civilizing mission" or "benign aid."

Huntington's "clash of civilizations" basically restates modernization terms in light of more recent developments. Tariq Ali points out that Huntington's work, first published in 1993, became a best-selling book and that, "thanks to Osama bin Laden," the author came to be viewed in some circles as a sort of "prophet." Ali argues that Huntington's "simple but politically convenient analysis [has] provided an extremely useful cover for policy makers and ideologues in Washington." Since the end of the Cold War, such policy makers and ideologues have claimed the need to engage in another kind of war, perhaps a "holy" one, on "terror." Huntington's views about culture may thus be seen in line with more material interests on the part of the Western establishment:

> Huntington's thesis argued that while the crushing defeat of communism had brought to an end all ideological disputes, it did not signify the end of history. Henceforth culture, not politics or economics, would

> dominate and divide the world. He listed eight cultures: Western, Confucian, Japanese, Islamic, Hindu, Slav-Orthodox, Latin American and perhaps, African. Why perhaps? Because he was not sure that it was really civilized. Each of these civilizations embodied different value-systems symbolized by religion, which Huntington argued was "perhaps *the* central force that motivates and mobilizes people." The major divide was between the "West and the Rest," because only the West valued "individualism, liberalism, constitutionalism, human rights, equality, liberty, the rule of law, democracy, free markets." Therefore the West (in reality, the United States) must be prepared to deal militarily with threats from these rival civilizations. The two most menacing were, predictably, Islam and Confucianism (oil and Chinese exports), and if these two were ever to unite, they would pose a threat to the existence of the core civilization. (Ali 273)

Ali argues that Western control of global resources, such as oil especially, is the objective of rhetoric about the struggle or clash between "democracy" and "religious extremism." The rhetorical "clash" occludes the materialism of oil and other pertinent resources by sounding the alarm about "threats" to Western "civilization." It follows, no doubt, that these threats must be "pre-emptively" struck down. A point similar to Ali's was raised by Edward Said in his earlier work, *Covering Islam.* Said anticipated an assault upon the Arab and Muslim nations by the West under the pretense of a putative "war on terrorism." He observed that the end of the Cold War left an ideological "vacuum" in U.S. foreign policy which might be readily filled by the "threat of militant Islamist fundamentalism" portrayed by the media and other opinion-shapers. Said, too, sees the oil resources of the Middle East as the real "fundamentalism" which underlies American hostility toward Islam. However one chooses to view the real motivations of the current "war on terror," one may recognize that the chief theatres are the oil-and-gas rich territories of the Muslim world in the Middle East and Central Asia. These resources, vital to "modern" production, cannot be dismissed as merely coincidental to the interests of the Anglo-American coalition and its partners. As one waits for "democracy" to be "installed"—the aim of the war alleged by Washington—one notes that new oil pipelines have already been installed, in embattled Iraq as well as in Near East Asia, from the Caucasus to the Mediterranean.[14]

"Modernization" is an opaque discourse which obscures material considerations and conflates various assumptions about the "modern" and the "traditional." But its most critical problem is that it portrays a hegemonic relationship among nations as a power-neutral, socially egalitarian, cultural liberalism. Modernization discourse thus supplants the "civilizing mission" of classic European colonialism. Instead it presents a kind of "capitalist realism" which portrays American intervention into the politics and economies of the East as progressive and benign. But "development" has been anything but benign:

> The massive efforts to develop the Third World in the years since World War II were not motivated by purely philanthropic considerations but by the need to bring the Third World into the orbit of the Western trading system in order to create an ever-expanding market for our goods and services and a source of cheap labor and raw materials for our industries. This has also been the goal of colonialism especially in its last phase, which started in the 1870s. For that reason, there is a striking continuity between the colonial era and the era of development, both in the methods used to achieve their common goal, and in the social and ecological consequences of applying them.[15]

Edward Goldsmith observes that despite the discursive cloak of philanthropy, U.S. interventions into the so-called developing world have reasserted the objectives of colonial production by another name, i.e., "modern," or lately, "global," development. The Americanization of colonial discourse has been well suited to the precepts of the increased global power enjoyed by the U.S. since the postwar era. This is perhaps the real meaning of the "Americanization" of Western development. "Modernization" can be called "Yankee-centric" in that, since the postwar era, the U.S. has largely directed the course of multinational trade agreements and organizations, financial markets, loans, "structural adjustments," and other means of development. Current debates among nations within the international finance institutions and trade organizations merely attest to the power held by the United States, which, although not monolithic or unassailable, is indeed hegemonic.

The discursive logic of modernization elides materialism, precisely because the recognition of such issues as hegemony and political economy, productive exploitation and state sovereignty, etc., would entail the critical regard of Western capitalism. "Modernization" would simply silence the interrogation of terms which would likely lead to the resistance, at the local levels, of its agenda. But modernization has not repressed resistance itself. Both in the "West" and the "East," in the so-called modern and traditional worlds, active resistance has risen to the concrete practices of "modernization." The so-called anti-globalization movement which has materialized in cities such as Seattle, Montreal, Miami, Cancun, Genoa, Prague, etc.—indeed which materializes in every city where the World Trade Organization or its task committees may meet—is one manifestation of resistance to the development practices which critics see as neocolonial and exploitative. For as Lerner said in his moment, "We speak, nowadays, of 'modernization'" (45), one observes that since the "fall" of the Soviet Union and the putative emergence of the U.S. as the single global "superpower," we speak, nowadays, of "globalization."

The active resistance which today confronts "development" may not be simply dismissed with rhetorical fallacies and obfuscation. Indeed, if one accepts the view of Jagdish Bhagwati, in his *Defense Of Globalization,* development is most trenchantly challenged by students of rhetoric and discourse, that is, by literature students at major Western universities. Bhagwati portrays the rise of anti-globalization as a campus "youth movement" partly attributable to the study of literary theory. Specifically he finds that deconstruction after Jacques Derrida, postmodernism after Michel Foucault, and post-colonialism after Edward Said, are the trends which have disrupted the summits of the WTO, the Free Trade Agreement Of The Americas, and the World Bank:

> Foucault's emphasis on discourses as instruments of power and dominance has led also to what is often described as an "anti-rational" approach that challenges the legitimacy of academic disciplines, including economics, and their ability to get at the "truth." There is little doubt that the language of power and the focus on it, feeds in turn the notion . . . that corporations will dominate and exploit the workers under the liberal rules that define capitalism, and by extension, globalization . . . Feeding the anti-globalization movement are also the post-colonial (poco) theorists, who, following Edward Said's pathbreaking writings, have a profound suspicion of Western scholarship as an objective source of interpretation and conceptualization of the colonial societies that were part of the global polity that European expansionism created. That suspicion breeds hostility both to Western disciplines such as economics and to the threat that they see from them to the cultures of the communities and nations that have succeeded the colonial rule. Thus the post-colonial theorists become the natural allies of the deconstructionists, the diverse post-modernists (pomos), the Foucault cultists, and the Marxists, in their anti-globalization sentiments in the literature departments. The cauldron draws its boiling waters from many spigots. (16–17)

Many students of literary theory would probably enjoy seeing themselves as central to what is arguably the most significant counter-cultural movement in the West today. Bhagwati is correct that literary analysis provides the tools to analyze and to challenge the discourse of development. However, the truth is that the anti-globalization movement is a diverse compilation of students, workers, professionals, housewives, artists, unemployed people, unions and collectives, public interest groups, consumer groups, human rights advocates, animal rights activists, ecology and wildlife conservationists, ethics observers, and others who see a need for either the oversight, reform, or eradication of the "globalization" project. Many who aggregate under the "banner" of anti-globalization are in fact peasants and workers, villagers and families, in the so-called developing world, as protests in Mexico and Brazil have shown. It is perhaps logic, not necessarily academic theory, which has brought these diverse groups together in the movement against globalization. Regarding Bhagwati's other ideas about academics, it may simply be noted that he fails to interrogate his own terms. One wonders how he concludes that literary analysis is "anti-rational" (he means to say, "anti-intellectual"); or that academic disciplines comprise the undoubtable record of human society; or that "economics" is defined by neoliberalism; or that capitalism is "truth."

Bhagwati mainly sees the anti-globalists as silly and his tack is to portray them as such. Yet his disregard does not dispel the threat posed by the anti-globalization movement, as he himself appears to recognize. Often the resistance to development, as in the case of the anti-globalization movement, is portrayed as diffuse, anarchistic, utopian, naïve, "luddite," or violent and destructive. Where resistance is radical or militant, it is usually portrayed as malice, sometimes as terrorism or just plain "evil." Of course there is actual violence which confronts so-called modern development and its architects. This violence is motivated largely by the conditions created through unequal development, though it is seldom recognized as such in the "developed" world. Mahmood Mamdani argues that the violence of "anti-Western" militants is political in nature, although it is usually portrayed in the Western media as "religious extremism." He, like Ali and Said, finds Huntington's view of a "clash" of religious civilizations to be reductive and opaque. In *Good Muslim, Bad Muslim,* Mamdani observes that Westerners typically misunderstand political violence; because they see it as "senseless," they attribute it to cultural, rather than material, motivations:

> Such violence gets discussed in two basic ways: in cultural terms for a premodern society and theological terms for a modern society. The cultural explananation always attributes political violence to an absence

> of modernity. On a world scale, it has been called a clash of civilizations. Locally—that is, when it does not cross the boundary between "the West" and the rest—it is called "communal conflict," as in south Asia, or "ethnic conflict," as in Africa. Political violence in modern society which does not fit the story of progress tends to get discussed in theological terms . . . By seeing the perpetrators of violence as either cultural renegades or moral perverts, we are unable to think through the link between modernity and political violence. (4)

The misperceptions about political violence can be seen as the result of modernization discourse's cultural logic. The notion that violent acts are outbursts of "evil," "senseless terrorism," or "religious fundamentalism," derives from the inability to consider material history, political economy, modes of production, etc.—i.e., the failure to consider what "modernization" has actually entailed for most people of the world. From that conceptual failure, or fallacy, arise the claims of essentialism—e.g., that religious extremism, Islamist fundamentalism, anti-Western "hatred," and the like, are in and of themselves the cause or reason for violence. The reductive media and official accounts of "terrorism" which have proliferated since the events of September 11, 2001, are a case in point. While the death of innocent people in the events was indeed terrible, the mindlessly reductive portrayal of the perpetrators as "hateful" extremists motivated by religious zealotry addresses the situation not at all. Given that the images of falling towers and a breached, four-sided Pentagon were repeatedly broadcast in the weeks and months after September 11, one wonders that so few observers apparently understood the symbolism of the targets. For "the Great Satan" was not attacked in his institutions of religion and culture, but in his centers of commerce and war: the World Trade Center and the Department of Defense. Because the logic of modernization discourse is bankrupt of material analysis, it cannot perceive the implications of these targets. Thus "modernization" offers no redress but the further exacerbation of the existing conditions.

I have tried to avoid ascribing intentionality to the fallacies of modernization discourse, choosing instead to examine its logic. That is because "modernization" is a kind of "living language" or a vernacular. Its intentions need not be made conscious in order for its views to be replicated. For this reason, modernization is embraced by liberals who sincerely aspire to its claims as a global panacea. One presumes the sincerity, for example, of C.K. Prahalad, who advocates the multinational development of a "new market" among the poorest of the poor in the Third World. He feels that the global "subaltern" has massive "purchasing power" as a class; i.e., the poor have huge market potential precisely because there are so many of them. In *The Fortune At The Bottom Of The Pyramid,* Prahalad writes that as one familiar with both the developed and the developing worlds, the contrasts between the two kept "gnawing" at him. The discomfort inspired him to find a way to help the abject poor through entrepreneurship:

> It started during the Christmas vacation of 1995. During that period of celebration and good cheer, one issue kept nagging me: What are we doing about the poorest people around the world? Why is it that with all our technology, managerial know-how, and investment capacity, we are unable to make even a minor contribution to [solving] the problem of pervasive global poverty and disenfranchisement? Why can't we create inclusive capitalism? (xi)

Why, indeed? Prahalad's account of how he spent his Christmas vacation is suggestive of Dickens. The good intentions, or at least the benign potential, of global capitalism have always been asserted by people who are no doubt just as well meaning. One presumes, however, that the agents who drive modern development—i.e., the directors of multinational corporations, the governors of the world finance institutions, the members of international trade organizations, the heads of state who enact development practices, and the like—are not unconscious of their own intentions. Modernization serves the objective of multinational capitalism to expand markets and to maximize profit regardless of the human or environmental costs. The obfuscation fostered by modernization discourse thus pertains not so much among the captains of industry and finance. Rather it accrues closer to the ground: in U.S. public life and civil society generally, where modernization discourse is the *lingua franca* of public institutions and popular culture, the academy and the media. But the consequences of modern development are readily recognized by critics. Those critics may not choose to simply respond discursively, but to make their resistance felt in material ways. In the end it is the proponents of modernization who are misled by their own fallacious logic. For this reason, otherwise intelligent Americans wrung their hands one fateful autumn day and wondered, "Why do they hate us?"

Many critics could have told them why. But critical analysis was largely neglected by the predominant media after the events of September 11, and it is still neglected today. Instead, several of modernization's discursive fallacies have been mobilized. One thinks, for example, of how the assailants' motives were ascribed to "Islamist fundamentalism" and to an irrational "hatred for the West," meaning the "hatred" of Western prosperity, secularism and liberal democracy. The claim was a reductive and essentialist portrayal which asserts Orientalist or Eastern "backwardness" in place of more material considerations. Conversely, one recalls the accusations, "anti-American" and "unpatriotic," which were directed at any serious critical inquiry of the event. These accusations had the effect of silencing dissent and censoring critical analysis in the public sphere.[16] Yet discursive fallacies and the lack of critical analysis may be more than theoretical issues. "The virtual outlawing of history by the dominant culture," writes Ali, "has reduced the process of democracy to a farce. The result is a mishmash of cynicism, despair and escapism. This is precisely an environment designed to nurture irrationalisms of every sort" (281). Ali speaks mainly in regard to the "fundamentalism" of Western modernity rather than religious extremism. That is, he speaks about the effects of "modernization" upon American civil society and public culture. But to continue to turn a blind eye or deaf ear to the actual practices and effects of "modern development," or "globalization," will surely perpetuate the conditions which produce resistance. "Development as usual" will likely mean that resistance, both in the "modern" West and the "traditional" East, will take ever more material shape. Resistance can be quite concrete at a hundred and ten stories high—as Americans, and the world, have witnessed.

1.2 CENTER AND PERIPHERY

Proponents of modernization typically invoke unarticulated notions about the technological progress, cultural liberalism, and economic growth, etc, which development brings to the "developing" countries. But an analysis should recognize that "modernization" elides the material relationship between the "West and East," or between the "First and Third Worlds." The history of Western development is also the history of colonialism. It has a rather generic quality, whether one speaks of the "developing" countries in Asia, Africa, Latin America, or the Middle East. The so-called Third World—a term which arose from development practices in the 1950s—comprises the former colonies and possessions of the Western colonial empires. The effects of colonial production upon the "development" of the Third World are not recognized by the modernizing view. Rather, "modernizers" take as a precept that "development" has simply not occurred in the Third World or has occurred only very slowly or "reluctantly." The "traditional" societies are often viewed as "reluctant" to give up their "backward" ways. Indeed, according to "modernization," there seems to be no history at all in the Third World. It is a realm conceived as pre-modern, static, and essentially ahistorical. The "absence" of history is seen to follow the "traditional" ways of Third World society and "inefficient" modes of production. Of course the real "absence" of history is in the perspective of "modernization."

What appears as "underdevelopment" to the proponents of modernization is the impoverishment of the Third World. They view the Third World as the less fortunate, less progressive, lesser part of humanity subsisting in the shadow of wealthy and progressive nations in the First World. But critics of modern development point out that the impoverishment and other abject conditions of "developing" nations are the result of colonial productive exploitation, as are the wealth and prosperity of the "developed" nations. With irony and error, "modernization" postulates that Western "development" will "pull" the Third World into modernity. But "modern development" mainly reifies colonial productive exploitation. That is, the "solution" proposed by "modernizers" perpetuates the same or similar practices which have produced the very problems of Third World impoverishment and instability.

There is a real need, therefore, to confront the fallacies of modernization discourse. One finds a useful tool provided by the center-periphery model of the world productive system. The model is key to the recognition and analysis of the global political economy inherent in the relationship of the "East and West," "North and South," the "First and Third Worlds." The center-periphery model is associated with and variously employed by Immanuel Wallerstein, Samir Amin, Fernand Braudel, and others in the fields of history, economics and political science. Furthermore, as Jagdish Baghwati might point out, it has been applied in the field of post-colonial literature by such theorists as Edward Said and Abdul JanMohamed. Postcolonial literary theorists have adapted the notion of "center and periphery," or "center and margin," to describe the cultural hegemony of the Western powers in the East or Third World.[17] Foremost the center-periphery model recognizes that "East and West," "North and South," etc., are not antithetical or polarized entities but interdependent features of the global political economy. While the view has obvious importance for a material analysis of post-coloniality, it has importance for historical and cultural analysis as well.

Because much of postcolonialist theory relies upon the center-periphery model, it is worth reviewing here before embarking upon the discussion of literature which follows in the subsequent chapters. The "world system," simply put, integrates the two spheres, the "center" and "periphery," and subsumes all production. In the terms of the model, nations whose economies are structured for an external, foreign, or world market form the "periphery" of the world economic system. They provide the produce, raw resources, labor, etc., to foreign production, typically Western, which is administered at the "center" of the world economic system. Production is aimed at "central" consumption as well as the consumption of a global market controlled by agents at the center. The center develops the resources in the periphery through capital investiture, trade agreements, treaties, loans, etc., and derives the surplus. Prices, trade, finance, exchange rates, loans, etc., are usually set by the world market. But this market is dominated by the industries, corporations, banks and trade associations which represent the interests of the "center." Within the world system, the center is at an obvious advantage. Peripheral economies are basically clients to the central productive forces. The client is often held hostage to a "monoculture," or an economy dominated by one product (usually agricultural). As "monocultural" production is aimed at the external, world market, other internal sectors of production wither. The client is therefore dependent upon the center for the import of goods which it cannot supply to itself under these conditions. The imported goods may often be the fruits of the client's own labor. The profits from this outward-oriented production generally do not accrue to the peripheral economy but to the foreign investors and their local *compradors* in government and commerce who facilitate these conditions. These are some of the practices of "development" which the discourse of modernization misrepresents as benign. The unequal relationship between the center and the periphery typifies what "modernizers" extol as economic growth and development.

That individual economies are connected is not the singular insight of the center-periphery model. Rather the concept makes several other important assertions. First, it regards a global phenomenon in which the conditions which characterize the center and periphery, East and West, etc., have been developed coextensively. As Fernand Braudel observes:

> The way in which the inequality of the world accounts for the progress and establishment of capitalism explains why the central region surpasses itself, taking the lead in every kind of progress; why the history of the world is an undivided procession, a cortege of coexisting modes of production which we are too inclined to think of as following one another in successive historical periods. In fact the different modes of production are all attached to each other. The most advanced are dependent on the most backward and vice versa: development is the reverse side of underdevelopment. (*The Perspective Of The World* 70)

While the histories of nations are typically depicted individually, Braudel sees them comprise the singular history of capitalism. He observes that nations do not really make autonomous progress in "successive periods" from primitive to advanced production. Rather the development of production entails coexisting modes which are "all attached to each other" through the interrelations of nations and peoples. These interrelations, further, are determined through an "inequality" which allows the "central region" to dominate the "periphery." Braudel thus sees a kind of "flip-side" world economy, with surpluses in the center dependent upon the repression of the forces of production in the periphery. This view refutes the characterization of the East or Third World as essentially a premodern, precapitalist, or "traditional" realm in apposition to the "modern," capitalist West or First World. The two are partners, if unequal ones, rather than binaries.

It might be argued that Braudel sees capitalism "arise" somewhat disinterestedly from the "inequality of the world," rather than that the rise of capitalism has developed the inequalities between its center and periphery, as in the views of Wallerstein and Amin. Braudel appears to attribute agency to the variant geographic factors which were instrumental to early production and commerce (*Mediterranean World*). However he sees it, his view does not preclude the recognition that Western capitalism has inhibited development in the periphery. Nor would he have seen his own thesis as preclusive, one presumes. There is a complexity and simultaneity in Braudel's conception of the world system which parallels the effects he describes. Importantly, in the work of Braudel and the others, it is clear that the societies which "form" the periphery were not "excluded" from "modernity." Rather they were engaged as much in the production of "modernity" as in modern production itself.

The center-periphery model also recognizes that the resources obtained from poor nations in the "East," etc., have produced the wealth and development of the "West," beginning at least with colonial production in the nineteenth century. It bears recalling that the history of capitalism, from its mercantile inceptions to its flower in the modern age, parallels the history of Western imperialism. Braudel stresses the role of the periphery in the growth of international capitalism. He sees this growth occurring as a "layering" of productive modes, induced by European imperialism:

> For this layering gives capitalism life: the outer zones feed the intermediate ones, and above all, the center. And what is the center if not the pinnacle, the capitalist superstructure of the whole edifice? Since points of view are reciprocal, if the center depends upon the periphery for supplies, the periphery depends upon the needs of the center that controls it. After all, Western Europe transferred—virtually reinvented—the ancient practice of slavery to the New World and "induced" the new serfdom in Eastern Europe [circa 1650] as a result of economic imperatives. This lends weight to . . . [the] assertion that capitalism is a creation of world

> inequality; in order to develop, it needed the connivance of the international economy. It was born of the authoritarian organization that was simply too vast. It would not have grown to be as sturdy in a restricted economic area, and it might not have grown at all if cheap labor had not been available. (*Afterthoughts* 92–3)

As with the chicken-and-egg conundrum of capitalism and inequality, Braudel apparently sees a mutual dependency between the periphery and center. His view is reminiscent of the Hegelian master/slave dialectic, a notion which was more or less common currency among the postwar French intellectuals at the time he was writing. Still one may see that the dependency of the periphery upon the center was less a "mutual" condition than one of hostage, induced through imperialism. Braudel recognizes, however, that peripheral dependency was contingent upon Western capitalist expansion. Amin and Wallerstein, comparatively, are more explicit that this economic expansion was facilitated through colonial means. In their views, Third World nations at the periphery of the world system fuel the production and profits of the First World. But the peripheral nations do so to their own diminishing returns. Prosperity at the "center" of the world system may thus be recognized as the product of Third World abjection.

The center-periphery model accounts for the material history which is elided by modernization discourse. According to the views of Wallerstein and Amin, that history, the colonial past, is present in the material conditions of developing nations.[18] The center-periphery model regards "underdevelopment" as the colonies' historic part in the global economy—to provide the raw resources for Western industries and, generally, to buy them back in the form of import commodities. Colonial "agribusiness," as well as colonial industry, inhibited the development of local production in the periphery. So-called "traditional" means of utilizing resources were considered "inefficient" for global consumption and so were displaced. Diversification was discouraged by treaties and by unequal foreign exchange rates. Import-substitution development, the bane of post-colonial economic self determination, was also typically inhibited by foreign trade agreements. The lack of an industrial infrastructure among Third World nations after independence was thus largely the legacy of colonialism. Decolonization had ended the overt coercion and direct administration of former colonies by the metropole. But the economic relationship characteristic of colonial exploitation persisted. This relationship is at the heart of what Wallerstein, Amin and other analysts call the "world economic system."

The history of capitalist imperialism makes a reply to the postwar development claims of modernization. "Modernizers" claim that development practices will eventually, gradually, produce a stable local economy in the Third World and increase the common wealth of "developing" nations. Yet these same, continually "developing" nations somehow never manage to attain the status of "developed" nations. After fifty years of postwar "development"—which follow at least three hundred more years of Western development—in the "Third World," one might surmise that the fully realized development of poor nations is not actually the aim of "modernization." Given the component function of the periphery in the development of First World profits, the actual attainment by the Third World of a societal status comparable to that of the First World would disrupt the world system. That is, actual development in the periphery would threaten the system which produces wealth and prosperity at the center. At the very least, widespread economic stability in the East or South would minimize the profits and influence of the West in those regions. Critics of "development" find it unlikely that the capitalist institutions at the world's center would overlook self interest in deference to more benign aims. Yet, as critics point out, these are the same institutions which administer "global development."[19]

The material history elided by "modernization" reconceptualizes East and West, North and South, First and Third. One may observe that there is no actual polarity between the so-called modern and traditional worlds—both are modern. Both have been developed through modern industrial production, just unequally so. For within the context of colonialism, the "Third World" had been an industrial world for about as long as the "First;" it had simply been alienated from the means of production. The modernizing view of the Third World as an impoverished, "traditional" society is therefore based upon—not the phenomenon of underdevelopment *per se,* but—again, alienation from the means of production. But further, the center-periphery model refutes the idea that poor nations, the former colonies, are at all "underdeveloped." Indeed they have been "overdeveloped" by the productive forces at the center of the world economic system. Real polarity lay not between "East and West," etc., but rather between those who control the terms of development—industrial production, technologies, capital, etc.—and those who are "developed" under unequal conditions. The situation is a historical polemic which observers after Marx have identified as the struggle over the possession of the means of production. Conceptually, if not literally, global "development" can be seen as that same struggle between the center and periphery. The struggle may or may not necessarily entail classic industrial production as much as it regards the terms of development in the Third World. Where modern "development" has been controlled and directed by the West, one sees the reification of colonial practices in the developing nations. Where development has been controlled and directed within the periphery, it has typically taken the form of state-centered policies enacted by the newly independent nations which emerged after decolonization. Such state-centered development, e.g., as with the typical endeavors of land reform, public works, diversification and import-substitution, have always been discouraged if not openly opposed by the West. Critics of modern "development" have long seen the Western policy of opposition to autonomous, local development in the periphery as "neocolonial."[20]

The center-periphery model has been criticized as "universalist" or reductive.[21] Yet the model rightly observes the rather generic history of development in the First and Third Worlds. It emphasizes the role of poor nations, rich in resources, in global production and thus recognizes the relationship of lack and excess in so-called development. Such insights are seldom made by modernization discourse. However, to define the function of the so-called Third World within international production is not at all the same as to equate the various cultures, societies, and traditions among "peripheral" nations. But one might see that there is a risk of doing so, if the center-periphery view is taken out of context. Again, that is a problem which arises when material phenomena is patently misunderstood as cultural. The cultural premise or logic of modernization discourse supplants materialism with such essentialism. Ironically, if any discourse proposes "economic determinism," modernization does so like no other, for it impossibly envisions foreign domination and the hegemonic patronage of client states as the "development" of cultural and social "progressivism."

Nevertheless, cultural and social phenomena may be seen to reflect material conditions in both the First World and the Third. In fact, this premise has long been argued by postcolonial theorists, such as Said, Frantz Fanon, Albert Memmi, and others who analyze the social and cultural effects of colonial subjugation upon Third World societies. Postcolonial theorists see a range of cultural and social features which characterize "peripheral" society. Their views mostly reject the cultural logic of modernization discourse, however. They regard cultural phenomena to follow upon material conditions, rather than identify culture itself as the material (or cause) of peripheral life. One may see that Western development has produced some general, material features in peripheral society, given one recognizes that these features vary among and within different nations and communities in the Third World. Some of the material features which characterize peripheral society are:

- the repression of local, autonomous development;
- foreign occupation (whether militarily or by "administrative advisors");
- a polarized local society in which, though there may be various strata or castes and a small bourgeoisie, there occurs an overarching split between the impoverished majority and a wealthy minority; and relatedly,
- the dominance of *compradors,* an elite variously composed of native or foreign "notables" who derive local powers from, and function to maintain, foreign control.

These features, which are the symptoms of colonial economy, are seen also to establish the "social formation" of the local society. One recalls that the term "social formation," after Louis Althusser, encompasses the economic, political, social and ideological organizations of a given society. Third World societies bear the mark of global production in the recognizable features of "peripheral social formation." One might add that such phenomena observable in the First World, such as unemployment and the closing of factories (which are relocated to sites of "cheaper" labor in the periphery), the rise of immigration to the "center," and the flood of standardized, "exotic" imports (e.g., produce) which destabilizes "central" small businesses, are also the recognizable features of global "development."

Anti-colonial writers such as Fanon, Memmi, Abdallah Laroui and others, recognized that the debilitating features of peripheral development, while imposed from without, take root within local society as institutions. Peripheral features thus may reproduce themselves and their conditions within the local society. For this reason, fundamental changes in peripheral or Third World societies are difficult to achieve. Yet the features of peripheral society are by definition "always already" linked to outside, or foreign, agency. In this way, Western global capitalism impacts the organization of peripheral society as a whole, or, the "social formation." Under these conditions, if change were to be achieved at all, local society must encompass a wholesale, systemic breakaway. This is the challenge which peripheral nations faced under colonialism and the conflict which they took up during the movement for decolonization.

Independence necessarily entailed a systemic break with the metropole; but it also posed a conceptual revision of local society, in all its aspects of formation. Anti-colonial works of the period, such as Fanon's *Wretched Of The Earth* and *Black Skin/White Mask* and Che Guevara's essays, "Man and Socialism in Cuba," and "On Creating a New Attitude," asserted that the transition to liberated society necessitated reciprocal changes in personal consciousness. Liberation, it was argued, entailed the rejection of value systems and cultural models which had for so long privileged the colonial hegemony and displaced populist or native models. Such arguments attest that the examination of "culture" has always been a part of postcolonial theory. To consider "cultural" imperialism, alongside the economic and political aspects, is integral to postcolonial understanding. A problem has arisen, it seems however, from the subsumation of postcolonial literature in disciplinary study. Academically, "cultural" phenomena are often split off from the material issues and fetishized as the defining features of Western Empire. The fetish of culture in postcolonial study has the effect of de-politicizing what are essentially very political and material phenomena. One recalls that Fanon and Guevara were not simply "armchair revolutionaries" but that to them "theory" necessarily implied a "praxis," that is, it implied the situational application of theory into material practice.

The reduction of "culture" in postcolonial study discourages consideration of the more material aspects of Western colonial enterprise. For that reason, many observers often fail to consider that "development as usual" may simply carry over from colonial times into contemporary globalization. But the reification of colonial practices by global development today ought to be a key area of inquiry in post-colonial studies—or so, at least, one presumes. The colonial past provides a great deal of insight into contemporary "development." One may observe that many of the same or similar concerns—about sovereignty, social justice, political and economic stability, etc.—as were voiced by the anti-colonial critics of the postwar era are extant in the criticism of globalization. Critics of development see the same or similar practices manifested by globalization as under colonialism. Indeed, even the "development" of a discourse of apology, "modernization," seems to follow in the footsteps of an earlier "civilizing mission." Thus it is necessary to reexamine and to analyze some of the phenomena which have characterized Western intervention in the Third World.

One briefly notes that an examination is especially relevant today, as the United States apparently retraces the path of earlier Western interventions, specifically those of Britain and France, in the East. Since September 11, 2001, the U.S. has embarked upon both a "terror war" and a "reform initiative"[22] conceived to "restructure" the Middle East according to American tastes. It is worth noting that in anticipation of Arab resistance to the deployment of the U.S. military in Iraq, the Pentagon reportedly screened the film, "The Battle of Algiers."[23] Gillo Portecorvo's 1965 French film depicts how the guerrilla tactics of Algerian rebels eventually won a long and bitter war for independence. The Pentagon viewing was intended to produce some insights about U.S. strategy for urban warfare in the Middle East. Militant resistance, now as during the decolonization era, is regarded by the Western protagonists as "acts of terror." The French, as portrayed in the film, were notoriously brutal with the Algerian guerrillas and with those even suspected of sympathizing with them. The colonial context of the "Battle of Algiers" may or may not have occurred to the Pentagon viewers. But it should not be lost upon postcolonial critics. Much of the phenomena which obtains today in the so-called "war on terror," and in the U.S. "reform" of the Middle East, replicates or reifies the late age of colonialism. Perhaps by examining some of the cultural and material aspects of Western intervention in the Middle East, one may arrive at a historically informed understanding of the objectives inherent in "global development" today.

Chapter Two

North Africa and the Anti-Colonial Critics

Fanon, Memmi, Sartre, Camus

2.1 COLONIAL VIOLENCE

The material history of colonialism attests to how the features of peripheral society were "developed" in the Third World. Western productive "development"—or rather, the repression of local development—was secured through military force or coercion. The features of peripheral formation stem ultimately from this basic condition. But under colonialism, coercion was not simply military; it was political and material, as well. Coercion took expression surely in military conquest and military occupation. It was evident also in many facets of public and private life in the periphery. Local society suffered the repression of universal (native) suffrage, of civil rights and civil society; the violation of human rights; the disruption of or intervention into native social forms; and, the unequal exchanges of an economic relationship based on treaties conceded through wars. The repression of local society, and therefore of local development, was achieved through coercion.

Jean-Paul Sartre maintained that coercion both explicitly and implicitly underscored all aspects of colonial society. He described this coercion as colonial violence. Writing about Algeria in 1957, he notes:

> Conquest was achieved by violence; overexploitation and oppression demand the maintenance of violence, which entails the presence of the Army. There would be no contradiction there if terror reigned everywhere on earth; but back in France, the colonist enjoys democratic rights that the colonial system denies the colonized . . . Racism is inscribed in the events themselves, in the institutions, in the nature of the exchanges and the production . . . Racism is *already there,* carried by the *praxis* of colonialism, engendered at every instant by the colonial apparatus, sustained by those relationships of production which define

> two sorts of individuals: for some privilege and humanity are one and the same thing; they assert their humanity through the free exercise of their rights; for the others, the absence of rights sanctions their poverty, their chronic hunger, their ignorance, in short their subhumanity. (50)

Sartre observes a cohesive, material system, one with component parts or features (or an apparatus), causes, effects, agency, outcomes. Colonial violence is a system which constitutes the features of daily life. It is an imposition, an artifice imposed upon local society and is underwritten by the proximity and the readiness of the occupying army. Thus the "subhuman" conditions for natives and the institutionalized racism in French Algeria were the local cognates of French democracy and largesse in the metropole.

The societal disparity between the center and the periphery was achieved through colonial violence. This is apparent in the double standards of French colonial society. One recalls that of all French North Africa, Algeria was considered by the French government to be topographically "a part of France."[1] "Algeria *is* France" was a French slogan during the Algerian war of independence (Stora 30). Of course the claim was ideological, but it emphasizes the double standard. For, apart from the obvious matter of historical and cultural criteria, how could there be one France composed of "Frenchmen" of varying degrees of citizenship and legal identity? Indeed, Algeria was not so much a part of France as its territorial possession.

The importance of Algeria to the colonists was its peripheral role in metropolitan French production. For it to play this part, the native Algerians were necessarily disenfranchised from French civil society and dispossessed of Algeria. After consolidating the territory during an initial period of French conquest and native resistance lasting from 1830 through 1871, France ruled Algeria through successive and coextensive administrative divisions (e.g., the *Bureau Arabes, communes du plein exercice,* and *communes mixte*) and by juridicial decrees, such as the 1863 Senatus Consultum Act and the 1873 Warner Act. These latter reforms were allegedly purported to protect tribal ownership of land, but historians subsequently have viewed them as flawed at best and at worst, as a swindle. Benjamin Stora recounts that by 1919, native Muslim Algerians had lost 18.5 million acres of land "which the state, individuals, and major companies had divided up among themselves," adding that, "The 'modern' agricultural sector was concentrated in the most favorable region, the Tell, where 98 percent of lands were appropriated" (7). Fergus Fleming relates the appropriation of Algerian land to the French military occupation in succinct terms: "Native farmers were pushed aside in favor of a competing class of white smallholders whose landgrabbing was enforced by an ever larger army" (135). He adds that a census taken in 1901 showed that the settler population had increased alongside a five-year build-up in French troops.

While French colonial methods in Algeria often had the semblance of metropolitan democracy, they were, in substance, intended to consolidate colonial power and precedence over native society. For example, a representative double electoral college system gave the patina of democratic inclusion to native Algerians, but in actuality it nullified the Muslim vote. A system of administrative segregation favored the European *colons* over and apart from Algerian natives. The *Code de l'Indigenat* of 1881 had established the French "subject" status of Algerian natives in opposition to the status of the European *colons* who enjoyed full rights of French citizenship. Thus, when Sartre refers to racism in the passage above, he means that the natives were proscribed by law a second-class citizenship:

> The political and social statuses reinforce one another: since the natives are subhuman, the Declaration of Human Rights does not apply to them; conversely, since they have no rights, they are abandoned without protection to the [putatively] inhuman forces of nature, to the "iron laws" of economics. (50)

This legalized racism was implemented through the apparatuses of colonialism, surely, "inscribed in the events themselves" of day-to-day life. But ultimately, it was French military power which enforced these apparatuses.[2] Thus, one sees that colonial violence underwrote the very concept of a French Algeria. It underpinned a basically economic relationship, and had far-reaching implications for the social formations of the local communities and the metropole.

A vivid portrayal of the relations between first and second-class "Frenchmen" is relayed by Mohamed Choukri in his memoir *For Bread Alone*. Choukri, a Berber native, immigrated from Morocco to Algeria as a boy to work on a large vineyard at Oran owned by wealthy *pieds noirs* or colonists. The cultivation of wine in Algeria was a French colonial imposition. French vineyards occupied the arable land in the north, which the natives had traditionally used to grow grain (*Maghreb in the Modern World* 36). Thus, Choukri worked, with other Berbers, on land which had once been tribal land. Their employment was not "economic development" or "jobs to the poor" granted to better their conditions; just as the French cash crop which replaced the native staples was not "modernization." Rather, these were exploitative conditions, artificially imposed through military coercion.

Choukri, then an illiterate boy of fourteen or fifteen years old, worked in the vineyard from five in the morning to six in the evening, usually with an hour break at lunch in a country where the longer, siesta break was likely to have been observed by urban *colons.* Choukri eventually got a reprieve from this labor and became a houseboy to the owners of the vineyard, a *pied noir* couple of French and Spanish origins.

One must consider the implications of wine production in a Muslim land where it is not likely to be drunk by a people whose hunger derived in no small part from the loss of their grainfields to support *pied noir* vineyards. The abject hunger and poverty which Choukri and his family experienced were common conditions in native society in North Africa. The infant mortality, chronic unemployment, and child labor which Choukri describes are the attributes of a second-class citizenship. They are the inverse aspect of the profits and commodities enjoyed in the metropole or by local *colons.* For Algeria, as for French North Africa in general, "underdevelopment" was a phenomenon reserved for the natives; it did not typically pertain to *colons* of any social strata, whether landowners or landless workers.[3] Thus it is important to understand that "Third World" underdevelopment was not merely an economic condition, produced solely by industrial alienation. It was engendered through military coercion or colonial violence. Military occupation and other means of coercion were fundamental to the social formation of the periphery. To overlook this basic fact is to suppose an essential, static condition of abjection in the so-called Third World. Indeed the term "Third World" serves as a repository for those suppositions.

What can be called the "violence of underdevelopment" is misrepresented by modernization discourse as "traditionalism." What Westerners see as traditional life in the Third World is often actually the features of colonial violence. Aspects of pre-capitalist societies such as village hierarchies, the peasantry and serf-like labor, which had mostly disappeared in the West relative to the degree of industrialization, were in large part artificially sustained in the periphery through the apparatuses of colonialism. These apparent conditions are seen by modernizers as the measure of a given society's "underdevelopment." But as Stora observes, modern Algeria had simply inherited the underside of the colonial legacy which had enriched modern France:

> In fact, in 1962 Algeria was heir to an outward-oriented economy set up in relation to the metropolis, and existed as a function of the million Europeans living there. In the first half of the twentieth century, the gradual integration into the French economy had brought about a rapid decline in local craft industries, which faced competition from French

> manufactured products. A dual and largely agricultural economy took shape. Side by side with a modern sector of large farm operations in the hands of the colons, a traditional sector with low productivity attempted to provide for the local population's subsistence. (123)

Traditional life in Algeria was misdirected, subverted, or artificially rendered static through the colonial inhibition of, or the intervention into, all aspects of local society: technology and industry; politics, law, and civil society; etc. The "traditional" social formation was thus an effect of colonial inhibition and intervention. Azzedine Haddour graphically describes the matter: "French colonialism denied the colonized participation in a diachronic history, it congealed their past and blocked their way to the future, it sclerosed and mummified the colonial society" (*Colonial Myths* 2). Haddour emphasizes the retrograde or stasis effect of artificially sustained "traditions." This effect was evident especially in local societies which were based upon an agrarian economy, such as Algeria or Egypt. In these cases, local agrarianism was shackled to central production in France and Britain. Stora recounts that not only was agricultural exportation overdeveloped in Algeria, but that the country's peripheral function as a market for products from the metropole destined its lack of industrial infrastructure: "The importation of manufactured goods was a condition for Algeria's being integrated into France, and all customs protection for eventual nascent industries was banned" (123). Consequently so-called modern developments, such as industry and its attendant phenomena, were retarded through the imposition of the peripheral role in international production. The peripheral role was not the result of "pre-capitalist" culture or of an allegedly objective global market. It was imposed by imperial force. The static "traditionalism" of native Algeria, which was characteristic of the periphery, had been developed by the modern, industrial West. Artificial stasis was the effect of an enthralled agrarian economy—that is, it was itself the effect of modernization.

Underdevelopment was therefore a two-fold problem; it was political as well as economic. Thus the solution to underdevelopment was not simply a matter of economic or social "reform." It involved a much deeper approach than mere reform. "The immobility to which the native is condemned," wrote Frantz Fanon about French Algeria, "can only be called into question if the native decides to put an end to the history of colonization—the history of pillage—and to bring into existence the history of the nation—the history of decolonization" (*Wretched of the Earth* 51). An end to stasis, or the beginning of real development, was conceivable only by eradicating the root cause of underdevelopment; real development made necessary full independence from the metropole. Gradual reform measures, or the proposed program of assimilation, which had been pursued by Algerian bourgeois nativist leaders for a couple of generations prior to the revolution there, had never accomplished much material change in native society.[4] This was the case also with "autonomy" in Egypt and Morocco, and with "Bourghibism"[5] in Tunisia. Gradualist reform rather ensured the *status quo,* with merely some concessions made to the nativist elite. For the rest of colonial society, conditions remained ahistorically "mummified."

Because peripheral society in Algeria was shaped and held through colonial violence, legitimate independence made revolutionary violence necessary. Revolutionary violence was required to undo at every level what colonial violence had made of local society. Fanon makes this point in *The Wretched of the Earth,* written toward the end of the Algerian War. Fanon argues that violence is the reality of colonial society and that when one recognizes that fact, as oppressed natives invariably do, one sees that colonial society must be, can only be, overturned by force:

> The naked truth of decolonization evokes for us the searing bullets and bloodstained knives which emanate from it. For if the last shall be first, this will only come to pass after a murderous and decisive struggle between the two protagonists [i.e., the colonizer and the native]. That affirmed intention to place the last at the head of things, and to make them climb at a pace (too quickly, some say,) the well known steps which characterize an organized society, can only triumph if we use all means to turn the scale, including, of course, that of violence. (37)

Fanon sees the peasant masses as the makers of Algerian independence, "for they alone have nothing to lose and everything to gain" (61). In his view, the impoverished natives have borne the full weight of colonial violence. They are outside of the strata of class privileges which the local bourgeoisie seeks to retain through compromise with the colonists. For the masses there can be no compromise, for there is only the reality of violence. Thus the use of violence, its application in armed struggle against the colonizers, is the material means of liberation.

Colonial society, as described by Fanon, is a "world divided into compartments" (51) or mutually exclusive zones occupied by the settlers on one hand and by the natives on the other. These zones are separate and unequal; the settler's zone is marked by excess and privilege, the native's by lack. Colonial society, thus compartmentalized, is a structural phenomenon. The structure is a reality which cannot simply be waived at will; it cannot be reformed through compromises or good intentions. It must be wholly dismantled through violent means: "The destruction of the colonial world is no more and no less than the abolition of one zone, its burial in the depths of the earth or its expulsion from the country" (41). The "abolition of [the] one zone" would be, in liberationist terms, that of the settler. Abolition of the settler's zone would summarily resolve the system of first- and second-class citizenry by eradicating its context, or the very structure of colonial life. Theoretically the native under class as such would be dissolved because the terms of its abjection, the privileged class of foreign elites, would also be dissolved. This process would not be accomplished without violence.

Violence is not reform. The call for militant resistance to colonial oppression departs completely from the "conventional" option debated in French and Algerian liberal circles, that is, the reformist pursuit of "assimilation." In comparison, it is interesting to consider how assimilation, or the proposed integration of local society into the metropole, was framed by the discourse of liberal reform. One may note that a large discrepancy existed between the liberal discourse and the colonial practice, however much "assimilation" was invoked by progressive voices among the metropolitan French and the moderate Algerian nationalists.[6] For example, John P. Halstead points out the disingenuousness of the French colonial concept in regard to the neighboring protectorate of Morocco:

> In theory, assimilation was a process whereby the institutions of a dependent people would become one with those of the metropole, to the mutual benefit of both, and natives (the elite, at least) would learn to become loyal Frenchmen. But the presupposition that natives wanted to, or could, become Frenchmen appeared to be ill-founded, and, in practice, assimilation amounted in Morocco, as it did elsewhere in the empire, to direct and often military rule, economic exploitation and acculturation of a very imperfect nature. (46)

As with Morocco and Tunisia, the other two areas of French North Africa, Algerian assimilation concerned the native majority in regard to the metropole. It was supposed that equality with the French would—gradually . . . eventually—be conferred to Muslim natives. This project could only be conceived in the context of colonial domination and colonial racism. For otherwise, it is absurd to speak of the assimilation of the vast majority population to the privileged legal status held by a small minority, *les pieds noirs*. Unlike the natives, the *pieds noirs* had representatives in the French parliament and full French citizenship. They opposed native assimilation for the obvious reason that it would have eroded their hegemony in local society. Indeed, Stora comments that the *pieds noirs* were "unanimous in defending their privileges, which made the most insignificant French government employee superior to any Arab. Their unity [in this regard] was due to a shared fear of the Muslim majority" (23). Ostensibly, the assimilation of the natives as French citizens would have lowered the settler's privileged status. But there was never a question of the assimilation of *pied noir* settlers into the mainstream of Algerian society. And given the colonial context, such a proposal would have been equally as absurd. Yet in the end, it was the settlers who were eventually assimilated by the "mother" country. Horne notes without irony "the way in which France *assimilated* [italics added] the over one million *pieds noirs* who flooded to her shores" (549). Henissart calls the flight of the settlers after Algerian independence "[o]ne of the biggest mass migrations in post-World War II history" and compares it to the (much larger) displacement of populations after the partition of India and Pakistan in 1947 (427 and n.)

The structural nature of colonial society suggests there could be no assimilation of the native community or "zone." If "assimilation" existed for some Algerians, it was to the degree which they functioned as a class to perpetuate the colonial system. Indeed such a tenuous position characterized many locals who Albert Memmi calls "colonials," those who held a conferred or conditional legal status in North Africa, typically European immigrants and their descendants and native Christians and Jews. "Colonials" derived some privileges relative to native Muslims, as did Muslim native elites educated in the French tradition (e.g., the Algerian "*évolués*") in regard to the poor and illiterate masses of the Maghrib. In Algeria, "[a]ccommodationist sentiment was particularly strong among members of [the] urban elite, a group that has come to be known as the 'reformists,' assimilationists, *évolués,* or Jeunes Algeriens, who fashioned themselves the occupiers' deserving partners" (Malley 45).[7] Yet the privileges of such locals were to be had only within the broader context of their own oppression within colonial society (*Colonizer and the Colonized* 13–18). On the other hand assimilation, whether political or cultural, would not have been possible for the whole of native society, even if it had been so desired. The liberal discourse about "assimilation," then, appears to have simply been a way to forestall or subvert the native struggle for independence. Assimilation seems, in effect, to have been a kind of "talking point," which existed in and of itself. As such, it would have served the purposes of colonial administration. Assimilation would ultimately have supported those parties which derived benefits from the *status quo,* i.e., local *compradors* as well as settlers and metropolitan agents. The pursuit of assimilation seems to have been a program apart from whether or not its objectives were ever truly intended to be implemented. Reform, at any rate, is not revolution.

The "abolition of one zone," regardless whether by revolution or assimilation, necessarily entailed "the destruction of the colonial world." This is why "assimilation" as it was conceived—"the pure and simple integration of the Muslim collectivity into the great French family" (Stora 17)—was not possible. It could only be a fiction promulgated by *status quo* interests or perhaps it was the utopian dream of local or metropolitan liberals. Its realization would necessarily have changed the fundamental structure of society; but that kind of change was never actually an aim of the metropolitan administration. The fundamental changes which occurred in Algeria were not brought about through liberal or assimilationist methods but by armed struggle. Algerian independence brought the dissolution of *pied noir* society, not native "integration." Yet the mass migration of the settlers was motivated by more than simply the threat of retaliatory native violence:

> Taking into account the huge discrepancy in wealth, property and land between the two communities—nine-tenths belonging to one-tenth—the excruciating land hunger of the Algerians coupled to their soaring birthrate, racial stresses and *pied noir* intolerance, and—perhaps above all—the accumulated hatreds of seven and a half years of war, could the Europeans realistically have remained more than a few additional years at best? (Horne 547)

The settlers' status had formerly been qualified through an apparatus of coercion; this apparatus was dismantled by Algerian nationalism, the outcome of the war of independence. The flight of the *pieds noirs* was therefore motivated by class slippage, and all which that implies, as much as by the war itself.

In their anti-colonial works, Fanon and Memmi articulate some general, or indeed "universalist," features of colonial oppression. To define, as both authors do, whole segments of society as "colonizers" and "colonized," or as "natives" and "settlers" or *"colons,"* suggests a paradigm in which certain criteria (e.g., ethnic or religious or gender differences) are flattened. Yet the paradigm makes the structural nature of imperialism more apparent. The latter is a point which both authors wished to emphasize: that colonialism is an institution, a structure, which determines one's life as a colonial subject, regardless of one's individuality or particular experience. The analyses of Fanon and Memmi imply also that, within an unjust society, oppression is not merely specific to one group; all groups, even privileged ones of greater or lesser advantage, are oppressed by an authoritarian regime, a police state, by the apparatuses of state or local power. For example, Sartre's discussion of the "colonials'" conflicted status underscores the artifice of privilege based upon colonial exploitation (48–49). For generally the privileged class of Algerians comprised people who were not themselves, nor were they the descendants of, French elites but of the lower classes.[8] They or their families had emigrated to North Africa for the usual reasons which immigrants leave their homes and settle someplace else: employment, quality of life, self-determination. But these things were offered to them at another's expense. Whether or not one recognizes the Algerian *pieds noirs* as an oppressed group, it is clear that they served much larger interests than their own, those of wealthy and powerful metropolitan agents. As Abdallah Laroui observes of the French *colons* in the Maghrib:

> But who were they? Diplomats, soldiers, businessmen, dealers in agricultural products and livestock, farmers, educators, missionaries—all were intermediaries. But their activity was neither action, or, in the strict sense of the word, reaction, but simply an actualization of ideas conceived elsewhere. (*History of the Maghrib* 323)

Literally, the predicament of the *pieds noirs* was one of exploitation by the metropole. Their presence and function in Algeria provided the premise for and maintained the colonial system. Like most oppressed people everywhere, they participated in the system which exploited them.

The position of the *pieds noirs* figured prominently, if controversially, in the French debate over the conflict in Algeria. Metropolitan liberals were not of one mind; but whether or not they favored the "integration" of Algeria or else like Sartre supported independence, they were critical of French colonial practices. Many leftists viewed *pied noir* society as the face of French imperialism in Algeria. Other observers saw *pied noir* activism or organization as a threat to the stability of metropolitan France. The *pieds noirs* were generally the lynchpin of contentions for both the left and the right. This rather suggests that, as a class, they were exploited by metropolitan society in various ways. Their exploitation is apparent in the contemporary national debate in France whether or not to handily "give them up." The latter happened, in fact; and the *pieds noirs* felt themselves betrayed by the man who had once assured them that he "understood" their cause: *"Vive l'Algerie française!"*—Charles de Gaulle.[9]

The views of Albert Camus, himself the son of French and Spanish Algerian settlers, are important to consider regarding the contemporary debate about French Algeria. Camus recognized the *pieds noirs* as a contingent feature of the French colonial system. But he felt that they were the less significant feature than that of metropolitan surplus:

> There have doubtless been exploiters in Algeria, but fewer than in metropolitan France, and the first one to benefit from the colonial system is the entire French nation. If some Frenchmen consider that, as a result of its colonizing, France (and France alone among so many holy and pure nations) is in a state of sin historically, they don't have to point to the French in Algeria as scapegoats [. . .]; they must offer up themselves in expiation. As far as I'm concerned, it seems to me revolting to beat one's *mea culpa,* as our judge-penitents do, on someone else's breast, unless to condemn several centuries of European expansion, and absurd to include in the same denunciation Christopher Columbus and Lyautey. (*Resistance, Rebellion, and Death* 119–120)

Despite the ironically Catholic moral overtones, Camus wanted to establish some ethical reason, or equilibrium, which he felt was lacking in the French debate over Algeria. The *pieds noirs* had much at stake in what was in many ways merely a theoretical matter in France. Camus stresses that metropolitan society benefited more from colonialism in Algeria than the *colons* who had shouldered it. The metropole derived a quality of life and an economy out of French colonialism, however distant appeared the means. His observation of the metropolitan agency behind the occupation of Algeria is a point well made. It clarifies the institutional—and impersonal—character of imperialism. He sees that, institutionally, French imperialism exploits the *pieds noirs* as it does metropolitan workers and Algerian natives. Camus doesn't want to see the *pieds noirs* scapegoated by a conscience-afflicted metropole which views the settlers as the problem. He advises the metropolitan French to "offer up themselves in expiation," if they feel a need to purge.

However, there are problems with Camus' reasoning. Although he clarifies the agency of the Algerian occupation, he elides the central conflict. The point of the Algerian conflict is not whether *colons* or motherland French are the authors or the benefactors of colonial occupation. Occupation is merely one facet of a broader system of injustice. This has many implications for colonial society on both sides of the sea. To establish the degrees of impersonal "guilt," however, is not one of the implications. Simply put, Camus' observation of metropolitan agency does not go far enough. It is a discursive sleight-of-hand. He takes as his interlocutors not so much those who call for an end to French dominance in Algeria. He addresses those who wrongly see *les pieds noirs* as the "site" or the "placeholders" of French dominance. Thus he fails to address the fundamental issue of French imperialism. Elsewhere, of course, he does address the larger issue, however much his views favor the claims of the *colons* in Algeria. While defending the settlers, Camus overlooks an important point. The *pieds noirs* may well have been an exploited class within the colonial system. But this does not negate their collaboration in the inherent injustice of local society. Neither does their collaboration negate the vested interest of the motherland French in preserving the *status quo.* Thus, Camus may trenchantly point out metropolitan agency in defense of the settlers. But his defense makes no reply to the fact of the occupation.

Again, it should be noted that French liberal guilt, the *"mea culpa"* which Camus criticizes above, has no function for a material analysis, except perhaps as a hindrance. The idea of guilt, blame, absolution, etc., is a rhetorical distraction. Such terms merely distort the material issues of the given conflict. Rather it is necessary to understand how classes or groups, whether metropolitan or local, function within colonial society. For this analysis one seeks not *mea culpas* but agency, method, apparatus, and structure, for these are material terms. Indeed as liberal guilt is irrelevant, so is liberal good intention. In a gesture toward *ad absurdum* argument, Camus mentions Marshal Louis Hubert Gonsalve Lyautey, who was the French Resident General of Morocco from 1912 to 1925. Lyautey was known for his "tolerance" toward native society. Camus suggests that the Marshal's honor cannot be tarnished by association with Christopher Columbus, who anti-colonial critics often regard as having paved the way for New World genocide. But the concept of a "good"—as opposed to a "bad"—colonizer again misses the point.

Camus invokes Lyautey because he was considered by the French to be the example of a gifted colonial administrator. Lyautey had established his military and administrative career in Vietnam (*Indochine*) and Madagascar. His approach in Morocco was seen as liberal and diplomatic. He maintained ceremonial recognition of various Berber chieftains as well as of the Sultan of Morocco, who he had appointed. He tactfully used the Makhzen (the indigenous Moroccan government) to rubberstamp the French policies of the protectorate administration, the Residency. As if the final say about his good reputation, after his death in 1934 Lyautey was buried at Rabat in a Muslim shrine.[10] Lyautey was also known to have personal fondness and respect for the Moroccans. A traveler who met him in Fez around 1922, records a sentimental moment:

> "But here," said he [Lyautey], taking up a little book concerned with the literature of the Mussulmans, "is a very charming volume indeed, upon a

> subject which interests me greatly," and he turned over its pages, resting his eyes for a moment upon a page of the Koran. "The Mussulmans are my friends." (O'Connor 113)

But if the "Mussulmans" were indeed his friends, one wonders what kind of friendship did the Marshal return? In North Africa, he oversaw the "pacifying" of tribal resistance to foreign rule. According to one of his generals: "The Marshal's policy is always: first to occupy their pasture-lands, and then, to compel their submission in the mountains, leaving those who are irreconcilable to stew in their own juice on the unprofitable summits" (O'Connor 125). It is a charmingly French turn of speech—to stew in one's own juice. But it refers to Lyautey's much less charming purpose: not diplomacy or cultural exchange but military occupation and the subjugation of Berber natives. It goes without saying that Lyautey's tenure in Morocco was not a diplomatic mission. His protection of Moroccan resources from outsiders has been seen by some as a disinterested act to preserve Moroccan integrity. But his protection, specifically of the phosphate fields near Marrakesh from the rival claims of Britain and the U.S., benefited French, not Moroccan interests, as one observer points out. During Lyautey's residency, the big French corporations acquired vast tracts of Moroccan land.[11]

If the Moroccan people are renowned for their hospitality, as colonial literature never tires of observing, it seems the other party was gravely remiss. Lyautey's respect for traditional Moroccan culture was, of course, in the context of French dominance. As a policy, the recognition and preservation of differences aimed at subjugation, not equity. Lyautey's ostensible deference to the mutual "autonomy" of town and country, of Arabs and Berbers, exploited the old internal divisions of native society to the benefit of French authority. Likewise, the legal and social separations between the Muslim and French communities, purportedly to preserve native traditions, instead supported a society of double standards. Indeed, however much the "Mussulmans" may have been Lyautey's friends, they were also his conquered "subjects."

Laroui observes that the French policy of "dualism" in North Africa allowed *colons* to enjoy privileges and freedoms in all aspects of civic and commercial life which were forbidden to Maghribis. Marshal Lyautey's respect for Moroccan cultural differences fits well with this policy. The objectives were intended to devolve native society for the better standing of the colony:

> This policy, one might think, ought logically to have enabled two societies to coexist. But in the eyes of the colonial establishment the coexistence

> was essentially provisional, for after going through a phase of enlightened despotism, the one society, it was thought, would transform itself into an adult bourgeois democracy, while the other, after a period of slow disintegration under the benevolent control of the military, would degenerate into an anthropological reservation. An aid to growth, on the one hand, a speeding up of regression on the other—this, the colonial ideologists tried to make themselves and others believe, was the judgment of history. (*History of the Maghrib* 344)

Dualism—two societies, separate and unequal—was a strategy of underdevelopment. The underdevelopment of local society was not simply an effect but an objective of colonial "development." Dualism, or the double standard, was never intended to "preserve traditions," as was claimed, but to destroy native society. Indeed, apart from Lyautey's personal admiration of Moroccan traditions and his friendly relations with native *compradors,* it was the Resident General's job to oversee the disruption and disintegration of local society. As Laroui observes, native abjection played out under "the benevolent control of the military." In Algeria, this control was not nearly as "benevolent" as in Morocco. Lyautey's regard of the Algerians was apparently quite different than his esteem for the Moroccans, likely because of the greater degree of Algerian resistance to French authority. Whatever personal good will Lyautey may have had—and it appears that he simply believed that French administration was in the best interest of Morocco—he served a function which was larger than his own intentions. But even his best intentions for Morocco were themselves structural concepts, shaped by the ideology which sees conquest as a greater good for the natives.

It would seem obvious that there can be no benevolent tyrants, no "good colonists." But the obvious bears mention if only because the material issues of colonial conflict are so often obscured or distorted in rhetorical ways. The ideas of guilt and blame, good and bad colonizers, etc., which Camus uses to deflect criticism away from the *pieds noirs,* only clouds the basic issues. It may well have been the case that colonial violence and social injustice were achieved despite only the best intentions of individual protagonists. But their good intentions do not really matter. As Memmi observes, "The distinction between deed and intent has no great significance in the colonial situation" (*Colonizer and the Colonized* 130). The irrelevance of personal or individual intent emphasizes the structural reality of colonial society. Lyautey's warm regard for the Moroccans, for example, had no effect upon his killing them. His function was to "pacify" their resistance. How he felt about it didn't alter the reality of an objective which was not, perhaps, his own, but which nevertheless was accomplished through him, through his own actions performed in the service of colonial agents. As with Laroui's observation about the French *colons* generally, his "activity was neither action, nor, in the strict sense of the word, reaction, but simply an actualization of ideas conceived elsewhere" (323). In this regard, Lyautey's reputation and intentions don't really matter. Thus Camus' invocation of the Marshal's good name makes no reply to the critics of French colonialism.

Marshal Lyautey's good will toward the "Mussulmans" of Morocco illustrates the ideology of Western development. The rhetoric bears little resemblance to the actual practices upon which it was based. Development rhetoric is comprised of notions about progress, traditions, and the "good intentions" of military-industrial agents who maintain they bring freedom, civilization and light into the dark but fertile recesses of the globe. These are the typical fallacies of modernization as surely as they are the myths of colonialism. "In colonial history," however advises Laroui, "one should judge results, never intentions. Beyond the motives and justifications of the colonizers and colonized alike, it is the logic of the world market that makes colonial history understandable" (*History of the Maghrib* 293). Indeed, rhetoric about good intentions and the "benefits" incurred by native society is intended to cover over violence and appropriation by claiming the opposite; thus, imperialism is said to be "democracy," dispossession is called "reform," and disenfranchisement, "assimilation." These platitudes offer a discourse of apology. For only through ideology could genocide be called "pacification" or could one's enemies and victims be called "friends." Thus to observe that a person's or a society's "good intentions" are rendered moot—by colonial violence, by a hostage economy, by the imposed rule of proconsuls and *compradors,* by the material conditions of abjection—is an important recognition. It regards what really matters in the colonial context; it also makes a cogent reply to the apologists for colonial violence. As the material reality of the colonial system can be discussed, referred to, analyzed, and understood, so the objectives and methods of decolonization can also be understood. One must be taken within the context of the other. This is the insight and usefulness of seeing colonial reality as a world system, composed of a center and a periphery.

2.2 TRADING PLACES

Liberation theory works such as Memmi's *Colonizer and the Colonized* and Fanon's *Wretched of the Earth* view colonial oppression as an impersonal, systemic institution. They portray the "shape" of local society as a part of that institution. Locally, colonial society functioned upon an internal logic based on colonial oppression. Therefore certain aspects of local society may be seen as largely self-perpetuating, independent of the ostensible garrisons of foreign coercion. Symptoms of underdevelopment such as poverty, political disenfranchisement, illiteracy, etc., for example, need no garrisons to reproduce the terms of their own conditions. To recognize the material base of discursive abstractions such as "poverty," "alienation," so-called "fatalism," and "illiteracy," and similar symptoms of oppression, goes a long way to address the problems of Third World "underdevelopment." These were the insights of the anti-colonial writers in the post-war generation.

Memmi and Fanon largely engage in a structural and cultural analysis of colonial society. They take as their model the Maghrib, the Arab "West" dominated mainly by the French, often called "French North Africa." Fanon, a Martiniquan, had been influenced by the work of Aimé Césaire and by the cultural nationalism of the Negritude movement. He saw the prospect of Algerian independence was based upon ostensibly similar principles: self-determination and a nationalism comprised of nativist and cosmopolitan features. Algerian revolutionary nationalism was a project he understood and with which he could empathize. Memmi, his contemporary, wrote about Tunisia, a part of the Maghrib which, along with Morocco and Algeria, comprised French North Africa. Memmi identified both as a native Tunisian and as a *colon.* He supported revolutionary nationalism, if with some reservations.

It can be generally observed that the nationalist movements in the Maghrib assumed a Muslim nativist tenor. The slogan of the Algerian reformists, for example, suggests as much: "Arabic is my language, Algeria is my country, Islam is my religion" (Stora 16). Even so, the slogan was invoked by moderates who early on saw the movement as culturally nationalist rather than as revolutionary. Laroui observes that the cultural character of the reform movement responded to the debilitated conditions of native life under French colonialism:

> Small wonder if at a time when his country escaped him, when he was losing the command of his language, when his religion was degenerating to meaningless gestures, the Maghribi should have begun to say to himself: my country, my religion, my language. Here indeed was an awakening, but at the historically lowest level. (*History of the Maghrib* 343)

But the character of the nationalist movement was by no means uniform. It was as much secular as religious. In some instances, it subsumed features of internationalist and metropolitan radicalism. These latter features typically have been seen as European influences and, ironically, as an unwitting consequence of cultural imperialism. Observers have often commented that the early nationalist movement in Algeria incorporated French concepts of liberty, equality, fraternity. As Malley observes, they also adapted the assimilation doctrine to native concerns:

> Turning the colonial discourse against itself, assimilationists would speak in the name of an Algerian identity that, in the image of its French counterpart, was territorially defined. Even as they accepted the premise of European presence, they developed an ethnonational narrative in which Algerian soil was particularly Algerian, possessing its own identity, its own interests, and, if followed, its own representatives (who, of course, were the assimilationists themselves.) In short, the assimilationists (along with others) contributed both to the territorialization of identity and to the notion that legitimate power meant the proper representation of the Algerians' common interests. (43)

But apart from such influences, Maghribi nationalism evolved after the Second World War toward the objective of actual independence.[12] The independence movement was generally reactionary toward Europeans, Jews, and local ethnic *colons*. Significantly, Memmi claimed all of these identities, as well as native identity: "I was a sort of half-breed of colonization, understanding everyone because I belonged completely to no one" *Colonizer and the Colonized* xvi). He saw revolutionary nationalism (i.e., independence) as the most logical course for local society.[13] He described how the local hegemony derived from colonial forces. It would only fall, he argued, when the apparatuses of coercion were repelled or removed. The disparities of colonial life were material, and were linked to the metropole as certainly as the "periphery" was shackled to the "center."

In *The Colonizer and the Colonized* Memmi describes the oppressive features which characterize colonial society. As he pursued his study, he writes, he found that his observations transcended his own experience as a French colonial subject in Tunisia and pertain broadly to all oppressed people, to "the fate of a multitude across the world" (ix). Though hesitant at first, he eventually came to recognize an "inventory of conditions of colonized people" (viii). He found as well that his depictions of colonial life also caught the imagination of a generation engaged in liberation struggle:

> It was my readers—not all of them Tunisian—who later convinced me that this portrait was equally theirs . . . So many different persons saw themselves in this portrait that it became impossible to pretend that

> it was mine alone, or only that of colonized Tunisians, or even North Africans. I was told that in many parts of the world the colonial police confiscated the book in the cells of the militant nationalists. I am convinced that I gave them nothing they did not already know, had not already experienced; but as they recognized their own emotions, their revolt, their aspirations, I suppose they appeared more legitimate to them. (viii-ix)

Memmi offers two "portraits," those of the two protagonists to whom the book title refers. Again like Fanon, he felt that the conflict of the colonizer and the colonized was the inherent tension in colonial society. Though he does not use the term, Memmi describes the peripheral "social formation" of colonial society. Implicit in his discussion is the idea that military coercion, or colonial violence, is always present in local society. This violence need not be overt. The society which is shaped by it perpetuates the colonial authority, its system of privileges and lacks, oppression and rule. The social formation of the colony has already shaped the relations of the two protagonists: they are antagonists. Their relations are inherently violent and opposed.

Memmi's views basically concur with those of Fanon and Sartre. Sartre, referring to the compatibility of Memmi's views upon colonial society and his own, makes the qualification that, "The whole difference between us arises perhaps because he sees a situation where I see a system."[14] All three writers saw a colonial world built upon violence which could only be remade through total revolution. If Memmi does not actually endorse armed struggle, he advocates the "process of liquidating colonization" (151), and he is nonetheless categorical: "The refusal of the colonized cannot be anything but absolute, that is, not only revolt, but a revolution" (150). This and not peaceable, gradual—ineffectual—"reform" was the means of liberation from colonial oppression. Militancy was the material option; ultimately it emerged from the conditions created by the colonial system.

The idea of violence, its necessity and inevitability in the struggle for liberation, was a concept shared by many liberation theorists of the postwar period, especially in regard to the Third World. An entire discourse was based upon it, and it was of necessity populist and accessible. Theory had evolved out of real struggle, or revolutionary *"praxis,"* as it was sometimes called. For this reason it is not surprising that Sartre, who had been an engaged observer if not a partisan of the French Resistance, recognized the place of armed struggle. If during the postwar, one mainly heard the merits of non-violence and passive resistance endlessly extolled, it was arguably a *status quo* response to the real threat of theorized, articulated, and mobilized revolutionary violence.

But ironically perhaps, the idea of *necessary* violence was as much a humanistic concept as that of non-violence. "The *guerrilla,*" observed Che Guevara in his handbook on the subject, "is motivated by love."

It was also a pragmatic recognition which saw that revolutionary violence was needed or inevitable. The anti-colonial writers acknowledged the pervasive violence of the metropole and the concretized, oppressive relations of colonial society. These conditions could not be "reformed" through passive resistance or good intentions. Memmi argues that within the colonial system, personal intention and individual will have no material consequence. The respective roles of both *colon* and native have been defined and concretized by the material conditions of local society. These conditions are categorical by design; the *colons* are imposed and the natives are denied. One exists at the expense of the other. Their relations themselves only exist at all within the context of exploitation. Neither the colonized person who identifies with European values, or who wishes to assimilate the metropole—nor the *colon* who would resist the exploitation of the natives by the mother country, or conversely, who believes he has "pulled himself up by his own bootstraps"—has any true effect, according to Memmi. The will and the choices of each protagonist are caught within the material framework of the colonial apparatus. Local life, whether public or private, conforms to categorical reality because injustice is inherent in nearly every conceivable aspect.

Or to put it another way, political self-determination is antithetical to colonial authority. Here is the old problem of reform versus revolution. Colonialism could not be reformed into a "just" system of patronage and "protection." The creation of a just society necessarily entailed the destruction of colonial "patronage." Memmi is correct to insist upon this point, as did Fanon and Sartre. Metropolitan hegemony exists *sui generis* upon the exploitation of a native under class in the periphery; it does not assimilate the oppressed into a "better" social position. Colonial hegemony would eventually have to go—if only because the metropole could not sustain the escalating commitment to repress the peripheral society. Thus Memmi observed that imperialism carries the seeds of its own destruction. But even that end is not so much accomplished by personal intentions as by dialectical effect, according to this view. Indeed in Algeria this is largely what happened. However militarily superior to the Algerian nationalist forces, France simply could not continue to allocate ever greater resources to fight a determined guerrilla war. One thinks also of the withdrawal from Vietnam after a similar anti-colonial struggle, culminating in the French defeat at Dien Bien Phu.

Given the structure of the peripheral social formation, then, individual will or personal intentions would have had little impact upon colonial life.

Both protagonists of colonial society could only try to take the other's place. Fanon discusses that the native longs to take the place of the settler.[15] The opposite would be true as well; the settler longs to take the place of the native. He or she may wish to take the place of the native not only in literal terms, but symbolically, as well. The symbolic assumption of the place or position of the native by the settler would suppose a cultural legitimacy where none otherwise exists. Colonial culture is organized around this pursuit. This is evident in many ways. For example, the very name of the Algerian settlers, *les pied noirs,* makes a nativist claim. The name is translated as "black feet," or "dirty feet." Sometimes it is taken to signify not the farmer's feet but his workboots.[16] "There are at least two schools of thought on the origins of *pied noir;*" comments Horne, "one, on account of the black polished shoes worn by the French military; the other based on the somewhat patronizing view of metropolitan Frenchmen that the *colons* had had their feet burned black by an excess of the African sun" (30 n.) Either way, the name *pied noir* refers to the Algerian landscape, the soil, and to the farmer's figurative and literal standing upon it. Symbolic references to the soil or land are called "autochthony." Structural anthropologists have identified these kinds of references in various myths and traditions as attempts to establish and define a native identity which is linked to land tenure.[17] Thus the discursive figure of the *pied noir* is an "autochthonous" concept which establishes a symbolic connection to the Algerian soil. The image of the settler in colonial culture is a mythic image. Memmi makes mention of it and its circulation in French North Africa:

> We sometimes enjoy picturing the colonizer as a tall man, bronzed by the sun, wearing Wellington boots, proudly leaning on a shovel—as he rivets his gaze far away on the horizon of his land . . . I don't know whether this portrait ever did correspond to reality or whether it was limited to the engravings on colonial bank notes. (*Colonizer and Colonized* 3)

The boots and shovel as much as the landscape in the icon described by Memmi characterize the figure as a *pied noir.* Memmi suggests that the image is a superstructural myth, as is evidenced by its replication on currency. This seems true enough; however, there is surely more than an economic motivation. Regardless of how the term, *les pieds noirs,* came to designate the French *colons* in Algeria, it is certain that their possession of the land, as well as their presence as landless workers in towns and cities, was an issue of disputed legitimacy. The *pied noir* image thus attempts to establish legitimacy for the colonizer by invoking a native identity through an autochthonous reference to the land. Ersatz nativism can be seen as an attempt to reduce *colon* anxiety. It seeks to erase the terms of colonial violence by which French Algerians inherited a privileged place in the land of their birth. It would dispel the claims of dispossessed Arabs and Berbers, i.e., the majority population of Muslim natives who were relegated to second-class citizenry by means of colonial violence. The mythic image of the *pied noir* is therefore motivated by the tension within colonial society. This tension arises from the double standard, the two zones separate and unequal, of the colonizer and the colonized.

In effect, the *pied noir* image attempts to normalize colonial society by disavowing the existence of the Algerian natives. The disavowal would allow the settler to assume the role of native.[18] Now it is the French Algerians who are the "natives," born and raised in the colony; after all, "Algeria *is* France," as the slogan went.[19] Yet however much the concept of *pied noir* nativism was invoked or promulgated, the claims of the majority population could not be refuted, nor, indefinitely, simply ignored. If the settler wanted to take the place of the native, then the native, as Fanon says, wanted to take the settler's place: "One step more and he is ready to fight to be more than the settler. In fact, he has already decided to eject him and to take his place; as we see, it is a whole material and moral universe which is breaking up" (*Wretched of the Earth* 44–45). The trading—or taking—of places in either case would occur through violence. Thus like violence, the tension of disputed legitimacy would have expressed itself within the everyday culture of colonial society. Symbolic and narrative strategies would have evolved to dispel the tension created by the material practices of colonialism—or what Sartre calls colonial *praxis.*

The tension of disputed legitimacy can be seen as the central theme of *The Stranger,* the novel by Albert Camus. *Pied noir* tension can be seen to motivate the actions and sentiments of the protagonist, Meursault, throughout the story. This motivation supplies a great deal of meaning to a narrative which has often been described as artfully meaningless, as an exposition in existential humanism.[20] But one might see that *The Stranger* illustrates Camus' ideas about the *pied noir* predicament and the need for social consciousness. The key scene in the novel in which Meursault shoots the native man on the beach is a telling moment for the position of the *pied noir* in Algerian society. It enacts a symbolic displacement of the native Algerian, the "Arab," by the French-Algerian *colon,* Meursault:

> Then everything began to reel before my eyes, a fiery gust came from the sea, while the sky cracked in two, from end to end, and a great sheet of flame poured down through the rift. Every nerve in my body was a steel spring, and my grip closed on the revolver. The trigger gave, and

> the smooth underbelly of the butt jogged my palm. And so, with that crisp, whipcrack sound, it all began. I shook off my sweat and the clinging veil of light. I knew I'd shattered the balance of the day . . . (76)

This dramatic portrayal of the landscape is significant to Meursault's act. The landscape is an autochthonous reference, and therefore has emphasis in the key moment. The intensity of the sea and sky seems to impel Meursault to shoot. The "balance of the day" he observes can be understood as the *status quo* of tensions between the two claimants of nativist legitimacy, and it is "shattered" by colonial gunshot. In a real way, the *pied noir's* nativist claims to Algeria are based upon such acts. *Pied noir* nativism is contingent upon the displacement of the Algerian natives.

In the beginning, Meursault himself does not understand his own act. It seems to have happened without his conscious will. He sees the confrontation on the beach as simply "a matter of pure chance" (110). But the weight of the sun on Meursault's trigger hand can be seen as the impetus of colonial relations. It illustrates Memmi's conviction that the *colon's* role is oppressive, regardless of one's intent, because the colonial system has already shaped the nature of social relations. Indeed, Meursault's intentions have nothing to do with the act of murder. He had not intended to shoot. He had no quarrel with the Arab. Rather he felt some sympathy for him and had restrained the seedy criminal, Raymond, from firing upon him. When Meursault fires, it seems to be a dissociative act; he didn't pull the trigger, but rather, "the trigger gave." Yet the four additional shots he fires into the "inert body" of the victim suggest the motivation of will, however much unconscious. This motivation is at the heart of Meursault's predicament, and by extension, of the whole of *pied noir* society. The problem with which the narrative deals is the bringing forward of that motivation to conscious self awareness—and the moral questions which consciousness necessarily entails. This is ultimately the question which underlies the magistrate's interrogation of Meursault:

> "Why did you pause between the first and second shot?"
>
> I seemed to see it hovering again before my eyes, the red glow of the beach, and to feel that fiery breath on my cheeks—and, this time, I made no answer. (84)

Instead of stating a reason for why he fired the subsequent round of shots, Meursault again recalls the landscape where the murder has taken place. The metanymic substitution of the landscape for a stated reason suggests that the landscape *is* the reason. The key event in the story is thus seen as paradigmatic of the struggle over disputed land. Indeed the landscape has been portrayed as the motive all along; it is that which impelled Meursault to fire the first shot. Here the autochthonous referent is apparent in the scene of the action. Symbolically, the *pied noir* man has shot the native over the pervasive colonial dispute about land. But Meursault himself cannot articulate this reason because it is too inherent to *colon* identity for him to recognize. He takes no responsibility for his act, but it attaches to him all the same. As Haddour comments, "Homicide expresses the colonizer's unconscious desire to eradicate the difference of the colonized Arab" (*Colonial Myths* 55).

The autochthony of the *pied noir* figure of *The Stranger* is problematized by the author. The *pied noir* Meursault is not simply associated with the landscape—but with the murder of the native, as well. Meursault's act reveals that murder is implicit in the *pied noir's* association with the land. This is an important observation for a reader to make. The implication of murder exposes exactly what the idealized version of the settler image seeks to cover up. The figure of Meursault critically opposes the propaganda image which Memmi observed on the face of colonial bank notes. Meursault is the settler in the very act of "settling" the colonial dispute over land.

If Meursault is unconscious of his motivation, the magistrate also fails to recognize it. Having secured Meursault's confession, he is yet unable to extract his penitence. Frustrated, he brandishes a crucifix at Meursault and launches into a religious lecture about repentance and salvation. This scene portrays Meursault's lack of religious faith, a lack which alleges his "criminality" in French Catholic *pied noir* society. His lack of faith also emphasizes agnosticism as a tenet of existential thought. But the interrogation scene has further significance. It establishes a symbolic link between the crucifix and Meursault, or, between the protagonist and the idea of a human sacrifice, a scapegoat, offered for the "sins" of the local society. Indeed, Meursault will be executed for acting out the crime in which all the *pieds noirs* have collectively participated. He will die, much like their own preconscious recognition, so that they will not have to admit their common crime. Meursault's withheld penitence implies the hypocrisy of the magistrate and of the state which he represents. Of course, Camus was an adamant critic of capital punishment ("Reflections on the Guillotine"). He would have noted the hypocrisy of a state which gave a nod to French Catholicism as it honed the guillotine all the while. But Meursault's interrogation also exposes and criticizes the hypocrisy of a local society which fails to recognize its own sins.

Indeed, the colonial state and society appear to be premised upon the sanctioned acts of murder. And in this regard, *pied noir* society would rather condemn one who might otherwise be a catalyst for self awareness. This is the meaning of Meursault's human(ist) sacrifice. As a scapegoat, his execution will purge both the guilt and self-conscious recognition of the collective crime of colonial society. This reading of the novel suggests that *pied noir* society itself is founded upon the murder and dispossession of the Algerian natives. The magistrate, the administrators, clerks, prosecutor, defense, witnesses, jury and spectators at Meursault's trial are all as guilty as he. Their outrage occurs partly because his act would make the murderous terms of their own existence obvious—for they are as unconscious as he. And they wish to remain unconscious. Otherwise they must come to know themselves as criminals, too. They resent Meursault for making themselves so apparent.

The event of murder had been predetermined by Meursault's position in society as a *colon,* though he is oblivious of it. He is oblivious in general to the other consequences of his existence. Even his filial relation implies a commitment about which he is indifferent. However, he is shortly made aware that his indifference cannot be tolerated by a colonial society so strongly linked to its own "mother." Indeed, Meursault's offense is that he understands himself as an autonomous man who exists in and of himself, separate from the society which has produced him. Meursault has acted without intent, yet consequence attends the act, rather than the intention. If his tragedy is his unconsciousness, he is victimized because he does not recognize his own, ascribed, role in the colonial system. He discovers too late the potential of his own will and only from the inside of his prison cell. But there is a deeper offense which Meursault has committed against the *pieds noirs.* Displacement is Meursault's crime, not because he has killed off the native but because he has taken his place too literally. As a French-Algerian "nativist," Meursault rejects allegiance to a metropolitan "motherland." For this crime Meursault incurs the death penalty because society—his society, "French Algeria"—negates him, existentially speaking. As a French-Algerian "native," he is a contradiction in terms. But moreover, he must be punished because his murderous act of nativism subverts French primacy. Camus' statement is telling: "In this society, all men who do not grieve at their mother's burial risk being condemned to death" (qtd. in Haddour 59 n. 57).

Meursault's rejection of metropolitan France is evident in his indifference towards his mother's death. Madame Meursault is a metaphor for the rejected mother country. The "old folks' home" in which she has died also refers to the metropole. This home for "invalids" likewise suggests the invalidity of metropolitan society to Meursault's own sense of identity. Even on the road to her grave, it is the Algerian sun and heat, autochthonous imagery, which preoccupy him. However, his lack of sentiment for his "mother" is an affront to the reactionary *pieds noirs,* symbolized by the audience and jury which attend his trial. To them, Meursault's indifference is evidence of his guilt:

> After asking the jury and my lawyer if they had any questions, the Judge heard the doorkeeper's evidence. On stepping into the box the man threw a glance at me, then looked away. Replying to questions, he said that I'd declined to see Mother's body, I'd smoked cigarettes and drank *café au lait.* It was then I felt a sort of wave of indignation spreading through the courtroom, and for the first time I understood that I was guilty. They got the doorkeeper to repeat what he had said about the coffee and my smoking. (112)

Meursault himself only realizes his filial "guilt" when the other *pieds noirs* make it apparent to him through their disapproval. They are indignant over his lack of emotion for his mother. But Meursault does not grieve her loss for she was already distant. His "mother" had long been unresponsive to him: "for years she'd never had a word to say to me, and I could see she was moping, with no one to talk to" (58). But for the other *pieds noirs,* this is tantamount to matricide.

Meursault's indifference toward his mother is similar to his lack of enthusiasm about the offer of a job transfer to Paris. He is unimpressed by the promotion—and notably, he regards the City of Light as "a dingy sort of town," inhabited by pigeons and pale denizens (54). Not unrelatedly, he takes no interest in culinary pleasures; he goes alone to a diner, the unremarkable Celeste's, or else he stands and eats from the pan (25, 29). He has no regard for the kind of bourgeois values which are seen as typically French, and after all, the importance of food is associated as much with the French as with one's own mother. As Tarrow observes, "*The Stranger* . . . constitutes an attack on the accepted norms of bourgeois society" (66). But further, Meursault's sentiments reflect his particular sense of *pied noir* estrangement—the predicament which he represents. The "dark courtyards" of Paris have nothing to do with the sun-drenched streets of Algiers. Meursault harbors no nostalgia because he is not in exile.

This interpretation sees a different sort of estrangement than the existential alienation which has long been attributed by critics to Meursault, likely following Sartre's reading in 1942. Sartre described *The Stranger* as "a classical work, an orderly work, composed about the absurd and against the absurd" (qtd. in Aronson 14). The protagonist's consequential act has often been overlooked for the universal humanist themes which regard "Man's alienation" in modern society. In the existential reading of the narrative, Meursault's guilt attaches not to the murder he has committed—but to his peers' outrage over his lack of sentimentality for his mother's death. His seeming lack of "natural" sentiment is the "crime" which makes him a social outsider, a "criminal." The protagonist himself considers this irony before and during his trial. Certainly, this irony is a central element of the text. But Meursault's estrangement can also be seen as symptomatic of his French Algerian "nativism." His sense of himself as a French Algerian is different than that of the other *pieds noirs.* His conception not only rejects the primacy of metropolitan France and posits the legitimacy of his "Algerianess." But it also contains the seed of ethical consciousness about *colon* society in regard to Algerian natives. The *pied noir* predicament is a singular issue which *The Stranger* addresses specifically, apart from its conventional reading as a hallmark text of existential humanism. To understand Camus' work in this way, as a work of *pied noir* representation, contextualizes it among the postcolonial writings of Memmi, Fanon, and Sartre, even as Camus arrived at different conclusions than his contemporaries.

This view of *The Stranger* also recognizes the "writerly" aspect of the work, to borrow a term from Roland Barthes.[21] The misplacement of guilt is an intentional narrative strategy on the part of the author. It is an important feature of the story. But this does not mean that the murder victim is meant to be inconsequential to the reader—though readers have often overlooked the murdered man for the existential act. Rather, the disregard for the native victim of *colon* society seems to be an important concept which the author wanted to portray. This is made apparent by a reading which emphasizes the particularity of the *pied noir* predicament—rather than the reading which regards the universal humanist themes. Camus' later writings directly address the *pied noir* predicament at the time of the Algerian War. Those works give additional weight to the interpretation of *The Stranger* as a work of *pied noir* representation.

Meursault's guilt in the murder of the native man is fundamental to the story's various themes, though it has tended to be misunderstood by many readers. Taking a postcolonialist view, for example, Edward Said discusses that the killing of the Arab has been overlooked because the universal humanist interpretation of the work is consistent with the French imperialist perspective upon the colonial subject (*Culture and Imperialism 169–185*). Said points out that the universal humanist reading elides a more critical, political recognition of the colonial world and its texts. Indeed, Meursault's predicament has been imagined by many critics in similarly abstract terms as by the blurb on the back-cover of the circa mid-1970s

English paperback edition: "A terrifying picture of a man victimized by life itself—he is a faceless man, who has committed a pointless murder . . ." An earlier edition of the same English text describes how "[l]ife begins to stalk [the protagonist] quietly and slowly, but inexorably," and calls the work "an indelible picture of a human being [i.e., Meursault] helpless in life's grip." The blurb quotes Justin O'Brien's contemporary view that Camus "has set himself among the moralists who discourse, for our edification, upon our most fundamental problems." In both of these editions, the protagonist, Meursault, is described as the "victim" of events. The murdered man, meanwhile, seems to be the unacknowledged catalyst of these events. (More recently Haddour, in a Derridean vein, sees the murder victim of *L'Etranger* as the actual "outsider" of the narrative text.[22]) These readings certainly support Said's point that the Arab's death has been overlooked in favor of a "universalist" interpretation, viz., "our most fundamental problems." However Said also contends that Camus himself probably didn't give the Arab's death much thought, either. Similarly, Ronald Aronson comments that "Camus never acknowledged that such violence was central either to his place in the world or to the society in which he was raised" (33). Yet one might disagree with the views that Arab death in Camus' novel is inconsequential both to the text and to the author. It seems instead to be the point: a criticism of colonial society and a questioning of *pied noir* legitimacy. Indeed, the record of Camus' opinions about the Algerian War attests to his grievous concern with colonial violence and the casualties of both natives and *colons.*

One may observe that the murder of the native man in *The Stranger,* and the flawed trial which results, are critical elements of the political subtext in the story and of the theme of conscious will. The author's intentional, discursive displacement of the murder victim is made all the more apparent as a textual strategy in light of comparison with another novel which employs the same strategy. Richard Wright also utilizes discursive displacement, for thematic purposes, in his novel *Native Son.* In both texts, the murder victim(s) and the flawed trial which results are literary constructions which critique an unjust society built upon class and racial oppression. Furthermore, both works criticize capital punishment as hypocritical, state-sanctioned murder.

Meursault's fate is much like that of Bigger Thomas, the protagonist of *Native Son.* Meursault, like Bigger, is tried and condemned not for the murder he has committed but for the social taboo which he is presumed to have violated. Both Meursault and Bigger have transgressed their respective societies' "normative" codes. For Bigger the transgression is miscegenation, an alleged sexual crime. For Meursault it is a sin of omission; he will not claim metropolitan France as do the other *pieds noirs* but instead claims a "nativist" identity. Indeed, Meursault's nativism is also a crime of miscegenation, one of origin rather than sexuality. And similarly, Meursault's actual murder of the Arab is deemed inconsequential to the symbolic matricide he is imagined by the jury to have committed—much as Bigger's actual rape of Bessie and his actual murders of the two women are deemed inconsequential to the crime imagined by the jury, the imagined rape of Mary, the rich white girl.

Both Meursault and Bigger are *apriori* criminals who exist "outside" of society and its so-called normative proscriptions. These norms disavow the violence and oppression upon which the society is sustained—racial violence and racial oppression in both cases. The social norms repress the public consciousness about material violence, for consciousness implies a threat to the *status quo.* The two criminals have therefore disrupted the social proscriptions—or worse, revealed them to be the illusions of the superstructure. In *Native Son,* the capitalist Dalton is implicated in the architecture of his own daughter's murder for he has helped to produce and sustain the conditions which led to the fateful meeting of Mary and Bigger. Similarly in *The Stranger,* Meursault's act has been pre-established by the very nature of colonial society, its social formation. Indeed the social formation is itself implicated in the acts of murder in both novels.

Furthermore, Wright's narrative shows that Bigger's guilt is less important than how it may be used by the prosecutor and the defense lawyer, Max, to hedge the "cold war" of their respective ideologies, American capitalism and American communism. One compares Meursault's case and sees that his death figures as well into the narration of colonial ideology. Meursault must be purged from society as the consciousness of a collective guilt engendered by the material base—and one may say the same also of Bigger. Meursault's execution will sustain the illusion of *pied noir* legitimacy where the reality of colonial usurpation would otherwise be apparent. Bigger's execution will allege that *his* violence, and not that which has created the impoverished under class—the violence of capitalism—is the bane of American society. Both protagonists therefore cannot exist materially within society, as the very terms of society negate their existence and make their identities impossible. But rather it is their actions which negate the illusions of the superstructure and which makes society's proscriptions impossible.

If some readers have missed the subtleties of plot in *The Stranger* or in *Native Son,* it is not because the authors had overlooked the implications of the protagonists' actions. Indeed subtlety of plot, or thematic irony, is the point in both cases. For example, Bigger, like Meursault, does not recognize or articulate his motivations even to himself. When troubling, preconscious thoughts threaten to emerge into awareness, Bigger "blots them out." He does evolve the consciousness which in the end redeems him, but as with Meursault it comes with irony and it comes too late. Bigger's gestures toward the humanist social collective are made from inside his prison cell, on the eve of his execution. Here is another similarity to Meursault.

Not coincidentally, Wright's friendships with Camus, Sartre, and Simone de Beauvoir in postwar Paris "exposed [him] to the core of French existentialism."[23] Works by Wright such as *Native Son* and *The Outsider* introduced existential thought into the American novel. Wright also wrote about colonialism and revolutionary nationalism in the Third World, as in *The Color Curtain,* his report on the Bandung Conference of 1955. Thus were the international issues of the day, which were also the topic of much Francophone debate, made accessible to American readers. The evident, Franco-American intertextuality of these contemporary authors is notable for many reasons. Certainly it stands to reason that if a writer's engagment with colonial politics were so deliberate, his fiction would unlikely skirt them. In both *The Stranger* and *Native Son,* the narrative compels the larger questions about the social formations which contextualize the protagonists' respective human conditions. Such questions were the fundamental issues of liberal humanism and of the liberation theories of the era.

In the text in question, Meursault had initially acted without awareness or intent. But through the consequences of his actions, Meursault evolves from a socially unconscious young man to become one painfully aware of his own position *vis-à-vis* society. He has not only found himself at odds with native society by virtue of who and what he is—a *colon.* But the nativist identity he has chosen for himself—through his act—has also put him at odds with *colon* society, a French Algeria which derives its cultural legitimacy from the metropole but which will not admit that colonial violence has authored it. But finally, he is at odds with his own *pied noir* nativism itself authored by colonial force, a "nativism" already delegitimized. Meursault is undone by the concrete reality of the colonial social formation. His fate ultimately foretells how the *pied noir* predicament will be resolved—for as the symbolic "mother" passes away, so goes her "native" son.

Although his protagonist was unconscious, Camus was not. The distaste with which Meursault regards the police and their liberties attests that the author recognized in colonial society the police state endemic to the Vichy fascism he resisted in France. Perhaps Meursault might have resisted his role as a collaborator in the colonial system, if only he had more than the nascent insight of an aversion to authoritarianism and bourgeois pretensions.

The possibility of resistance seems to be suggested by the narrative, but not without irony. The mechanism by which Meursault develops consciousness is his own systemic exploitation. He suffers and thus becomes aware; but isn't it too late? Is his self awareness pointless? Or does it confer meaning upon his life and his actions? The novel may beg these existential questions; but the narrative tells of the necessity of consciousness. After all, it is not too late for the reader.

The last point, the relevancy of the reader, is an aspect of all the works by the authors considered here. Fanon and Memmi, Sartre, Camus and Wright were not detached observers of the issues about which they wrote. They addressed a literate and informed readership and sought to influence opinions about critical issues such as totalitarianism, racism, and social injustice. This immediacy is apparent with the works of Fanon and Memmi, and in an American context, with those of Wright. It is also explicit in the journalism of Camus and Sartre, if dealt with more conceptually in their novels. However, the context of their works and their many shared assumptions about the human condition did not mean that their thoughts in all ways concurred. Disagreement over communism ended the confraternity of Sartre and Camus. However, the Algerian War and the question of Algerian national independence was as well a key issue which divided the thought and opinions of the two modern moralists.

Chapter Three

Camus, Djebar, and the "Non-Color" of Nonviolence

3.1 "A CASUISTRY OF BLOOD"

The notion of human will is variously problematized in the works of Fanon, Memmi, Sartre and Camus. The former two felt that the inhibition of will was a primary feature of oppressive, colonial society; and yet they recognized this same will as the very force which would create the new conditions of independent nationhood. Importantly for Fanon and Memmi, this force was not the good will of reform but the liberatory will of revolution. Camus also felt that human will was a creative force. But he differed with the others over the application of will in revolutionary violence. If the others saw that local violence was the inevitable response to imperial violence, to the violence of underdevelopment, Camus did not concur. Yet ultimately, the four thinkers upheld the notion of human will as the force for material change.

Camus shared with his contemporaries the criticism of colonial injustice. But he saw the colonial conflict differently, at least in regard to Algeria. Unlike other critics, he felt that the system could be reformed. He held that social justice in Algeria could be achieved through willful, peaceful means—whereas Fanon had observed, "That affirmed intention . . . can only triumph if we use all means to turn the scale, including, of course, that of violence" (37). The point of departure essentially lies in how each one saw decolonization. Camus believed in the proprietary role of metropolitan France, even as he condemned the injustices of the colonial system. Fanon and Sartre recognized the role of armed struggle to achieve nationalist self determination, even as they did not readily embrace the object of bloodshed.[1] Memmi, too, recognized the material reality of the independence struggle. Ultimately, native independence was at the heart of Camus' differences with his contemporaries.

Camus' views about the "Algerian question" seem to break also with the tenor of existentialism which places primacy upon acts of will.[2] Sartre, typifying the existentialist credo, had written that "Not only is man what he conceives himself to be, but he is also only what he wills himself to be . . . Man is nothing else but what he makes of himself. Such is the first principle of existentialism" (*Existentialism and Human Emotions* 15). Yet Camus did not consider himself to be an existentialist and on occasion publicly articulated his rejection of the linking of his name and work to Sartre's. Aronson discusses some reasons for Camus' demurral; but he points out that the similarities between the two men were sufficient and reasonable criteria for them to be linked (58–61). Indeed it seems moot to deliberate whether or not Camus' work is in keeping with the tradition of existentialism. Still, it is interesting to observe how his views about the Algerian War may alternatively inform or revise the conventional view of the author as an existentialist.

Contrary to the act of self will, Camus seems instead paralyzed by the implications of the Algerian struggle. He feels that the intellectual cannot or should not advocate one or another protagonist in the bloody conflict. His denunciation of the violence committed by both sides appears to sidestep the larger issue of the colonial oppression which has motivated the conflict:

> To justify himself, each relies on the other's crime. But that is a casuistry of blood, and it strikes me that an intellectual cannot become involved in it, unless he takes up arms himself. When violence answers violence in a growing frenzy that makes the simple language of reason impossible, the role of intellectuals cannot be, as we read everyday, to excuse from a distance one of the violences and condemn the other. This has the double result of enraging the violent group that is condemned and encouraging to greater violence the violent group that is exonerated. If they do not join the combatants themselves, their role (less spectacular to be sure!) must be merely to strive for pacification so that reason will again have a chance. (*Resistance, Rebellion, and Death* 116)

Camus' concern that increased violence will result if the intellectual takes sides seems patently outside the existentialist notions about individual actions and social consequences.[3] The existentialist acts upon his values and thus creates the terms to which he will subsequently respond. He or she does not refrain from action out of fear for the possible consequences, for new acts will account for new consequences. Camus seems here to be removed from such a notion. But of course, his inaction is also a choice or reflects an intention, if a passive one. It is not merely the possibility of unfavorable results which gives him pause. Rather, he cannot endorse the actions of others because he cannot also act on their behalf. He cannot endorse actions which he himself would not take up. He commits not to action but to inaction, to an end to the violence. This choice seems to be a compromise of conscience. But there is a leap of faith between his position and an end to the armed conflict. He admits that he wrestled with his own convictions regarding the Algerian War (*Resistance, Rebellion, and Death* 111–112).

Camus' opposition to violence was not solely a matter of conscientious objection. He was opposed not just on moral grounds but also because he opposed Algerian nationalism. He was not, however, opposed to native demands for civil rights and for an end to colonial oppression. But he thought these demands could be fulfilled within the context of French Algerian society. He envisioned reforms in the legislative and juridicial terms which pertained to Algerian natives and in the inclusion of natives in the wider French nation, i.e., the metropole. Unlike Sartre and Fanon, both who supported full independence for Algeria, Camus did not support independence from metropolitan France.

In "An Appeal for a Civilian Truce in Algeria," a lecture he delivered in Algiers in 1956, Camus proposes that all participants in the conflict refrain from acts of civilian terrorism, as a single step toward peaceful negotiations. He would like to see the end of the conflict altogether, but fears that a call for a moratorium would undermine his proposal and thus the objective to avoid civilian casualties. The proposal of a truce addresses the "two Algerian populations," French and Arab, as Camus describes them. One may assume he appealed to the French Algerian irregulars as much as to the native guerrillas, though he does not name them. Apart from the issue of civilian death, Camus maintains he would not discuss the terms of the conflict or the demands of the various parties. In the lecture, he recognizes that both French and Arabs "have a right to security and dignity on our common soil" (*Resistance, Rebellion, and Death* 137). Though he refrains from political discussion, Camus' position is apparent. He sees one nation, unified by "our love of our common soil, and our anguish" (133). This nation is French Algeria. He describes it as a dysfunctional family, as a country where the French and Arabs are, ironically, already in solidarity—whether it be the union of death or, if they choose, that of life. He also sees it as a "community of hope:"

> On this soil there are a million Frenchmen who have been here for a century, millions of Moslems, either Arabs or Berbers, who have been here for centuries, and several vigorous religious communities. Those men must live at the crossroads where history put them. (136)

Camus' hope for fraternity was apparently sincere. However, there is a blind spot in his vision and it disregards a fundamental matter. His assertion that the peoples of French Algeria must live where "history" has put them rather dismisses the very agency which has brought them into conflict, if together. This agency is French colonialism. Camus' gesture thus equalizes the social status of the "French and Arab" peoples of Algeria and their claims to the land. But in fact their respective statuses and claims were anything but equal. Their inequality, even on the day of Camus' lecture, was significantly imposed through French colonial law. Nor was the historical tenure of Berbers, Arabs and Frenchmen in Algeria analogous, and this not only regards their disparate numbers or their length of residency but many other social and cultural factors as well.

Moreover, a couple of referents in Camus' speech raise the flag of Western modernization discourse. This important observation points out the contradictions in Camus' ideas about colonial "reform." One recognizes that the decontextualized, abstract referent of "history" in the passage above is typical of "modernization." Indeed, Camus also refers to the "ancient and deep origins of the Algerian tragedy" (134). As was discussed in the previous chapter on "modernization," discursive abstractions such as "ancient ethnic conflicts," and the like, obscure the material bases from which conflicts really derive. They simplify the conflict over land to the irreducible, essential notions of "history" and of "ancient hostilities." They also obscure the claims and positions of the protagonists in the conflict. The problem occurs in Camus' speech; it conveys the sense of an essential old battle between old essential rivals. But in fact, the conflict of Frenchmen and Muslims was not so ancient, while the local communities of Berbers and Arabs were not so much in conflict.[4]

Camus felt that independence would economically destroy Algeria: "our two peoples would separate once and for all and Algeria would become for a long time a mass of ruins, whereas a mere effort of reflection today could still change things and avoid catastrophe" (140). As a measure of reflection which would stay the course of peace, he holds out the potential of European-directed economic development: "floods of riches will cover the continent and, overflowing even to us, will make our problems out of date and our hatreds null and void" (142). Camus seems to advocate the forfeiture of sovereignty for trickle-down economics. In fact, his ideas about the necessity of the metropole to Algeria are belied by the typical fallacies of modern development. Modernization portrays the impoverishment of the local society as a static, essential condition, rather than the effect of metropolitan exploitation. It offers a putative, "trickle-down" economic agenda. Indeed, Camus sees a flood of European riches trickling into Algeria and sweeping away the Algerian conflict, native poverty and peripheral "backwardness."

It seems that he might have known better. Camus ascribed to socialist principles although—or perhaps, consequently—he was staunchly critical of Soviet "internationalism." His intoning of the empty platitudes of capitalist development seems to conflict with a mind so intent on universal ethics. He understood the oppressive nature of European imperialism, but failed to recognize its reification in the capitalist bloc of the post-war West. One may be tempted to categorically attribute his failure of perspective to a vested interest as a *colon* in the preservation of French claims in Algeria. Memmi, contemporarily, had said about as much about Camus' ethical paralysis.[5] And Camus' own comment, an aside made at a lecture in Stockholm after having received the Nobel Prize for literature in 1957, can be (and has been) seen as a fundamental compromise of ethics in regard to the so-called Algerian Question: "I believe in justice, but I will defend my mother before justice" (qtd. in Stora 50). But one should also consider that Camus was writing out of the conditions of post-war France after a decade of capitalist reconstruction. He had seen what can be accomplished when "development" is applied to the infrastructure of a "local" society. Having witnessed the reconstruction of France after the devastation of war, Camus may well have thought that Western economic development would do the same for Algeria. This is suggested in his idea that "overflowing" riches would accompany peace there.[6]

The Marshall Plan had redeveloped the French infrastructure and, ostensibly, without compromising French sovereignty or French dignity. But Western capitalism has never seriously taken the infrastructure of the "Third World" as the object of development. Third World infrastructure has mainly been the object of "First World" hindrance; to develop a truly viable local infrastructure would only encourage local autonomy from the central interests. A well fed, well developed colony is no colony at all; for surfeit is an attribute of sovereignty just as lack indicates dependence. Rather the hindrance of local infrastructure is an apparent objective of Western development, in order to retain the central corporate interests and the patron-client relations. France was a First World country—this is why it was deemed important for reconstruction, among other reasons. But nothing about its own reconstruction would make it refrain from acting in Western self-interest in regard to "French Algeria." Thus development practices, as had been implemented in post-war France were quite a different matter than those which would be implemented in French Algeria. The kind of broad-scale reconstruction which characterized the Marshall Plan was never intended for Algeria. And of course, development in either case was not analogous because of the materiality of colonialism. World war was not the cause of political and economic adversity in Algeria as it had been in France, and this

Camus knew. The Algerian War was rather a consequence of colonial rule. Indeed to pursue an analogy, one would better see that the French Resistance and the Algerian guerrillas were acting respectively upon the principle of self-determination. Sartre recognized the principle in the Algerian conflict, even though he too, like Camus, had witnessed the reconstruction of France.

The war in Algeria was perhaps mostly a catastrophe for the minority classes which had prospered or which at least had lived better than the masses. Conversely, as Sartre points out, terror and violence, not peace and stability, were the everyday conditions for the native majority who lived under colonial rule: "there would be no contradiction there if terror reigned everywhere on earth" (50). Camus' hope for "pacification," for peace in Algeria, largely had resonance for the *colons* who experienced the war as an interruption, figuratively or literally, in their lives. But for oppressed natives, who suffered most of the human costs of war, it also brought an opportunity—however violent or fractious.

Camus' prospect of a "united" Algeria where the security of French *colons* was assured misses the point of nationalist struggle. As Halstead comments in the Moroccan case, "Even the most ardent French critics of colonial policy . . . believed that the roots of the [nationalist] movement were to be found in the perversion of the protectorate arrangement rather than in the arrangement itself" (29). Halstead might have been speaking of Camus in regard to the Algerian situation.[7] But aside from Camus' vested interest, there seems little doubt that he really did hope for a fraternal "French Algeria," where the commonwealth would be shared by the native majority and where native human rights would also be assured. These intentions were apparently at the heart of his vision. But Memmi would have observed that such good intentions really amounted to nothing in the face of the material interests of metropolitan power. Camus himself saw that his hope for peace was likely to be unrealized. Later, after withdrawing from public debate on the matter, he admits that: "[s]uch a position satisfies no one today, and I know in advance how it will be received by both sides. I sincerely regret it, but I cannot do violence to what I feel and what I believe. Besides, on this subject no one satisfies me either" (111).

3.2 NEW ALGERIA

Camus' vision of a French-Algerian peace accord, and ultimately, of social reform in Algeria, is based upon his positivist view of human will. Camus affirmed the primacy of individual will, even within the context of an oppressive colonial society. Moreover, Camus saw the collective will as the means of social reform. His views in this regard depart from Memmi's, who held that colonial society inhibits individual will. For Memmi, as for Fanon, the aim of collective will is to depose—not to reform—colonial society. The problematic of human will is central to the works of these authors, as it is for Sartre, in *Existentialism and Human Emotions.*[8] Human will, of course, is at the heart of existentialism. Yet if Camus is to be regarded as an existentialist after all, it seems that Fanon and Memmi pose a rather post-existentialist response to his thought. Importantly, the different ways in which these thinkers understood human will is reflected in their writings about colonial society.

Camus envisioned a new society created through assimilation rather than through violence, reform rather than revolution. He was frank about his interest in preserving French Algerian claims; he admitted that his views were those of a *pied noir.* But his ideas about assimilation and reform were hardly typical of reactionary *pied noir* society. Rather, he invoked socialist principles and reflected the attitude of Francophone progressives. Most other *pieds noirs* apparently saw assimilation, if not also socialism, as anathema.[9] Camus proposed a "New Algeria" transformed by land reform and the redistribution of wealth, among other initiatives, into a just and equitable society. Inclusion for the *pieds noirs* would therefore depend upon their willingness to disengage from the apparatuses of colonial violence—i.e., the military garrisons and the police—and from caste society which the metropole had created and sustained in Algeria. These criteria—land reform, redistribution of wealth, universal suffrage, etc.—were similar to that of contemporary advocates of non-aligned decolonization in Africa. But Camus was not for non-alignment, let alone for Algerian independence. Still his vision of materialist reform was well beyond the pale of most assimilationists. He understood that his proposal would not be readily embraced by *pied noir* society nor embraced by the French left. As a young journalist, he had already incurred reprisal from the Algerian branch of the French Communist Party for his "apostasy" (he was expelled). His peace proposal would not be accepted by the protagonists of the native struggle, the FLN (National Liberation Front) and other militants, because it dismissed Algerian national independence. Least of all would his proposal be accepted by the *"ultras,"* the *pied noir* extremists who committed violence (or acts of terrorism) upon the natives in retaliation for the Algerian guerillas' revolutionary violence (or acts of terrorism) upon the French *colons.* Camus saw his position as some kind of middle ground between two groups of violent extremists. But it had the effect of putting him between a rock and a hard place, in regard to the main parties in the Algerian conflict.

Camus was also critical of the established liberal position, which would have held out French citizenship for select Algerian natives. He felt that the issue of assimilation had been debased through continual postponement. The implementation of actual, egalitarian assimilation was an endlessly deferred moment of truth. He calls it: "[t]he perennial lie of constantly proposed but never realized assimilation, a lie that has compromised every evolution since the establishment of colonialism" (*Resistance, Rebellion, and Death* 144). He felt that the assimilation of Algerian natives, in fact rather than abeyance, was necessary for the continued existence of the French nation—an idea which suggests that he adhered to the "Algeria *is* France" conception, incidentally. Camus wanted to see assimilation established through the extension of full French rights to Algerian natives, including their fully proportional representation in the French Parliament.

However, even the latter tenet, proportional representation, demonstrates why assimilation was a dead letter proposal. The actual, egalitarian assimilation of Algerian Muslims would have posed an enormous threat to French primacy. For simply the demographic majority of Muslims in Algeria would illustrate the absurdity of native "assimilation" to French government. If assimilation were to serve the purpose of social reform, it would have had to take a different direction altogether. But the assimilation of minority French *colons* into Algerian society was never a plan. Of course, to entertain French assimilation in this way would presuppose Algerian independence.

Even the very idea of assimilation, in the way that liberals envisioned, was a fallacy. For the material history of the French assimilation of Algeria had been anything but egalitarian. In material terms, the assimilation plan had been the appropriation of Algerian land and property by the French government. Camus' own ideas about Algerian assimilation reflect the liberal fallacy. Moreover, his vision of an egalitarian kind of assimilation project is connected to his concept of *pied noir* nativism. One would seem to enhance the other, in his view. This may be observed in "The Silent Men," which is ostensibly a story of the class struggle (*Exile and the Kingdom*). Here, Camus presents a hope for the new, integrated society which will create the terms of a "New Algeria." The *colon* and native workers in the story are portrayed as the artisans of egalitarian fraternity.

In the story, a group of coopers return to their workshop after an unsuccessful labor strike. They are mainly French and Spanish Algerians, with the exception of an Algerian native, "Said, the only Arab in the shop" (69). The workmen feel humiliated and defeated. Their work has ethical as well as monetary value to them; it gives them a sense of validity. But now their trade itself, cooperage, is growing obsolete; and they have been coopers too long to learn another trade. "Changing trades is nothing," reflects the protagonist Ivars, "but to give up what you know, your master craftsmanship, is not easy. A fine craft without employment and you're stuck, you have to resign yourself. But resignation isn't easy either" (66). It seems to the men that they are no longer valid; they derive not only a sense of pride from their trade but also a sense of identity. They capitulate, fearing they will soon have no work to which they may return. Their protest has been figuratively silenced; and the men keep up a literal silence as they return to work in the shop. The solidarity of their silence is the focus of the story.

The erosion of the workers' livelihood presents an analogy to the privileged position of *colons* in Algerian society. Both seem to be slipping away through the forces of progressive history—and not through militant violence, one notes. The analogous situation seems to be one of impotence against stronger, objective forces. Against these forces, the men fall silent. However, their silence, initially an expression of defeat, develops a more profound meaning. It becomes a triumph of human solidarity. The failed strike is irrelevant to the great effect of will which the men manage collectively. Their silence expresses their solidarity in the struggle for justice. This struggle asserts the potential of a broader solidarity, one which will assimilate both *pieds noirs* and Algerian natives. Thus by analogy, the *pied noir* may make a place in the future not by resisting the progressive forces, but by letting himself be subsumed by them. He must commit himself to the future society of his own making.

The *pied noir* predicament is symbolized in the figure of the foreman who opens the shop to the workers upon their return. In the passage below, Camus describes the man's taciturn dignity and the tension of his unresolved allegiances:

> Ballester, who was the oldest of all, disapproved of the strike but had kept silent as soon as Esposito had told him that he was serving the boss' interests. Now he stood near the door, broad and short in his navy-blue jersey, already barefoot (he was the only one besides Said who worked barefoot), and he watched them go in one by one with his eyes that were so pale they seemed colorless in his old tanned face, his mouth downcast under his thick, drooping moustache. They were silent, humiliated by this return of the defeated, furious at their own silence, but the more it was prolonged the less capable they were of breaking it. They went in without looking at Ballester, for they knew that he was carrying out an order in making them go in like that, and his bitter and downcast look told them what he was thinking. Yvars,

> for one, looked at him. Ballester, who liked him, nodded his head without saying a word. (70)

Ballester is loyal—to a fault. He is beholden both to the boss and to his fellow workers. This is certainly a conflict of interests. It has made him refrain from either criticizing or joining the strike. His silence supports the others, but he disapproves of them on behalf of the boss. Ballester's double consciousness suggests that the allegiance of *pied noir* society is torn between the metropole and its own interests. Camus sees the interests of metropolitan France and French Algeria as not only separate but conflicted. Ballester's loyalty represents the problem which the *pied noir* must resolve. He must choose between the validity of *his* Algeria over the presumptive authority of the metropole.

Importantly, Camus' description of Ballester draws upon nativist signification for the *pieds noirs.* The men in the story are not farmers, yet there is similarity between Ballester and the settler image described by Memmi. Ballester is unpretentious and has the integrity of a work ethic, much like the booted settler on colonial bank notes. Ballester does not hold himself above his fellow workers; though he has seniority among the others, he is "of them" as well. In essence, these qualities of "good character" distinguish him as the foreman of the shop and as a *pied noir.* Camus' portrayal of Ballester is not propagandistic like the settler image described by Memmi. But one sees that the qualities of industriousness, integrity, honesty, simplicity, etc., were implicit in the *pied noir* ideal, as with the nativist, heroic images of other Western societies. Similarly, for example, the cowboy embodies American nativism because of his association with the lands of the American West and because of his "rugged individualism." Cowboy nativism, however depends upon the absence of actual Native Americans. The ideal cowboy image covers over imperial violence, i.e., the genocide of native people which made way for settler society in the American West. The French Algerian settler engraved on colonial money does this also.

Ballester's portrayal, like the other nativist images of settlers, conveys the ideal qualities upon which the nativism of *colon* society was supposed. These ideal qualities displace the violence upon which settler society is founded. Hard work and integrity stand in for genocide and theft. This is true of the imagery, regardless of the referent upon which the image is based. Ballester and Yvars, the protagonist, are after all sympathetic characters. They were likely based upon real people in Camus' youth for whom he had affection. The uncle who was his guardian, for example, was a cooper.[10] These real life referents are not at issue; it is the *pied noir* image which is analyzed here. Indeed, Camus deals with the *pied noir* image strategically, i.e., in a "writerly" way, as a narrative figure to express the social themes important to his thought. This strategy has already been discussed in regard to *The Stranger.* There Camus had touched upon the native genocide implicit in *colon* nativism. But the figure of Ballester presents a much different *pied noir* predicament than that of Meursault. Camus chooses to express not the alienation of Meursault, but the—necessary—hope and solidarity of Ballester and Ivars. If *The Stranger* presents the problem of colonial violence, upon which *pied noir* society was predicated, "The Silent Men" seeks constructive reform through willful effort and communality.

Moreover, specific features connect Ballester with the Algerian landscape and indicate that he is an autochthonous figure. He is tanned by the sun, and significantly, he works barefoot. The sun is an important motif which recurs in Camus' portrayals of Algerian life; here the sun is apparent in the foreman's tanned face. The other detail, Ballester's bare feet, is a patent reference to *pied noir* identity. It connotes a nativism which draws not only upon the land but also upon the only actual native in the shop: "he was the only one besides Said who worked barefoot" (70). Ballester derives nativism through metonymy; he and Said are connected in this very significant metonymic detail. Said's name, in fact, is a reference to nativism; its Arabic meaning denotes a rural person, connected to the land.

Camus' use of autochthonous imagery claims nativism for *pied noir* identity. But significantly, here the claim is established not by displacement, as in *The Stranger,* but by synecdoche or metonymy. This small detail implies that Camus saw *pied noir* nativism through equality with Algerian natives, or assimilation, rather than through usurpation. His conception of nativism is substantially different than that imagined, generally, by *colon* society. Nevertheless, any idea of *colon* nativism could be called an oxymoron. Indeed, in the passage quoted above, what the metonym connotes is disingenuous. After all, Ballester may choose to work barefoot, but Said probably has no shoes. The material positions of the men in colonial society are not analogous. Their origins, materially speaking, can never be equalized, even through assimilation. It is notable that Camus does not refer to Said as a native, though that is clearly what he is. He calls him an "Arab," meaning that he is a Muslim, but differentiating him from other Muslim natives, i.e., Berbers. While this may reflect colonial convention of the time, it does obscure the identity of natives as such. It is that very native identity which is disputed in colonial society.

One can therefore read "The Silent Men" as more than a story of simple class struggle. Rather, it portrays the conflict of the center and the periphery. This struggle is at the heart of the coopers' predicament. *Pied noir* identity appears to be in conflict with the metropole as much as it refers to it. The "silent men" seek the resolution of this dilemma. The story suggests that resolution may be found by claiming the "native" Algerian identity which is, if not the *pied noir's* birthright, then his fact of birth. This resolution can only be accomplished through a concerted effort of will. The "silent men" must not only be willing to disengage from the metropole but also to share in an assimilated Algeria in which they no longer hold class privileges.

The "silent men" are the casualties of colonial production. The men's strike has been broken not by the employer's resolve or power, but by the dissolution of craftsmanship in global industry. The destruction of crafts in the periphery is a symptom of colonial production.[11] It is not merely the coopers' labor but their trade itself which has been devalued. Cooperage has become anachronistic in the modern age in which commodities are mass produced. The coopers themselves are merely hold-overs of a by-gone era:

> Fewer and fewer barrels and large casks were being made; work consisted chiefly in repairing the huge tuns already in existence. Employers saw their business compromised, to be sure, but even so they wanted to maintain a margin of profit and the easiest way still seemed to them to block wages despite the rise of living costs. What can coopers do when cooperage disappears? You don't change trades when you've gone to the trouble of learning one; this one was hard and called for a long apprenticeship. (65)

As a class, these peripheral craftsmen are in conflict with the metropole. The metropole has created the terms of their obsolescence as well as their exploitation. The "central" conflict of labor and management therefore seems irrelevant to the situation described in the quoted text above. Lassalle, the boss, is also oppressed. His livelihood is tenuous and fated, too, just as the workers he employs. The story intimates an exegetic event; Lassalle will, for one reason or another, have to close down the shop. Not only has cooperage been made an obsolete trade, but Lassalle apparently has no one to whom he may pass on the family business. His only child is a very young daughter and she is gravely ill. While she might reject typical gender expectations and follow her father into cooperage, it is uncertain whether the child will even recover to grow into adulthood. The girl's illness, as well as the foundering business, has put Lassalle in a difficult position. Yet his pleas for the workers' understanding are as ineffectual as the strike. Indeed, the silence which rebuffs him demonstrates where the submerged power of production really lies. But the workers' power cannot be realized in this situation because its aim is misplaced. The class struggle has been transposed onto the terms of center and periphery. The coopers' labor strike has no effect within the colonial system. This impotence has left the workmen speechless, for how may they protest?

Ironically though, conflict with the metropole has significance for *pied noir* nativism. The opposing interests which are inherent between the workers and Lassalle, and between Said and the others, are ultimately made moot—or mute—by the larger, imperial context in which all the men are oppressed. In effect, the colonial system has "assimilated" the coopers as a peripheral people. It puts them in the position of the "native." This is suggested by the workers' eroding conditions. Truly, the other workers are better off than Said, just as Lassalle is better off than the other *pieds noirs* whose labor he employs. But these conditions are symbolically equalized by the events in the story.

The peripheral condition thus finds Yvars in the position of any North African migrant. He considers leaving the country with his wife to find work in the metropole: "If only he were young again, and Fernande too, they would have gone away, across the sea" (84). This alternative, migration, is symptomatic of peripheral production. Yvars would have to immigrate and become an urban proletarian in France. That is because local industry and commerce are repressed in the periphery by international production. But Yvars fears he isn't young enough to uproot. He appears to choose inaction; but really he makes no decision. He seems to simply know that he will stay. Yvar's actions—or his inaction—could be taken as resignation. Camus has portrayed him with a limp, a classical symbol of impotence, which implies something not only for Yvar's will but also for *pied noir* standing in colonial society. Yvar's lameness is a motif which corresponds with Ballester's bare feet. All this seems to confirm Memmi's claim that individual will and intention have no consequence within the colonial system. But Camus, whether or not he considered himself to be an existentialist, felt differently.

Camus sees that the men's oppression also offers the potential for their self determination. Thus, Yvar's consideration to leave the country is a telling moment—not of defeated will but of nativist potential. Yvars will stay in Algeria because it is his home. For him, leave-taking would be an emigration, not a return, across the sea to France. But for Yvars to remain in Algeria, he will not merely see the loss of his class status. He will also see the erosion of the criteria which legitimizes his cultural identity: his labor, that which makes him not so much a Frenchman as a *pied noir*. Yvars sees in this destruction the realization of an alternative. His rejection of emigration therefore proposes not inaction but resolution. He aspires to a native identity, based upon new criteria, which can only be had through the dissolution of the old. His identity would issue from an assimilated society shared by *pieds noirs* and Algerian natives. This would entail the recognition of the *pied noir* as a native Algerian and of the "Arab" native as an equal. It implies the dissolution of class and caste. *Pied noir* nativism would therefore be established not by exclusion and exploitation but upon new criteria of communality and equality.

Camus' vision of an assimilated, "New Algeria," appears to be an egalitarian vision, if not a socialist one. This is evident when, at the lunch break, the men share their food. What makes the narrative definitive of Camus' prescription for Algeria is the inclusion of Said, the Arab:

> [Yvars] was beginning to eat when, not far from him, he noticed Said lying on his back in a pile of shavings, his eyes looking vaguely at the windows made blue by a sky that had become less luminous. He asked him if he had already finished. Said said that he had eaten his figs. Yvars stopped eating. The uneasy feeling that hadn't left him since the interview with Lassalle suddenly disappeared to make room for a pleasant warmth. He broke his bread in two as he got up and, faced with Said's refusal, said that everything would be better next week. "Then it will be your turn to treat," he said. Said smiled. Now he bit into the piece of Yvar's sandwich, but in a gingerly way like a man who isn't hungry. (77)

The lunch scene suggests the Marxian notion, "from each according to his ability, to each according to his needs." Because each cooper shares what he has, all may have a meal. But Said has the least of all the men and thus has nothing to share. He is hesitant to take the ration from Yvars because it could be construed as charity. His dignity is at stake. Yvars assures him that the food is not charity but fellowship, and that Said will have a turn to provide in the future. The workmen's communality therefore includes Said as an equal. Of course, this scene neatly inverts the actual, colonial relations of French Algerian society, in which *colons* of all strata were greatly outnumbered by the native majority. Despite the actual demographics, the *colon* minority owned the majority of wealth and means. The largess of a few coopers toward their single native co-worker is a distortion of the numerical reality and the inequality it represents. And yet Camus' basic idea and intention do recognize the need for *colon* society to yield to native demands for equity. For him, assimilation would offer all a share in the common wealth of a common nation. That nation would not be Algeria, however—but France.

Camus' vision of a New Algeria falls short of national independence, on the one hand. On the other, it ignores the violent underpinning of *colon* society, a society which cannot exist without militarism, without force. He sees violence not as Sartre does, as endemic to the entire formation of colonial society. Rather Camus sees the Algerian conflict as the perpetuation of local conflicts between local protagonists, a "casuistry of blood," a snake which swallows its own tail. In his view, it is a violence which has taken on a momentum of its own. But this kind of violence can be abated, he feels, through society's collective act of will:

> I know that the great tragedies of history often fascinate men with approaching horror. Paralyzed, they cannot make up their minds to do anything but wait. So they wait, and one day the Gorgon devours them. But I would like to convince you that the spell can be broken, that there is only an illusion of impotence, that strength of heart, intelligence, and courage are enough to stop fate and sometimes to reverse it. One has merely to will this, not blindly, but with a firm and reasoned will. (*Resistance, Rebellion, and Death* 141)

Although the prose is aesthetic and inspiring, it misrepresents Algerian violence as a universal essence. Camus has detached the violence from its material cause—it appears to be simply the same inhumanity which plagues any society of any era. As in his "Appeal for a Civilian Truce" Camus invokes the rational, humanist "essence" of society. But he fails to address the factors which have engendered conflict. That conflict is not about one's will or intentions but about land and sovereignty. The regard of "will" is an abstraction which makes these more material considerations moot.

For Camus, human will is the essence of society. This is, of course, an existentialist notion—and it is striking how differently Camus and Sartre pursued an existential logic in regard to the "Algerian Question." But if Camus thought that a "firm and reasoned will" could put an end to violence, he did not think it would be easy to summon. For this will would not only have to lay down arms, it would have to remake Algerian—and ultimately, French—society into something entirely new.

3.3 ALGERIAN PLIGHT

If Camus himself doubted the feasibility of non-violence, yet he did not lack the courage of his convictions. Assia Djebar recounts how the French Algerian author, "pale and tense, but determined," made his address for a truce while reactionary *colons* threw stones and threatened violence outside the lecture hall in Algiers. Camus may have abjured violence, but he apparently didn't flinch in its presence, not even as an angry mob called for him to be lynched:

> In the *Place du government* just around the corner, thousands of European extremists—the *ultras*—shout slogans: "Mendès France au poteau!" ["Mendès France to the gallows!"] and "Camus au Poteau!" [Camus to the gallows!] Inside the hall (some of the windows soon shattered by volleys of stones from outside), Albert Camus, pale and tense, but determined, reads the text of a speech calling for a truce. On the platform, Ferhat Abbas, the moderate Nationalist leader (who will only join the F.L.N. a few months later) listens to the writer. Nationalist Muslims and liberal Frenchmen mingle and fraternize. Later on, this scene would seem to belong to another epoch. (109)

Djebar portrays Camus' 1956 "Appeal for a Civilian Truce" in the context of the moment's heat which had produced it. He stands in stark relief to the *ultras* whose violence represents the pitch of *pied noir* reaction to native rights. Moderate Algerian nationalists are represented in this scene by Ferhat Abbas, who for a time negotiated between the Algerian guerrillas and the French government. Camus' appeal for tolerance was framed by these circumstances. Djebar sees his appeal as occurring within a window of opportunity, so to speak, which was subsequently, irrevocably lost. The violent conflicts in Algeria escalated soon after, culminating in the Battle of Algiers a year later (vividly portrayed in the film by Gillo Portecorvo).

Two generations afterward, Djebar also entertains the creation of an integrated, if utopian, society in her book *Algerian White.* She contemplates a French-Algerian fraternity in the way proposed by Camus. Like him, she is mainly concerned with the graphic effects of violence. Like Camus, she sees human will and good intention as an alternative to bloodshed. This alternative would seem to offer potential for social change:

> And yet this dialogue might have led to an Algeria which, like its neighbors, claimed independence without too bloody a price. All Franco-Algerian links would not have been smashed in a single blow [. . .] But instead the law of arms prevailed (hundreds of thousands of French soldiers, including reservists, on one side; and on the other, a few thousand *maquisards* in the *djebels,* a few hundred "terrorists" in the towns). Holding sway over heaps of civilian dead. Nineteen-sixty-two was to see the constitution of an independent and sovereign state, but one which had been bled white. (109)

Djebar has an apparent sympathy for Camus' political position—assimilation—which seems anachronistic given her own recognition of Algeria's need for independence. Thus one wonders what she means by "all Franco-Algerian links would not have [had to] been smashed in a single blow." (In fact, they were not.[12]) But the object of national independence implies that the links which bind the colony to the metropole must be broken; for political and economic links, if not cultural ones, are the apparatuses by which colonial dominance is established. One sees that colonial dominance may be maintained over peripheral nations even when they possess nominal "autonomy," such as was the case with Algeria's neighbors, Morocco and Tunisia,[13] and with Egypt, said to be independent by Britain when the protectorate ended in 1922, though it remained under British control for another thirty years. Thus to pursue anything less than the sundering of exploitative political and economic links would mean to relinquish sovereignty in favor of an ersatz "autonomy" administered by the metropole. Indeed, the degree to which any former colonial nation had "sundered" such links to the former metropole, or to the "center" of the world system, was the bane of the era of decolonization.

Djebar's conjecture might suppose that the ostensible break with the metropole, brought about through decolonization, has meant a fundamental break as well. The presumed rupture is consistent with a view which sees imperialism as mainly a political phenomenon. But one has seen, throughout the entirety of this discussion, how that which links the center to the periphery is a much more complex arrangement of overt and subtle phenomena than simply the unilateralism of metropolitan government. Of course Djebar recognizes this subtlety. In the same work she explores the cultural imperialism inherent in her own French speech, and cites the intolerance of the French authorities for Algerian nationalists, whether moderates, militants, or mere suspects. These are observations which follow the views of Fanon and Memmi; by observing the psycho-linguistic and material effects of colonial oppression, Djebar addresses the deeply structural facets of colonialism. Indeed, Djebar's French speech in the company of her intimate Algerian friends, decades after the last French soldier had departed, is evidence of the subtle ways of imperialism. Cultural links are not so easily broken.

Despite her concerns, however, Djebar does not attempt an analysis of the violence which she condemns. Yet *Algerian White* vividly portrays the violence which has beset Algerian society since the latter days of colonialism until today. It seems that she is mainly interested in representing the tragedy and graphic qualities inherent in situations of violence, rather than portraying the motivations which underlie such conflicts. She does not evaluate the particular conditions of violent conflicts, although to do so might pose some considerations about their abatement (her implied objective). The lack of analysis in a work which is so emphatically about violence—which is otherwise an extremely moving and insightful account—is problematic. The result is that her representations of Algerian violence appear somewhat as spectacle. Her lament of the unrealized potential for peace misrepresents the materiality of the decolonization struggle as well as the later conflicts.

Like Camus, Djebar fails to recognize violence as a colonial apparatus in local society; nor does she represent it as the expression of material issues. She understands that violence and poverty in Algeria were characteristic of French colonialism. But she appears to see these conditions as obstacles which could have been overcome through good faith on the parts of the protagonists, French and Arab. The kind of colonial fraternity which she considers disregards the material, systemic reality of violence and underdevelopment in the periphery. Her view ignores the institutional violence which has created French Algerian society, a society materially based upon an apartheid system.

Djebar's credence to goodwill departs from the earlier observations of Fanon, Memmi, and Sartre. One has already considered the views of the latter three and that the material conditions of colonial society render personal intentions and good will moot. Individual will and intentions were irrelevant in the French Algerian context because the social formation had concretized the roles of colonial protagonists. The roles of colonizer and colonized were fundamentally opposed, according to the liberation theorists, i.e., Fanon, Memmi and Sartre, regardless of the desire of social progressives for fraternity.

Memmi had considered the kind of fraternity which would "assimilate" North Africans into French civil society. His view was contemporary with Camus' if not conciliatory with it. Unlike Camus, who felt that the assimilation project had been subverted and could thus be remedied, Memmi rejected the idea altogether. He saw it as utopian in the least and, ultimately, as culturally imperialist. Importantly for the present discussion, Memmi anticipated the discursive revision of North African liberation as a failed attempt at French assimilation. His comments seem to anticipate Djebar's hindsight:

> Now that colonization is reaching its end, tardy expressions of good will are heard asking whether assimilation was not the great opportunity missed by colonizers and mother countries. "Ah, if we had only agreed to it! Can't you imagine!" they daydream. "A France with one hundred million Frenchmen?" It is not forbidden to reimagine history, and it is often consoling, but only on the conditions that you discover another meaning to it, another hidden reality. Could assimilation have succeeded? Perhaps it could have at other periods of history. Under the conditions of contemporary colonization, apparently not. It may be a

> historical misfortune, and perhaps we should deplore it altogether. Not only did it fail, but it appeared impossible to all parties concerned. (*Colonizer and Colonized* 125)

Memmi's insight that it is consoling to reimagine history goes right to the heart of Djebar's portrayal of a potential truce between the French and the Algerian nationalists. For why else would Djebar, who was conscious of Algerian self determination, imagine that sovereignty could have been negotiated on "fraternal" terms? She entertains an inclusiveness which was not possible in Algerian society, given the prevailing material conditions.

Perhaps Djebar's retrospection actually pertains to a different social dialectic than the one which Memmi confronted in Tunisia a generation earlier. She seems to confront not the conflict of the metropole and local society, but that of the so-called modern and the traditional. In fact, her views seem to transpose the latter conflict onto the former. Both conflicts, ultimately, are rooted in colonialism. But there seems to be a lack of specificity in her regard. As we have seen with the rhetoric of modernization, this lack of specificity elides material history.

Djebar has seen significant material changes in post-colonial Algeria: state independence from Western colonialism; the shift away from revolutionary nationalism as the organizing principle of the state and the fragmentation of the authoritarian regime which had been based upon that principle. These changes have entailed demonstrable reactions in local society. Such reactions address the material conditions which have undergone, simultaneously, here rapid transformation and development, there exacerbation and further attenuation of stasis. Algeria, like Egypt and the Maghrib countries, had grafted together a "modern," urban, and typically secular elite and a broader, "traditional," impoverished society. These are the conditions which characterize the "unequal development" of modernization.

Like other leaders of revolutionary nationalist states during the decolonization era, the leftist elite in independent Algeria had responded to the conditions of unequal development by pursuing Western-style modernization, or, "more development" (utilizing socialist paradigms). The apparent failures of this pursuit to produce better living standards and a more open society for the nation as a whole is regarded by observers as the impetus for the populist appeal of the post-independence "Islamist" movement in Algeria. The Islamists' agenda is often seen to embody religious or cultural motivations rather than economic motives. Yet to see it purely this way is a cultural reduction of a popular movement which does respond to material conditions of privation and repression:

> Political Islam [in Algeria] emerged as a major factor, and took its place in the void left by Arab nationalism. The populations were barely gathering up the detritus of modernity. They felt that yawning gap—between the "North" and "South"—as an injustice. The rise of Islamism, experienced as the hope for a return to ethics, in combination with the bankruptcy of the single-party system, brought about a need for individual responsibility, which would go hand in hand with the search for a new kinship. (Stora 202)

The Islamist movement in Algeria has been resistant to "Westernization" and to the secular government, which again like those of other decolonized nations has replaced its socialist policies in favor of *laissez faire* capitalism. Hugh Roberts' observation that the Algerian Islamists have failed to articulate a comprehensive position on economic policy, however, suggests that development itself is less the issue than how it is applied.[14] The recent conflict of these protagonists—that is, the secular Algerian government and the Islamist movement—is often described as a conflict of modern and traditional forces: the push toward and pull away from so-called Western development. In Djebar's 1995 account, *Algerian White,* one can see the tension of both these forces upon local society.

What appears as a bit of nostalgia about Franco-Algerian fraternity, then, seems rather to be Djebar's own response to the real subject of her book: the recent conflict between the government and the Islamists, which she portrays rather as an essential, inter-generational violence that has plagued Algeria since the late days of French colonialism. This is an interpretive reading by which one may "discover another meaning, another hidden reality" (Memmi 125) to Djebar's historical re-envision of a potential Franco-Algerian truce. She suggests that if Algerian reaction against the French had not been so pronounced, perhaps the legacy of violence would never have been engendered. But this understanding of conflict seems willfully simple, if not willfully opaque. It is not forbidden to reimagine history, as Memmi points out. But such historical revisions are prey to misappropriation by any kind of agenda. One finds that "modernization" supplies its own "hidden rationality" to the revision of Third World liberation. That rationality is not so generous or inclusive as the one considered by Djebar.

One has already considered previously (and no doubt will again) how abstract concepts serve the ideological superstructures of the material base of power. But it is important to remember that superstructural narratives rather assume a life of their own, through dissemination, through discourse. The appropriation of ideas and concepts is not always clearly or consciously motivated. But lack of motivation does not imply lack of interest. This is why it is important to critically analyze discourse, especially liberal discourse, which presumes a consensus for the greater good. One usually finds that there is no actual "consensus," just as there is no "greater good."

Djebar herself considers that historical revision may serve the self interest of established power. In one interesting turn of her narrative, she tells of the "nationalization" of the body of the Emir Abdelkader, an Algerian notable who led native forces against the French in the middle nineteenth century. The independent government sought out his burial remains and promoted his image as an icon of Algerian nationalism.[15] Djebar portrays this project as an empty gesture which only emphasizes the failure of legitimate governance and the betrayal of nationalism by self-interested rule. Algeria's newly independent government sought to be identified with Abdelkader, who was popularly esteemed as both a folk hero and as a marabout (saint). Abdelkader was seen, in an organic sense, as the forebear of Algerian nationalism.[16] At the height of his resistance, he had carved out an independent zone, not exactly a state nor a kingdom, in west-central Algeria. He staved off the French for about 10 years, from 1837–1847, until his defeat and subsequent exile in Syria.[17] At the time of independence, his remains had long rested in a Damascus mosque.

The repatriation of Abdelkader's body became an issue of cultural nationalism during independence. It was a symbolic gesture, meant to invoke populist and nativist legitimacy for the new government. The emir's body was thus a kind of icon which the government would have wielded for its various associations. Possession of Abdelkader's body, or his image, ostensibly signified the government's legitimacy in a number of ways. Foremost, Abdelkader's resistance of the French prefigured the FLN guerrilla war for independence.[18] To transpose the image of the emir onto the independent government, which was composed of former FLN leaders, would have heightened the notion of an authentic, organic leadership. Furthermore, Abdelkader had not only the authority of his own armed struggle, but he was also the descendant of a notable religious family. His name was therefore associated also with religious and social, or "traditional," prestige. Because of the prestige of his family, Abdelkader had been approached by local tribes to lead the resistance against the French. The emir was thus imagined or portrayed as a figure who had unified the local tribes in a *nativist* struggle. As this struggle was later re-envisioned as a *nationalist* one, Abdelkader would also have been seen as a figure of nationalist unification.

The idea of nationalist unification was important to the FLN throughout the war and certainly afterward, when it assumed the offices of government.

The FLN had sought to consolidate and represent the independence struggle under its own leadership, by either incorporating or excluding other groups, leaders or dissidents. These efforts were largely successful and the FLN represented Algerian independence at the Evian Accords, when France agreed to end colonization. But the FLN's dominance among nationalists was not without discord and intrigue.[19] Nor was the party itself free of internecine struggles. Abdelkader's repatriation was accomplished by the Algerian government in 1966, the year after Houari Boumediène had displaced Ahmed Ben Bella, the first president of independent Algeria, in a military coup. Both men had been FLN compatriots. Thus one can see the urgency to invoke solidarity where factionalism and resentments would have presided.

The "nationalization" of Abdelkader's body may be seen as the appropriation of "history" for a specific political agenda. The fate of Abdelkader, or rather his body and his legacy, illustrates how a concept, especially one regarded by general consensus, can be easily divested and reified as an object of manufactured consent. Thus again, it is important to recognize that there is a substantial difference between an actual person or an original meaning or intention and a simulated one which merely refers to the original in some way. For example, it seems that Abdelkader's image would have quite organically affixed to the FLN in the struggle against the French. Nationalist propaganda would only have enhanced an analogy which likely already existed in the popular imagination. However, the propagated image would have been a useful gesture to cover over political and social divisions among the Algerians. This would have been true especially during the early years of independence when representation and leadership were contested by various agents.

Post-independence struggles were typical of the newly independent nations of the period, e.g., Egypt, Morocco, Cuba. The strategies which arose there often took the form of cultural nationalism. The use of nativist imagery was one such strategy. It aimed at cultural cohesion, conformity or legitimacy, in the establishment of the independent state. In Algeria, the independent government was invested in establishing itself as a legitimate presence in contrast to the colonial rule which had preceded it. The new government was a secular government influenced by French models. Thus the identification with a native Muslim figure, such as Abdelkader, who caught the popular imagination would have been especially useful. It would have connoted, or been intended to connote, a nativist legitimacy for an independent government fashioned, arguably to a high degree, upon foreign political models. It would have conferred, or aimed to confer, cohesion upon a government which bore the marks of internecine conflicts and old wounds.

Abdelkader's body was courted in the service of Algerian cultural nationalism, or in the creation of a kind of nationalist mythology. His image was the sign of a distinct cultural continuity and identity. It attempted to restore what had been interrupted by the French. Thus one may say that the figure of Abdelkader, if not his body, was engaged in the process of simulation.[20] The mediated process of simulation had a separate reality from the actual, living person to whom it referred. The repossession of the emir's remains came to represent first the legitimacy of the independent government, and then the cohesion of a nationalist identity. And then, as portrayed by Djebar, Abdelkader's "relic" became the empty sign of authoritarian control.

While Abdelkader's image was promulgated by the government, Djebar notes that his own views were not. The emir's writing and poetry, she observes, were never so much an object of the independent "official culture;" only his body, silent and objectified.[21] It was thus the *idea* of Abdelkader, detached from his own thought and motivations, which was important—important because useful—to the new government. In this regard, Djebar compares the repossession of the marabout's remains by the Algerian government with that of St. Augustine's relic by the Lombard Kingdom in medieval Italy. She sees both Abdelkader and Augustine, the Algerian-born Christian patriarch, as:

> Two paternal bodies transported—moved in spite of their secular sleep . . . alas less their work, their words, their preserved light than what remains of the body: a skeleton, a nail, a hair, some relic that will allow for statues to be erected, for the flow of speeches, for any ceremony at all. (221–222)

The body of Abdelkader, as of Augustine, was made a useful icon. It became a simulacrum, divested of content and reified as the ideogram of institutional authority. The sign-cum-body was rendered functional for new content, "for the flow of speeches, for any ceremony at all." These speeches and ceremonies serve an altogether different agenda or intention than the one presumed to have animated the living person of reference.

Djebar sees the "nationalization" of Abdelkader's body as a hollow gesture—as a gloss which easily peels away from the emir's actual legacy and from the living native dissidence which his reified figure was invoked to mask. She tells how Algeria's revolutionary government negotiated with the Syrian grandson of the Emir Abdelkader, the man she calls his heir in the text below, to have his remains exhumed and repatriated. The man's son, also a descendant of the emir (i.e., his great-grandson), has met with notably less esteem from the same government which courts his forebear's legacy of dissent:

> They describe to him the people who are waiting, the planned festivities, the statue commissioned in Italy, the ceremony . . . Abdelkader's heir listens to it all; does not flinch. Ends by saying:
>
> "My son. One of my sons is in your country!"
>
> "In Algeria?" they are surprised.
>
> "Yes."
>
> "Where?"
>
> "In one of your prisons; he's been there for more than a year!"
>
> Complete surprise. No one knew. The president didn't know. One of the direct descendants of the great resister in the prisons of Algeria? Astonishment. But the only ones arrested were Communists or others of the same ilk—arrested to keep them from doing any harm.
>
> "Exactly. My son is one such. He has been incarcerated for his ideas (they are not my ideas, but he is my son); he has been tortured!"
>
> It's a mistake, a ghastly mistake, they say. It is true that the [youth] did not reveal himself as [Abdelkader's descendant], but only as an activist with a cause.
>
> "Set my son free and you may return my grandfather to your country!"
>
> It seems those were the terms he used: "You may return him to your country!" That is why the old man, who will not leave his office in Damascus for the splendors of the Bay of Algiers, who has negotiated the freedom of his youngest son, smiles; he knows that returning the bones of Abdelkader is pure show. (224–225)

Djebar portrays the dark irony of the situation. The nationalist authorities court the corpse of Abdelkader and meanwhile abuse his living legacy, the emir's young descendant, who is tortured and imprisoned for political dissent. The Syrian heir knows that the prestige of his grandfather may be useful to the new government. He plays some politics himself and secures the release of his son. Significantly Abdelkader's great-grandson, his imprisoned descendant, represents the first "modern" generation of "free" Algerians. This is Djebar's own generation, which has found the ostensible forms of national independence emptied of content, detached from the ideas which they supposedly represent, reified as the icons of authority and institutional power. Abdelkader's legacy, both in a conceptual and corporeal sense, is thus greatly abused by its appropriation as the "insignia" of an oppressive, institutional authority. Djebar's own telling of the story emphasizes this point. Politicization has transformed the sign-cum-idea into an object of veneration, an object of distraction manufactured for mass consumption. The possession of this symbolic object would confer prestige, authority, legitimacy upon the state which cynically aspires to its own self interest.

The story about Abdelkader's repatriation has thematic relevance for Djebar's account of Algerian violence. The image of Abdelkader as a dead body, a dead letter, connotes the corruption or desecration of the idea of Algerian nationalism. Djebar sees the death of "free Algeria" in the violence which has engulfed the nation. In *Algerian White,* Djebar recounts the political violence spanning three consecutive periods in Algeria: the late colonial period, new independence and the recent civil unrest. Her book denounces violence and struggles to assert a hope for peace. The title refers to the color of purity, of the death shroud, white, which is also the color of Muslim clerical and traditional native dress.[22] Independence and the inter-generational conflicts it has wrought, she contends, have "bled [Algeria] white" (109).

Violence appears to be the thread which holds together Djebar's various accounts of Algeria before and after independence. This thread supplies cohesion to the numerous, disparate events which she narrates. It humanizes the features of a continuous struggle which has often tended to be portrayed in superficially ideological terms. Like Camus, Djebar is concerned with the death of innocents. She tells of the tragic deaths of intellectuals, writers, artists and teachers; she tells of assassinations, executions, murders; of suicides and accidents, suspicious illnesses and traumatic, fatal dissipations. She indeed recognizes that the circumstances of individual demise have arisen from the political conflicts which have produced violence. But her focus upon violence as the linkage of events does reduce their complexity. It inhibits the view of the deeper issues which have motivated the conflicts. Thus for all the historical detail and specificity of her work, she declines to offer an explanation of the social conflicts which have taken the lives of her subjects.

Djebar's abhorrence and denunciation of violence are legitimate and humanely motivated. Yet there is a basic problem with her perspective. It is basically non-materialist. Indeed, like Camus' historic address, she has chosen to focus upon violence itself as the primary issue, rather than upon the root causes which have produced the violence. Her work, not unlike Camus' proposal of a truce during the Algerian War, laments the waste and cynicism of what appears as an unthinking, mechanistic kind of trans-generational violence. But while her sentiments are entirely sympathetic, they offer no analysis. Some particular features of her writing contribute to this problem. First, her accounts of the events are told in a third-person, descriptive narration which has the feel of a filmic "voice-over," rather than that of an eyewitness account. A reader is unsure which of the events she has actually witnessed herself—if indeed the book is a memoir—and which are anecdotes she has researched or received second-hand. For example, Djebar's account of Camus' 1956 speech in Algiers adds no additional or personal details to a scene which has been chronicled by other authors.[23] The "voice-over" style of her narration throughout the book need not be considered a fault, however; the events are portrayed with a visual immediacy which is powerful. Djebar is, of course, a film maker as well as a writer. But the style does connote a removal from the events which is not made up by the author's reflection or analysis. Thus one gets a sense of the events mainly as spectacles about which one may emote but may not try to understand. Stora comments that the French public has looked upon media representations of the recent conflict in Algeria with a mixture of detachment, horror, and even some spite born from memories of the 1954–1962 war: "In fact, when one fails to make Algerian suffering a television spectacle, one makes demonstrations of emotion or consensus more difficult" (237). Djebar's portrayals likewise give primacy to an alienated, spectacular emotion.

Another feature of Djebar's writing, however, does contribute more essentially to the immaterialism of her account. Her technique of parallel narrative places together the acts of French soldiers, those of the nationalist *fedayeen* and, more recently, those of the Islamist guerrillas—so that they all seem nearly interchangeable. It is a rather "universalizing" treatment of individual events which does little more than to describe or show the graphic, inhumane nature of violence. There are also many tragedies to which she refers but seems to attribute only to the anonymous reactions of the time. The effect of these narrative strategies is to equalize and thus to fetishize the violent social conflicts which she describes. The conflation of anti-colonial with postcolonial events of violence suggests that Djebar conceives of the recent conflict along the lines of French popular conception as the reification of the earlier war. Yet this popular conception also lacks materialist understanding of both conflicts and foregrounds essentialist notions about "Third World" inscrutability and backwardness:

> "The second Algerian war": that expression has been much used in France since 1992. More than the historical principle of "repetition," (of the first conflict against the French presence), it is the notion of *recidivism* that is invoked: Algeria is a land destined for war, struck by a curse, embarked on a perpetually tragic destiny. The violence may have calmed for a time after 1962; then it resumed, unleashed with even more energy. It is erupting today, incandescent, unpredictable, with

> infinite cruel variations. Under the French "spectators'" gaze, everything lies in the words, the account; the images are almost impossible to look at." (Stora 236)

Since the late 1980s, Islamist militants have been seen as the source of instability and unrest in Algeria. This is certainly the view taken by Djebar. Yet she fails to analyze the conflict, one presumes, because the methods of the militants are violent methods. It seems she wants to transcend literal meaning to stress a universal truth. This is likely a symbolic choice which she has made:

> In Algeria today, following the serial murders of writers, journalists, and intellectuals, against which increased repression is the response—the only policy brandished against a religious fundamentalism that has decided to take power at any cost—faced with these convulsions that submerge my country in a nameless war, once again referred to as "events," in this return to violence and its anaesthetizing vocabulary, what is "white" (the white of dust, of sunless light, of dilution . . .) and why say so here? I can only express my disquiet as a writer and as an Algerian woman through a reference to that color, or rather that non-color. "White acts on our soul like absolute silence," Kandinsky said. Through the reminder of abstract painting, I have here begun a discourse that has in some way swerved. (226)

Djebar is rightly critical of the "anaesthetizing vocabulary" which frames Algerian violence. It is a discourse which reduces violent conflicts to a simple euphemism, to "events." One recognizes only the troublesome events, but never the conflicts which motivate the violence—not really, not in any material way. In discourse it is always the violence which overshadows the cause expressed through the medium of violence—for violence is merely a medium, however terrible. But though Djebar is critical of the discursive "whitewashing" of violent conflicts, she capitulates to it herself. Who can say anything for certain, she asks, "and why say so here?" (226) She claims to make camp with the abstract expressionist painter, Kandinsky, and to render a kind of symbolic truth through a reference to the color white. But this is an intellectual cop-out. To conjure Kandinsky merely substitutes aesthetics for analysis. It makes no attempt to understand the motivations of violent conflict; rather it tends to make them opaque. Since her book is, after all, a powerful and emphatic denunciation of violence, it seems disingenuous to portray violence as merely its own end, as a thing without reason or rationale upon the parts of its protagonists. To make the attempt to understand that reason or rationale can only cast the terms of the conflict in greater clarity for all who presume to have a stake.

Djebar is adept at representing the individual, human details of what may be understood as the paradigmatic shifts of postcolonial history. Nevertheless, the perspective offered in *Algerian White* tends to isolate the experiences of individuals apart from the broader social dynamics or processes of the period. Rendered as a series, Djebar's portraits of innocents are so composed as to be decontextual. As a result, her account seems atomized, too closely focused upon specific events isolated from their motivations. Paradoxically, the events which the author so carefully renders become interchangeable features of a meaningless, immaterial "violence." Thus she does not transcend the immediacy of her subject, even as she well conveys its terrors. Essentially, her lens replicates the reductive view upon postcolonial society which is all too prevalent in the West. Djebar's view is subsumed by the modernizing perspective which sees the "Third World" as the site of undifferentiated, rampant, senseless violence. She would likely dismiss such an opaque view of the Algerian conflicts as is often regarded by Western observers. Yet her own account capitulates to it, for lack of material analysis. Rather, her "universalist" denunciation of violence, which does not differentiate motive or condition, is subsumed by the discourse of modernization.

The fetishistic reduction of "violence" in Djebar's view is essentially the modernizing view. Djebar's account is, in effect, "gutted" of any real understanding which it might have conveyed about the conditions which perpetuate the conflicts in Algeria. Her "universalist" denunciation of the violence simply equates the occasions of its expressions. Thus any insight into her own implied objective—how peace and stability may be attained—is likewise inhibited. Yet Djebar's intentions are progressive and liberal. She has deliberately chosen not to be polemical (13) in order to serve the cause of peace. She rejects factionalism itself, as it fuels the ongoing conflicts in Algeria. The attempt to avoid polemics is a discursive strategy meant to provide rationale and equity to a heated contest. But the result is that it elides any consideration of the conditions which produce factionalism and conflict. The failure to recognize the cause of conflicts can only exacerbate and perpetuate the existing violence.

Djebar's "neutrality" reflects some of the problems with liberal panaceas such as "nonviolence" and "development." Gutted of material analysis, the denunciation of violence is open to discursive appropriation for any agenda. Ironically, this is the kind of misappropriation which Djebar trenchantly portrays in the story of Abdelkader's body. There, an ostensibly recognized "sign"—a native folk hero—was subsumed by the discourse of a vested interest—that of a rival faction within the national leadership which sought to secure its own power. This vested interest was far from the original referent, its original meaning or intent. As we have seen, the image of the "great resister" was reified as an icon of repressive institutional power.

An analysis may recognize strategies such as the appropriation and simulation of signs. It is an important recognition, for much is presumed to be warranted in the name of any platitude and its variously interpreted signs. As was discussed previously in the example of Marshal Lyautey, the best intentions may very well accompany the meanest practices. Certainly, Camus' call for Algerian "pacification" was intended as a far thing from the actual French practice. Camus wanted to see an end to bloodshed; this is what his kind of peace called for. But as a material practice, "pacification" meant quite simply native submission by colonial force—it was little more than a *pax Romana.* This was the kind of peace which Lyautey was in charge of establishing, despite his good will toward his Muslim "friends." Thus a large problem with Djebar's will toward peace is that it may be so easily appropriated by practices which aim to suppress dissent and resistance to Western "development." The denunciation of violence implies the will to end violence, surely. This will typically invokes greater authority, more control, increased security. And often by extension, the will to "end violence" authorizes a state of emergency, the suspension of civil liberties, the ratification of "temporary" extreme measures, a policy of aggressive "prevention" or "pre-emptive" action. After all, Abdelkader's descendant and his fellow activists were only "arrested to keep them from doing any harm" (225). Their arrest, incarceration and torture were actions ostensibly justified by the same invocation, the will to preserve the peace and the rule of law. Yet such tyranny is far from the good intentions of would-be pacifists.

Djebar's denunciation of violence, the premise of her book, is undoubtedly sincere. Like Camus, she is motivated by humanistic values. Her objective—as was his—is to end Algerian "fraternal" violence and restore the peace. But one may also evaluate Djebar's premise as a thing apart from her intentions. That is, her call to end violence apparently intends to serve humanistic aims. But in practice, like "pacification," to invoke "state security" may actually sanction state repression and institutional violence, and act to increase militant resistance or "irregular" violence, i.e., "terrorism." For example, a fundamental source of violent conflicts between Islamist militants and the Algerian army was the suspension of elections in 1991 and again in 1992 (when candidates of the Islamic Salvation Front were expected to lead), followed by the declaration of a state of emergency. A continuing series of terrorist attacks and murders of policemen, civilian professionals, and prominent citizens, the events referred to by Djebar in *Algerian White,* burgeoned into civil war. "The attacks and murders attributed to the Islamist groups, and the actions of reprisal by the Algerian security forces, caused some thirty thousand deaths between the installation of the state of emergency in February 1992 and December 1994" (Stora 215). The 1993 report of Amnesty International denounced the Algerian government for the widespread use of torture upon detained militants since the state of emergency had been decreed.[24] Abdelaziz Bouteflika inaugurating a period of reform, disarmament, and amnesty upon his election as president in 1999, claimed that 100,000 people by then had died in the civil war.[25] Clearly, state "security" measures had done nothing to abate the violence or to repress the Islamist movement or the militants. In effect the call to end violence, if left unexamined, may simply serve to privilege one type of violence—that of the state or the oppressive authority—over another kind of violence—that of militant resistance. The privileging of one over the other simply exacerbates the problem of conflict. The weakness of Djebar's view, therefore—which otherwise presents a riveting and detailed portrait—is that, like Camus, she entertains a fetishized notion of violence as an essence, as something itself to be abated—but presumably at a human cost. An evaluation or analysis, therefore, can offer some insight into how liberal good intentions are so often misappropriated and distorted in the service of other, less generous, interests. Perhaps, as at the behest of Memmi, one may "discover another meaning" to Djebar's admission, "I have here begun a discourse that has in some way swerved" (226).

Chapter Four

Paris on the Nile, Egypt on the Plantation

Development after Muhammad Ali

4.1 MUMMIFIED HISTORY

The unequal relations of the First and Third Worlds, in which the former's surpluses are derived from the alienated conditions of the latter, are indeed the relationship of lack to excess. When this system is recognized as an integrated system of international production, as by the center-periphery model, it becomes clear that Western "modernization" is an obfuscating and disingenuous theory. Rather with the global view, one sees how nations which comprise the former colonies have been engaged participants in industrial modernity throughout the history of international production.

"Modernization" relies upon an assumption that "development" or "progress" is the peculiar essence of Western societies. It is further assumed that "progress" may be or should be generously conferred by the West upon "traditional" nations "willing" to "modernize." But as we have seen in the previous sections, assumptions about the "essence" of the East and of the West are fallacies. It is a typical modernizing fallacy, for example, to see the suppression of developments in the formerly colonized world as an expression of "traditional" lifestyles. Rather, the suppression of local development by external agency is not a local cultural tradition—and this is a key recognition of the center-periphery view. The development of local economies and so-called modern institutions in formerly colonized nations did not occur at a pace and tenor as in the West because they were not allowed to develop. Rather, under colonialism, independent activity was suppressed throughout all levels of society. Local, autonomous, independent development is what Azzedine Haddour refers to as the "diachronic history" of the "East" or "Third World." When he says that diachronic history in the East was "sclerosed" or "mummified," he means that independent, autonomous development was suppressed by the West (*Colonial Myths* 2).

In the previous chapter, one considered how Algeria was underdeveloped by means of colonial violence, or through French military force. One may also consider how underdevelopment may be achieved through methods other than, primarily, military force. North African nations such as Morocco and Egypt, for example, never shared with Algeria the pervasive degree of colonial management and administration, nor did they share in as bloody a struggle for independence. Of course these differences owed to the unique historical and societal factors inherent in each of these particular nations. Yet all three nations bore the marks of suppressed local development to the advantage of metropolitan surpluses. During the late colonial period in Egypt and Morocco, it was primarily economic means rather than military occupation by which unequal relations were retained with the West. This was so even though both North African nations could regard the presence of a local sovereign and of an ostensibly autonomous administration. Such "home rule" was especially disingenuous in Egypt. There independence had been formally granted by Britain in 1922. Yet Britain continued to dominate Egyptian political and economic life until 1952. The situation could be called "neocolonial," perhaps, after the end of the Protectorate era because of both political and economic ties to the metropole. Clearly, such bondage pertained regardless of formal independence.

It is important to recognize that economic means may bind so-called underdeveloped or "lesser developed" nations in the East to the Western nations at the world economic center. Much of what is called "progress" or economic development in "underdeveloped" or "lesser developed" nations rather exhibits the features of peripheral economic bondage. Specifically, a couple of peripheral features which are reified as "modern development" are:

- the "development" and maintenance of an elite class (*compradors*) in commerce and government which is beholden to foreign investors and outside agents, and accordingly,
- the disenfranchisement of the impoverished majority, regarded as the locus of "backward" or retrogressive "traditions" which are said to conflict with "modernity," and for whom benefits are predicted to—eventually—"trickle down" from "modernized" elites.

The tenuous position of the local petty bourgeoisie may hover between these two extremes, as described above. The stratifications of social class may not be an entirely imposed phenomenon in and of itself, of course. But marked class polarity is a telling feature of so-called economic development in "peripheral" nations.

In response to the fallacious claims put forth by modernization discourse, an important example to consider is that of modern Egypt. There so-called "modernization" has assumed many forms throughout the last two centuries. Egypt's role in international production, from the rise of Western industrialism in the nineteenth century through postwar independence bears the features of peripheral exploitation. Specifically, the split between a *comprador* elite and the disenfranchised majority defined Egyptian cultural, economic, and political life throughout the late colonial period.

The modern history of Egypt, though unique and having evolved through a particular set of factors, yet illustrates the peripheral problematic. The actual, material development of formerly colonized nations is at odds with the world economic system dominated by a handful of Western institutions and agencies at the so-called center. This is exemplified by the kind of economic and societal developments which occurred in Egypt after Ottoman decline gave way to European power there. Although modernization was aggressively pursued over several generations by the heirs of Muhammad Ali, what was "developed" in Egypt was quite far afield from the European models to which Ali's successors aspired. Egypt's pursuit of "modernization" in this period developed instead a mode of agrarian capitalism akin to feudalism and bonded to industrial agents in Western Europe.[1] It is exactly such history—the material history of formerly colonized nations—which is elided by the fallacious logic of modernization discourse.

It is ironic that Egypt, a land synonymous with the very idea of "history" in the Western imagination, should appear so conceptually impoverished. But the very notion of "ancient history"—the problematic term which so frequently recurs in modernization discourse—reflects a selective memory, particularly in regard to Egypt. Perhaps few other nations than Egypt have been so selectively imagined. The elision of colonial history, as has been discussed previously, is a tenet fallacy of "modernization." Modernizers supplant colonial history with a fiction about "traditions" and backwardness alleged to be essential qualities in the East. To confront the materialism of colonial history upturns the fiction about a retrograde, "traditional" Eastern essence. Egypt's long, unbroken cultural identity and the independent nation's role as a catalyst of Arab political development in the late twentieth century belies the modernizing view that "progressive" or diachronic history is the exclusive possession of the imagined West. Indeed, to regard material history dissolves the illusory fetish which modernizers make of "history"—ancient or modern, "Eastern" or "Western."

It is interesting to consider for a moment the truncated view with which Egypt is regarded by Western popular conceptions. At least in the

U.S., popular conceptions about Egypt typically regard a vaguely conceived "age of antiquity"—sometimes portrayed as Biblical, sometimes as Hellenic. One easily recalls the popular film images of 1960s Hollywood—of Elizabeth Taylor, splendid in eye make-up and Richard Burton, her ill-fated consort (*Cleopatra*); of pharaonic Yul Brenner defying seven plagues to pursue Charleton Heston in a chariot (*The Ten Commandments*). Such stylized images of Egypt endure and are simulated continually in the American imagination—e.g., as recently in a children's film by Disney. The promulgation of these images creates the impression that Egypt once embodied a glorious, glittering, pagan antagonism to Judeo-Christianity—and was therefore, in the Western imagination, duly smote, in Technicolor. Even today, a visit to just about any bookstore will turn up many books about the "boy-king" Tutankhamen or about dynastic Egypt. But works which deal with more recent Egyptian history, even with Ottoman history in Egypt, let alone the modern period, are much less readily accessible. Surely there is no dearth of published material about modern Egypt. But the wide commercial availability of material about the "antique" in comparison with the lesser accessibility of the modern is rather telling of American popular consumption, if not our popular conceptions, of Egyptian imagery.

Lately, popular conceptions about Egypt have evolved somewhat. This is due to recurrent media portrayals of Arab terrorism or Islamic fundamentalist militancy, especially after the September 11 events in 2001. Some of the alleged hi-jackers on September 11 were identified as Egyptian nationals. The photos of the hi-jackers were shown repeatedly on television news broadcasts and in newspapers in the weeks after the events. True, the photos of the young men did not merely reveal their nationalities. Still, their apparent ethnicity and the repeated references to terrorism forged a strong visual link between Arab men in general and the concept of terrorism in mediated public discourse. Prior to the 9/11 representations, there was the event of the EgyptAir flight 990 which crashed into the Atlantic Ocean under mysterious circumstances in 1999.[2]

Separate investigations of the crash conducted by American and Egyptian authorities issued conflicting findings. The American report concluded that one of the pilots, Gamil al-Batouti, had willfully brought down the plane in an act of murder-suicide.[3] As proof of the pilot's intentions, the investigators pointed to his last words, retrieved from the black box recording: "I put my faith in God." The pilot's use of the Muslim expression was portrayed in the American media as characteristic of religious extremism. U.S. media reports implied, if not overtly stated, that the latter had motivated his alleged act of murder-suicide. The American portrayal was disputed by the Egyptian authorities, who attested that the pilot merely invoked a common prayer in his distress. The Egyptian investigators attributed the crash to a mechanical problem with the Boeing-made aircraft. Nevertheless, the U.S. media's repeated references to the pilot's last words and alleged intentions portrayed him as an unbalanced Islamic extremist. The portrayal dominated the U.S. media, regardless of the contrary finding of the Egyptian report and the testimony of the pilot's family and friends. Generally today one finds the U.S. media is no less biased in regard to Arabs and Muslims. Recent events in the so-called "war-on-terror" seem to provide "sanction" for the racist images of "Islamist terrorists" simulated in the American media.

The truncated view of Egypt in the American popular imagination may be dispelled, at least theoretically, by even a cursory review of the history which is typically elided by "modernizers." The retrieval of this history for the current discussion will hopefully shed light upon what Western development in the East has historically entailed. Egypt had figured into the world economic system, it can be argued, from a very early age—as early, perhaps, as depends on how one would define the terms, "world," "economic" and "system," or indeed, "center" and "periphery." Therefore, the present discussion will focus upon Egypt in the age of capitalism. Contrary to the claims of modernizers, one sees that Egypt had participated in modern industrial production from the rise of industry early in the nineteenth century. Egypt's own pursuit of industrialization and new technologies produced some features of modern society, such as those seen in the West. This autonomous, local development progressed until the intervention of the Western powers.

Early development in Egypt was initiated not through rapprochement with the West but independently, on Egypt's own terms, even within the context of Ottoman rule.[4] Much of this early activity took place under Muhammad Ali (1805–1848), an Ottoman general who, though not a native Egyptian, may be considered as a forerunner of the modern Egyptian nation state. Although Egypt was an administrative unit of the Ottoman Empire, centralized rule was by then much in decline. Ali was a strong provincial ruler and his reforms were aimed at local autonomy. His modernization plan was to develop and maintain the local infrastructure. Ali created a national army and sought to build civil society through public works, public education and state reforms. Importantly, he sought to establish the political conditions for civil society by disempowering religious authorities and traditional elites. The disempowering of such notables may have also been self serving, as this class would have mitigated Ali's own authority. Nevertheless his reforms are those typically associated with the development of the modern, sovereign, secular state.

Muhammad Ali established many features of so-called modern society in Egypt, but not without political costs. His reforms brought conflict with the European powers allied with the Ottomans. Egypt's military and its expansionist aims in other parts of the empire posed a threat to the Ottoman Sultan. This situation elicited Western intervention on behalf of Istanbul in 1840. British influence in Egypt is seen by historians as dating from this time (Finkel 446), eventually manifesting in the 1882 occupation and the establishment of the Protectorate in 1912. Britain essentially took over Ottoman control of Egypt with the turn of the century. Egypt's colonial relationship with the West can thus be said to have begun in the late Ottoman age. The Ottoman Empire's weakening authority and its dependency upon Europe—ultimately the "sickness" described by colonial writers—established the conditions which were later capitalized upon by the West and by Britain in particular. Indeed, Ottoman weakness was the very condition which had allowed for the autonomy of Muhammad Ali and his proto-nationalistic reforms. British administration undermined this direction.

With successive "capitulations"—i.e., diplomatic and commercial concessions to the foreign powers, Egyptian development stagnated. Muhammad Ali's nationalistic gains were lost. Ali's modernization plan was eroded, both by colonial administration and by his successors, whose modernizing efforts substantially differed from his own. Notable in this regard was the Khedive Ismail, grandson of Muhammad Ali, whose pursuit of modernization ultimately led to debt and dependency. In the passage below, Amin describes how autonomous modern development was interrupted in Egypt through colonial intervention:

> In Egypt there had already been in the eighteenth century, with Ali Bey, a first attempt at modernizing the Egyptian state, something which required its emancipation from the Ottoman yoke. The circumstances following the adventures of Bonaparte's armies led to a second attempt being made, by Mehemet Ali Pasha [Muhammad Ali]. The Egyptian ruling class—of foreign origin (Turkish, Albanian, Circassian)—was the Pasha's military bureaucracy, which levied tribute from the peasantry, made up of families of small holders. Their surplus was used by the Egyptian state to finance modernization in the form of irrigation works and the establishment of a national army and of industry. The Anglo-Turkish alliance in 1840 dealt a blow to this attempt at modernization. Europe, hastening to the rescue of the Ottoman Sultan, whose armies had been beaten by the Egyptian Pasha's forces, compelled Mehemet Ali to submit to the Capitulations, thus putting an end to the effort to

> develop industry. The Pasha's successor's from 1848 to 1882, gave up this independent policy, in the hope (in the case of the Khedive Ismail) of Europeanizing and modernizing Egypt with the aid of European capital, integrating the country into the world market (by developing the growing of cotton), and appealing to the financial houses of Europe to find the capital for this outward-oriented development. (*Unequal Development* 302–303)

Amin points out that Muhammad Ali's early, independent program supported local industry and was financed through levies and military expansion. This program was replaced by a "modernization" dependent upon foreign capital and the world market throughout the later nineteenth century. Local industry was hindered in Egypt for the development of a peripheral economy that exported surpluses to central (or, foreign) agents. The modernization program of the Khedive Ismail was thus qualitatively different from the reforms of Muhammad Ali. Ali had aspired to Western-style technologies, etc., without the posture of prostration to Western culture and ideology. But Ismail wanted to create "a Cairo to rival Paris." Toward this end, he acquired huge loans to finance a series of large-scale cultural, architectural and landscaping projects. Under Ismail the Suez Canal was opened but would remain under foreign control until 1956. Meanwhile the local economy became increasingly dominated by a single factor—the production of cotton. Egypt benefited from the halt in U.S. cotton supplies to the world market during the American Civil War; but the "boom" ended after the war, and Ismail's projects incurred outstanding debts. Western banks had indulged him in what might today be called, "debt gorging;" but later they summarily recalled the loans at a heavy advantage. In this way, much of Egypt was "privatized" by foreign banks. Ismail's modernizing aspirations played largely into the hands of his creditors.

Modernization under Muhammad Ali had some substantial differences from that under Ismail. Ali's efforts to develop civil society, such as the creation of public works and education, did not so much aim at lavish prestige or urban aesthetics but at the reform of Egyptian society as a whole. Furthermore, his efforts to industrialize served the aims of national autonomy and expansionism. It is also significant that Muhammad Ali's reforms were financed independently. Conversely, the efforts of later Egyptian leaders such as Ismail, Fouad and Farouk, fostered an economic dependency upon the West. Their reforms pursued what might be more accurately called, "Europeanization," with the colonial connotations (rather than Lerner's "parochialism") of the term. It was largely because of the dependency upon European financiers that

Egypt developed into a peripheral society, with a peripheral economy, rather than an industrial society with a so-called "developed" economy.

The "Europeanization" of Egypt under Ismail and his successors tended toward the imitation or appropriation of European cultural forms by the local ruling elite—rather than the development of economic solvency such as that associated with the European nations which had provided the credit. It also entailed European guidance in economic pursuits which did not so much develop Egyptian society as line the pockets of the ruling elites and their foreign bosses. But while a largely Europeanized, cosmopolitan elite derived some outward trappings of a modern Western lifestyle, the larger native society bore the abjection of colonial exploitation. Thus it is important to understand the direction of Western-led development, at least in a historical sense. That is because "globalization" today is quite similar to early modern development practices in the colonial periphery. This can be seen in the emphasis of globalization upon loans, privatization, and market or "structural" reforms which privilege foreign investors. Such "structural reforms" typically neglect local infrastructure and inhibit local entrepreneurship in favor of multinational enterprise. Today, proponents of globalization claim that "development" will bring "modernity" and "democracy" to the Middle East. But such privileges have—as in early modern Egypt—historically accrued only to the small class of elites or "compradors" who assist foreign ventures. Western development has merely "trickled down" poverty and disenfranchisement to the local majority.

What "modern development" ultimately meant for Egypt after Ismail was, in fact, peripheral economic bondage. Under British rule, Egypt became an agricultural supplier to Western industry, primarily British textiles. In this way, Egyptian cotton and some other raw resources fueled the economic development of the West. Once linked to the "global economy," Egyptian production—which had formerly pursued some local diversification and industrialization—was basically limited to agrarian production. This production exported both resources and surpluses, that is, profits, to the "global" market, i.e., to capitalists at the "center" of the world economy. This Egyptian agrarianism was "monocultural," which means it was dominated by one crop (cotton) cultivated for export. Egypt's monocultural economy was aimed at and in the service of the development of Western capital. To see Egyptian agrarianism in this light is to make an important recognition. The discourse of modernization posits that agrarian production in the global "periphery" is a "traditional," pre-modern mode. But plainly, Egyptian agrarianism in the modern age was not "traditional" as much as it was an aspect of peripheral economic exploitation. Peripheral agrarian production was thrust upon Egypt through colonial violence.

Monocultural production formed the economic base of Egyptian society during the period of British administration. This had profound effects upon local society as a whole. The predominance of cotton production not only hindered the development of a diversified economy. But given the nature of agrarianism in this case, the cotton economy produced what can be called para-feudal conditions for Egyptian society as a whole. These para-feudal conditions, in turn, impeded a wide array of social developments. Such impediment is, again, what Haddour means when he refers to the "mummification" of diachronic history. He means that social development is repressed through the colonial apparatuses.

Class polarity is typical of colonial society. Widespread economic abjection and the alienation of the masses is usually commensurate with the expropriation of local surpluses and resources, and the excessive wealth and privilege of a small elite beholden to foreign powers. These attributes characterize what is termed by Wallerstein, Amin and others as the "peripheral social formation." Implicit in the term is the recognition that exploitative economic factors shape—or if you like, determine—the oppressive conditions of colonial society. These factors may shape or determine the conditions of local society as much as, if not more than, foreign military oppression.

The peripheral economy itself, especially one engaged in monocultural agrarianism, is one of the repressive colonial apparatuses. This was the case similarly, more or less, in French Algeria. There the arable land was granted to *pieds noirs* farmers in order to supply the metropole. An elite class, comprised mainly of French and European *colons,* was structured and sustained through this arrangement. The majority of Algerian natives, rather, lived disenfranchised lives. Many performed serf-like labor on foreign-owned farms and vineyards or else worked itinerantly in cities and villages. French "development" in Algeria before independence had merely developed native poverty and abjection. These are the conditions about which Fanon spoke and to which Haddour refers; Memmi, too, discusses how colonial production affects or shapes local society in the periphery.

Egyptian agrarianism, as a peripheral function in the world system, developed and supported a para-feudal society. The Egyptian *latifundia* of the period is symptomatic of this mode of production. The *latifundia* were landed estates owned by a small number of elites and worked by serf labor, with all this situation implies in terms of feudal class relations and production. It is important to note, however, that this "modern feudalism" was in fact the product of international capitalism:

> This was the setting in which the ruling class of Egypt was to undergo a change of structure, taking possession of the land, with the help of the state, and transforming themselves from a mandarin-type bureaucracy [as under the Ottomans] into a class of latifundia-owners. This did not mean "feudalists," as has often been said, but agrarian capitalists, whose prosperity depended on the world market. Egypt having thus been made into a cotton plantation for Lancashire, when the British threat to Egypt's independence materialized, the Egyptian ruling class quickly agreed to submit, on being guaranteed the maintenance of its privileges. It was well repaid by the British and became the biggest beneficiary of the opening up of the Nile valley. (*Unequal Development* 303)

Amin points out that Egyptian production eventually took the form of an "agrarian capitalism." The term, "agrarian capitalism," emphasizes Egypt's peripheral role in the world productive system. It is a term which at once recognizes and belies the notion of feudalism. With the concept of "agrarian capitalism," one sees that Egypt had always participated in the kind of production which is associated with "modern" society. But this participation was confined to colonial, or peripheral, production. Early local industrialization in Egypt had been interrupted in favor of cotton production to supply British textile mills. Had it not been for the British (or for any of the host of Western foreign agents) Egyptian society would presumably have developed of its own accord and after its own fashion. But this autonomous development was interrupted and an artificially "feudal" society evolved instead.

Amin, importantly, distinguishes agrarian capitalism from the feudalism it ostensibly resembles on the basis of its link to the capitalist world system. One might think of "agrarian capitalism" as the modern reification of classic feudal production. (This would not imply that the two modes are identical, but that they are comparable based on certain criteria.) Whereas European feudalism had been eroded by the capitalist mode of production, Egyptian para-feudalism was contemporaneous with accelerated global capitalism; indeed it was a function of it. Egyptian agrarian capitalism characterized the peripheral role in international production, or global capitalism.

The clarification about agrarian capitalism—that it is a modern rather than a feudal mode—shows that para-feudal conditions in the periphery were a synthetic phenomenon imposed through European capitalist imperialism. This is a significant observation for those who wish to understand the material stakes of contemporary development practices, or "globalization" today. The para-feudal conditions in the agrarian "periphery" are said by modernizers to be the conditions of "underdevelopment." Yet one may recognize that these conditions nonetheless bear a link to multinational capitalists at the global "center." With today's global "agribusiness," serf-like conditions in the periphery feed productive surpluses to the center. Again, where one sees "modern serfs," one recalls Haddour's assertion about the repression of diachronic history inherent under colonialism. Therefore one must question what is truly intended by those who promulgate the policies of economic "structural reforms"—or globalization. Similarly one must question the intentions of "modernizers" who today wish to develop so-called "democracy" in the Middle East. Modernizers, globalizers and reformers—all largely ignore or elide the history of Western "development" in the region. What that history has actually entailed has very little to do with democracy or local development. Egypt's early modern period is a case in point. The development of local society there was hindered by Western agency. Autonomous, local development in Egypt was replaced by the pursuit of Western-style—and Western-oriented—development. The latter pursuit was financed by Europe and entailed excessive loans, dependency on foreign capital and technologies, the inhibition of native enterprise, the patronizing of *comprador* elites, and programs aimed at cultural "Europeanization."

Western "development" in modern Egypt precipitated a downward spiral. Egypt had entered the nineteenth century poised to develop itself into a modern nation state. Industry, secularism, civil society and national defense (which implies sovereignty) were the recognizable features intended to establish modern statehood. But under Western "development" Egyptian society assumed para-feudal conditions. The unequal development of modern Egypt was characterized locally by a small class of beholden elites and an impoverished, disenfranchised majority. These conditions are characteristic of what is called the "peripheral social formation," or of a colonial society shackled to peripheral production in the global economic system.

The material history of modern Egypt briefly summarized above may provide some perspective for those who wish to understand globalization today. That is because many of the same features which characterize that history are extant in the so-called developing world even now. Development encompasses similar policies and rhetoric whether during the late age of colonialism or the current age of globalization. Western development, then as now, has led not to economic, social and political progressivism in the East, but to instability, dependency, debt and tyranny in local society. Thus it is important to review the "development" of colonial Egypt, as we ostensibly embark upon a well-worn road, paved with the rhetoric of good intentions.

4.2 DEVELOPMENT FOR THE FEW

To emphasize how economic factors shaped modern Egyptian society is not to ignore the role of colonial violence. Society of the periphery in Egypt was developed and maintained, ultimately, through the threat of British military force. The threat of violence had strong-armed successive generations of political "capitulations" on the part of local leaders. One such concession was the continued occupation of Egypt by British soldiers after formal independence was declared in 1922. Egyptian independence before 1952 was not independence at all, but was rather a limited "autonomy," subject to British authority.

Commercial production was not the single object of British interests in Egypt. Because of the strategic location of the Suez Canal, Egypt served another important function, besides cotton production, in maintaining the broader objectives of British imperial power. These objectives were geopolitical as well as commercial. The Suez Canal was an artery of British naval power. Its strategic importance was similar, say, to that of the Panama Canal to the United States during the same period. Egypt's compromised sovereignty—its "autonomy" rather than "independence"—was of utmost importance to Britain—and ultimately, Western—interests.

Yet the British administration of Egypt was different from that of the French in the Maghrib. The very scale of military occupation, for example, was much more limited by comparison. British forces tended to be concentrated in the Suez Canal Zone. In Algeria, foreign military garrisons were present throughout the country. French troops basically provided security for *pied noir* communities and local colonial government. Indeed, this aspect of formal colonization—the foreign colony or settler community—raises another significant difference. There was no British settler community in Egypt comparable to that of the Algerian *pieds noirs.* British authority in Egypt, by comparison with French North Africa, was ostensibly less invasive. In Algeria and in Morocco, respectively, a French Resident General assumed ultimate military and administrative command. But the British administration of Egypt took the semblance of "advisors" to an autonomous local government. This was somewhat the case as well in Morocco; however, it seems that the Moroccan sultans had a more troubled relationship with their advisors than did their Egyptian counterparts.

Peripheral society and economy in North Africa was developed and sustained through the imminent threat of violence inherent in foreign occupation.

British militarism, or colonial violence, was the backdrop of modern Egypt as was French violence the backdrop of French Algeria and Morocco. Occupation, though different by degrees—if such a "difference" has any meaning—nevertheless had similar results for local society. It created mass economic abjection and a second-class position for most natives, both in relation to the metropole as well as to local *comprador* elites. Such poverty and alienation were, in fact, considered by Sartre to be facets or examples *per se* of colonial violence. But it can be argued that economic domination rather than military domination characterized British rule in Egypt. Exploitative economic relations with Britain and other Western countries limited Egyptian sovereignty and profoundly affected Egyptian society. Because of this, and because of the relatively smaller scale of foreign troop deployment, modern Egypt was in effect a colonial society by economic rather than by primarily militaristic means. To say this is not to dismiss the British military occupation, but rather to recognize the interrelated facets of the colonial system, the relationship of "center and periphery."

Perhaps because colonial militarism was less attenuated in Egypt than in Algeria, one may better observe the self-sustaining functions of the peripheral social formation. In Egypt, as in colonial societies generally, local society itself—or, the "peripheral social formation"—perpetuated the features of the colonial condition. These features are often taken as signs of cultural "essence," yet they may be recognized as materially constructed by the conditions of colonial life. The plantation economy which evolved in Egypt under the British maintained much of the old power relations between the native peasants and the landed, Ottoman aristocracy. The latter was a foreign ruling class which had been established under the Ottoman Empire. As Amin points out, this class saw its own vested powers as holders of large cotton-producing estates and was therefore concessional to British rule (*Unequal Development* 303). Successive foreign rule had been the case in Egypt historically. But after the Ottomans, the presence of Turkish, Balkan, Circassian, European and Levantine elites continued to characterize the society. By the industrial age, Ottoman "foreigners" throughout class society had assimilated culturally, but generally retained "caste" privileges at all levels in relation to most "native" Muslims. The cultural signs of material privilege were marked by light skin, legal status, honorifics, etc. This situation created a plainly visible social polemic between what was, at least ostensibly, the "foreign" and the "native" classes.

The criteria upon which "native" or "foreign" identity is attributed, of course, is a slippery slope. However, to emphasize the ethnic identity of certain groups and to acknowledge their relative powers within the class system is to gain some perspective upon colonial society in late modern Egypt. One assumes, perhaps erroneously, that one may generally call "native" the majority of Egyptians across the class strata who were either Muslim or Christian and who were not largely of Ottoman, Levantine or European bloodline. Admittedly, this definition of native identity is problematic—since what constitutes bloodline or pedigree is necessarily collapsible criteria—yet it is a useful definition for the present discussion. Native Egyptians comprised a small bourgeoisie and, more largely, the peasantry (i.e., including landless peasants, the village hierarchies, and the rural "notables"). The Copts, a native minority which traces its lineage to the "original" Egyptians and to the earliest Christians, shared sometimes in elite class privileges, sometimes in the receipt of xenophobic hostilities, sometimes in nationalist activism.

One may conjecture that to the degree which ethnic elites of greater or lesser strata were matriculated throughout the generations into Egyptian society, they were perceived likewise to a greater or lesser degree as "foreign" or as "ethnic minorities." Muslim Turks had more deeply assimilated than had Sephardic Jews or Levantine Christians, for example, two groups whose presence in Egypt was at least as old if not as dominant. Ottoman rule had encouraged much Levantine, Jewish and Armenian immigration to Egypt. Greeks, Italians, and other Europeans were less assimilated and were often referred to collectively as *khawāgat,* a somewhat pejorative term which one observer likens to *gringo* (Rodenbeck 130). Ethnic minorities played a significant role in Egypt's peripheral production beginning in the nineteenth century when a small industrial class, ancillatory to the plantation economy, was formed. They participated both as invested agents at all levels of class strata and as colonial subjects, acted upon by external and internal forces. Their roles may be understood as a structural feature of colonial society.

This social phenomena, so marked by the trappings of cultural identity, was engendered and maintained through an outward-oriented economy which exported profits and resources to the "central" Western agents, e.g., British textile production, European shipping, banking and commerce. One scholar observes the colonial agency of Egypt's chronic social divisions and notes "an almost inverse relation" between economic power and native identity:

> We have thus, on the one hand, those who pulled the strings: the Liverpool import firms and the British, French and Belgian banks; and on the other, tied to the soil, the colonized human being. Between the two extremes there were intermediary rungs: branches of the different Agencies, local firms, brokers, subcontractors, large, middle and

> small producers, landless peasants and labourers. Between one rung of the ladder and the next, differences not only in power and in living standards, but in dress, language and appearance, in an almost inverse relation between economic potency and Egyptianess. (Berque 290)

The local hierarchy which governed commercial life was characterized by ethnicity and religious affiliation. Such "identity politics" was also a legally inscribed aspect of colonial society. It was supported by international commerce and the world market which needed a custodial class in the relations of production. Not only big landowners but ethnic small businessmen as well enjoyed the privileges of class or caste power to the disadvantage of most natives. Minorities, even those of relatively modest means, tended to support the *comprador* administrators and foreign agents who represented their own interests. Their supportive function as a class, if not so much as individuals, had been codified by generations of foreign rule.

Egypt's "capitulations" to the West had legalized the social stratification of ethnic and religious identities. As in French North Africa, separate tribunals were established for Muslims, Jews and Christians, respectively. Various ethnic groups also enjoyed the protection of their foreign consuls in civil matters. Resident holders of foreign passports or dual citizenship ("third nationals") were likewise protected by their consulates. Commerce laws and trade agreements favored foreign business generally and that of ethnic minorities specifically. Thus a small retailer of goods, a latter-generation *colon* from Italy or Greece, say, while certainly not a member of what is typically considered as "ruling class," nevertheless figured in the constellation of imposed rules and shared in legal and economic benefits. Similarly, Muslim Turks, Christian Arabs, Syrians, Armenians and other Levantines derived through legistlative means commercial and other benefits to the exclusion of the majority of native Egyptian Muslims. While there were native Muslims who figured among the elite, the legal privileges of Muslims generally as a class tended to accrue to the social castes which were identifiably "non-native." The "Ottoman" court of King Farouk provides one example of the latter.

Drawing upon trade journals and municipal documents of the period, Jacques Berque speaks of the commercial power of ethnic minorities before independence in his study, *Egypt: Imperialism and Revolution:*

> [T]o consider the details of economic life, we realize that here again the cosmopolitan element prevailed over the Egyptian. We have only to glance at the lists of contractors and tradesmen published by specialist journals or the bulletins of the Chambres of Commerce. Let us

> examine, for instance, a list of contractors in building materials: out of fifty names, only three are Eastern, let alone Egyptian. Even when the business in question deals with such natural produces as eggs, gum arabic or sesame, collected by the fellahin [native peasant] and thus implying a direct contact with him, we find only four local names among the twenty-five exports registered in Alexandria. The proportion is even smaller in the liberal professions: out of twenty chemists' shops in Cairo, only two bore Eastern names. The grocery trade was the exclusive province of the Greeks. Almost everywhere, in the import as well as in the export trade, the dominant figures were foreigners, with a handful of Levantines . . . Out of the hundreds of cloth manufacturers and merchants, and of tailors, we can hardly find a dozen Arab names. (293–294)

The municipal records cited above relate the caste privileges of ethnic minority and foreign small businessmen, grocers, contractors and tradesmen. This group was by no means an aristocracy or a ruling class in terms of political power or wealth; yet they were an elite in relation to most of native society. Although caste privileges were certainly not uniform, even the lesser strata obtained them, presumably in a no less stratified distribution. Even small businessmen who set up shop locally and catered to local markets ultimately participated in the system of outward-oriented production, simply by virtue of the constructed nature of their competitive advantage. They were likely not to have recognized this advantage as an aspect of global production. As in racialized society in the U.S., the petty bourgeoisie rarely acknowledges its own circumstances, ignoring its own ethnic and caste attributes while (loudly) proclaiming its labor, its merit, and its self determination. Yet even in the U.S., the position of the local petty bourgeoisie is becoming more starkly apparent as tenuous and as parasitic upon underpaid labor in the Third World—a recognition fueled by the growing export of white collar jobs, such as in computer programming and telemarketing, to so-called "developing" nations.

One recognizes that class, ethnic and religious identities are shifting signifiers and do not concretize any kind of uniform experience, in Egypt or anywhere else. Yet there were broad tendencies toward class power, or lack of it, characterized by religious, ethnic and cultural signifiers, which can be observed and which figured materially within modern Egyptian society. These signifiers and their implications for material life were important to Egyptians of all castes and strata as they had been for the foreign imperial powers. As a result, modern Egyptian society was deeply polarized between the cosmopolitan upper classes—which included the native bourgeoisie—and the large native peasantry.

The Egyptian upper classes tended to identify culturally with Turkey and Europe, and to see their own interests in terms of empire rather than nation. This was characteristic of the ethnic minorities and so-called "third nationals"—Egyptian holders of foreign passports and foreign residents—among the elite. Muhammad Ali himself, though an early force for Egyptian nationalism, had been an Ottoman army general and was of Albanian descent. Egyptian leaders after Muhammad Ali who sought to "modernize," notably Ismail, sought for their elite constituency the mainly cultural facades of European life, such as opera houses, Continental cooks and tutors, Francophilia and other attributes esteemed in a somewhat derivative fashion from the Ottoman Turks. Under the patronage of Ismail, Giuseppe Verdi composed *Aïda* while the Cairo Opera House was built for the production (Rodenbeck 133 n.). Meanwhile, the newly dug Suez Canal was owned and operated by foreign interests, an arrangement which would later be a catalyst for Egyptian independence.

It was generally viewed in Egypt that the class interests of Ismail and his heirs, and of the ruling elites who supported them, coincided with colonial rule. The problem of political and economic dependency, in the nativist view, lay in the preservation of foreign power by these local collaborators. Westernization (or, Europeanization) was most often seen as the mark of foreign interests and foreign sympathies. And yet at the same time, it was also understood as a class distinction, a sign of upperclass status, a measure of wealth and prestige. This sort of discrepancy is often cited by postcolonial critics and is sometimes called "double consciousness." Fanon described the phenomenon in his work, *Black Skin, White Mask.* "Double consciousness" is an esteem for the outward signs of oppression because in the colonial context they signify local prestige and power. Again, it may be noted that such regard derives from the peripheral formation of local society. Like the roles of minority elites, "double consciousness" functions, albeit more abstractly, to support colonial hegemony.

The commercial and social features of Egyptian society before 1952 are characteristic of colonial production; to identify them as such is not mere economic determinism, a reduction which one would understandably want to avoid. Rather, to fail to recognize the—basically economic—infrastructures of colonial society is to ignore much of the meaning of history. Moreover, to identify these features as structural lends an appreciation of the predicament of decolonization. After independence, there remained the old colonial problem of the peripheral dependence of the "traditional," agricultural economy upon the Western industries at the world's "center." This problem is often referred to as "neocolonialism," the perpetuation of colonial submission not through military means but through peripheral economic ties to the metropole.

The material conditions of peripheral economy produced many effects which appear as and were in fact local cultural expressions, as we shall see. However, it would be reductive to take the signs of peripheral social formation as essentially cultural phenomena. Cultural expressions, however particular, are not things independent of the material conditions from which they arise. One may consider how certain cultural phenomena reflected the conditions established through colonial production. Or, in other words, how did certain cultural phenomena reflect the peripheral social formation? By "cultural phenomena," I refer to ethnic and religious group identification, or lack of identification, and the coexisting and competing manifestations of nativist, nationalist and transnationalist thought or inclination. Such "identity politics" figured strongly in the inner relations of Egyptian class society.

Nativism, nationalism and transnationalism and group identity in colonial or formerly colonized nations are constructs which have typically been the subject of postcolonial theory. However, much postcolonial theory, especially in the academy today, skirts the economic underpinnings of these constructs. Instead, what can be described as a "decontextualized racialism" prevails as an orienting concept of much postcolonial theory. That is, much postcolonial work foregrounds a kind of racialized "identity politics," detached from materialism. I refer here to the work of Homi K. Bhabha, Arjun Appadurai, et al. It is important to consider the materialism of so-called "identity politics." To do so would add another dimension to much postcolonial thought in the academy today. With the current example, one may see that certain cultural features of modern Egyptian society contributed to a politics of identity. These features were obviously rooted in peripheral production, i.e., in agrarian capitalism. The maintenance of a class of *comprador* elites, and the much regarded "cosmopolitanism" of this social class were symptoms of agrarian capitalism as much as the cultivation of cotton. Also symptomatic was the development of Cairo and Alexandria, and a few wealthy suburbs, as the administrative centers for government and commerce. In those places a European "veneer" was established by the ethnic minorities who dominated the means of production. Conversely, the outlying areas and provinces, removed from the seats of power, were "traditionally" native and chronically impoverished. In Upper (Southern) Egypt, peasant life was dominated by rural and village "notables" who owned large cotton and sugar cane plantations. The "underdevelopment" of the rural precincts, except as related to crops and shipping, was another telling feature of peripheral production. Like the cosmopolitanism of elites, the "traditionalism" of most natives, especially in the rural areas, were "cultural features" which stemmed from the colonial economy. The "overdevelopment" of the peripheral "centers" such as Cairo and Alexandria, the domain of *comprador* elites, were commensurate with mass native lack, or so-called "underdevelopment." Of course in real terms, neither elites nor the masses were simply "over" or "under" developed, but the conditions of both were symptomatic of modern global production. The fissure of modern Egyptian society into, basically, a society of "haves and have-nots" is typical of colonial societies in general. Egyptian society was likewise visibly divided by class interests and associations. That much would seem apparent.

It seems a comprehensive view, therefore, to examine how certain cultural features developed as local responses to economic factors in modern Egypt. Ethnic group identification and the inclinations toward nativism, nationalism and transnationalism were some of the defining cultural phenomena of the period. To see these cultural tendencies as responses to material conditions makes an important semantic distinction which, again, is all too often lacking in postcolonial studies. Rather, many postcolonialists simply skirt economic materialism in favor of a "racialist" or culturally essentialist hypothesis. This is probably due, in no small part, to the imminence of "modernization" as a discourse which "presumes to know" about former colonial or "developing" nations. "Modernization" is predicated upon cultural essentialism.

Modernization discourse inevitably posits economic phenomena—whether "Western" or "Eastern"—as wholly cultural. Modernizers' big fallacy is that economic abjection in poor nations is the result of, or is itself the expression of, culture or religion. This had been the "mantra," so to speak, of the Western authors of empire. One recognizes that "mantra" in the works of modernization pundits today. Correspondingly, the other big fallacy invoked by modernizers is that the wealth of Western nations results from inspired entrepreneurship in a "free" market. The latter myth has imparted religious-like fervency to the cult of individualism so characteristic of Western capitalist societies.

Too little of the postcolonialism in vogue in the academy today addresses the fallacy about Western wealth and the so-called "free" market. Rather, the "free market" seems to be accepted as a self-evident "truth." And while postcolonialists are quick to attribute the former fallacy, about Eastern or Third World backwardness, to colonial racialism, it is too often a "decontextualized racialism" which assumes "race" as an end in itself, at least discursively. That view is rather short-sighted, in my opinion. Contrary to the claims of modernizers then and now, that is, of either the imperial or the "globalized" age, native poverty and disenfranchisement in modern Egypt were not the self-evident symptoms of Eastern backwardness. Nor was the cultural Westernization of Egyptian elites reflective of "modernization." Both may be recognized as the attributes, rather, of peripheral social formation, or more specifically, of Egyptian agrarian capitalism.

Chapter Five

Letters of a Lost Generation

Alhadeff, Aciman, Said, Durrell, Mahfouz

5.1 COTTON TRADED FOR SILK

The class power of ethnic minorities in Egypt had been developed under Ottoman rule, when much foreign immigration to Egypt had occurred. The positioning of foreign nationals from elsewhere in the empire into military, administrative and commercial capacities was an Ottoman tactic to secure hegemony. Western colonialism in the nineteenth and twentieth centuries fostered the expansion of an Egyptian industrial class of *émigrés* from throughout the Mediterranean region. The series of political and national upheavals in Europe and the Near East from the early to middle twentieth century further induced emigration to Egypt. A trajectory of diaspora or transnational exile was shared by many Egyptian minorities, such as Sephardic Jews, Palestinians and Armenians, who had elsewhere been displaced or dispossessed. Ethnic minorities from Europe and the Levant, in addition to ethnic Turks, eventually comprised an elite class, one which was well known for its cosmopolitanism and urbanity. As the later kings of Muhammad Ali's line endeavored to "modernize," this elite class bore the effects of Westernized modernity and prosperity.

The commercial and institutional privileges of ethnic minorities were maintained under European and British colonialism and cultivated toward global production. This situation bears Amin's observation that the "mutilated nature of the national community . . . confers an apparent relative weight and special functions upon the local . . . bureaucratic and technical groups" in the periphery, or in this case, upon the minority elites who fulfilled these functions (*Unequal Development* 202). The class power of Egyptian minority elites had accrued because of their "relative weight and special functions" when compared to the agricultural subsistence of most Muslim natives. Amin's observation stresses that it was the colonial repression of local development and of the native masses which allowed elites to prosper. The prosperity of minority elites—which accrued by strata to a greater or lesser degree—was engendered through a colonial hegemonic system which, in the modern period, derived from peripheral production in the world system. Minority elites in Egypt comprised an administrative and managerial class beholden to foreign colonial powers in Britain and Europe.

Yet at the same time, the system of colonial hegemony which favored minority elites in Egypt also inculcated among them a dependency upon external agency and a tenuousness of position locally. The status of Egyptian minorities was dependent not only upon external support, but also upon legislation regarding citizenship, nationality and commerce. The legal criteria which favored minority elites were shifting and unstable. Elite status was impacted by varying political and economic forces within Egypt and, externally, by forces which pertained throughout the wider British Empire and throughout Europe. The privileges and the fate of Egyptian minority elites were dependent upon the favors and susceptible to the vagaries of the world system.

The position of minority elites in Egypt may be observed in the memoirs of the contemporary authors, Gini Alhadeff, Nawal El Saadawi, Andre Aciman and Edward Said. Interestingly, all four authors lived in Egypt more of less contemporaneously, in the period after the Second World War, in Alexandria and Cairo. There they spent the formative years of their youth, though they differ in age and generation. For example, Said and Aciman attended different campuses of the same boy's school, Victoria College, at different though pivotal times in the institution's history; i.e., respectively, shortly before and not long after the Egyptian Revolution in 1952. Alhadeff and Saadawi both write about plantation life in rural Egypt, albeit from different perspectives; whereas Saadawi takes as her subject the lives of the *fellahin,* Alhadeff provides an insider view of the planter elite. Edward Said is, of course, the late literary scholar, postcolonial critic and political activist. Andre Aciman is an author whose essays and autobiography have done much to chronicle recent Egyptian history and to contextualize it for an American understanding. Gini Alhadeff, a travel writer and novelist, has published a memoir of Egyptian life which is remarkable for its highly imagistic writing and its unflinching candor. Nawal El Saadawi is a doctor and feminist who helped bring the issue of female circumcision to international attention. She is also a novelist and human rights activist.

It will be interesting to consider these four writers and their works in a "materialist" context, that is, apart from the mainly "cultural" perspective inherent in much postcolonial study. Of the four, Said and Saadawi are well known in the fields of postcolonial and feminist studies. The other two, Aciman and Alhadeff, are younger and have recently garnered critical appreciation for the caliber of their fiction and travel writing. To discuss the memoirs of these four authors in materialist terms is in no way meant to reduce their individual experiences to a purely structural formula. Rather the following discussion will consider historical, material and societal aspects in order to provide additional insights into the experiences recorded by the four authors. This effort, I think, is actually in keeping with what the memoirists themselves intended to accomplish. Collectively Said and Saadawi, Aciman and Alhadeff, represent a unique historical vantage with which to view the last generation before actual Egyptian independence in 1952. The four memoirists appear similarly conscious, though with varying effects, that their experiences obtained within a kind of window of history in which the shade was soon to be drawn.

The four memoirists considered here were Egyptian elites of varying strata. While Saadawi is a native Egyptian from a petty bourgeois family of professionals and Muslim clerics, the other three authors typify the *émigré* experience of minority elites. Alhadeff and Aciman were "third nationals," that is, Egyptian-born holders of foreign passports. Said, who was born in Jerusalem and resided in Egypt, held American citizenship. The Alhadeffs were a planter family and were longer and better established in Egypt than other *émigré* families. They were Sephardim from Italy, Rhodes and Turkey who settled in Alexandria and Cairo in the nineteenth century. The Acimans were neither landed nor as well established as the Alhadeffs. Like the Saids, Aciman's family were more recent *émigrés* and successful entrepreneurs. The Acimans were Sephardim who had come to Egypt mainly in the twentieth century, some to escape the Holocaust in Europe. Said's family were Palestinian Christians who settled in Egypt when the British mandate in Palestine was dissolved.

Aciman, Said, and Saadawi tend to historicize their accounts and thus provide a context within which to view the lifestyles of the Egyptian upper classes, however much varied their strata. More importantly, their accounts allow a reader to observe how class privileges, or class inequities, contributed to the broader polarity in Egyptian society before 1952. One might say that the latter three authors recognized the existence of "two Egypts," one a transnational scene for elites, the other a nation of second-class citizens. In their own ways, and from their individual experiences, these three memoirists attempt to engage or account for this polarity. Alhadeff, by comparison, leaves room for a reader's own interpretation; though it may be noted that her style overall seems to favor tongue-in-cheek observations. However her account of family life does not really historicize or situate the subject within the contemporary movements of local society. Still her narrative gives easily to such an analysis.

The Alhadeff family played an active role in Egyptian agrarian capitalism. They owned large estates and an important company, Pinto Cotton. According to Alhadeff, the Egyptian Chamber of Commerce had cited the family firm in 1940 as "one among those which rank highest in the export of Egyptian cotton" (151). Alhadeff's maternal grandfather, Silvio Pinto, was a municipal administrator and a planter who had been decorated with an insignia by the Egyptian minister of finance. Pinto held the title, Commander of the Royal Order of Cotton, a commercial title of quasi-royal significance. Pinto's decoration, as well as his administrative tenure, attests to his stature among Egyptian planters. In a real way, he figured among the local agents which facilitated peripheral economic production in Egypt.

Alhadeff's memoir, *The Sun at Midday,* subtitled, *Tales of a Mediterranean Family,* portrays the lifestyle maintained by her family and other Egyptian elites of haute bourgeois status. The upper echelon, typically wealthy commercial agents and big landowners, had access to the ruling aristocracy—an important signifier for their social status, if not also for their commercial and class privileges. Cotton production, rather than "noble" bloodline, was their *entre* to a prestigious inner circle which Alhadeff calls the rarefied "Atmosphere" (36–37) of Alexandrian society. The lifestyles of Egyptian elites were inextricably linked to cotton. It was, according to Alhadeff, a lifestyle of silk based upon cotton, of cotton traded for silk.

Yet the cotton life was one which Alhadeff never actually shared. A series of political upheavals throughout the 1940s and '50s led to her grandfather being "impoverished in wealth as well as in status, having to sell his house to settle his debts" (156). The family lost their Egyptian assets but resettled abroad to comfortable, if less expansive, means. Although born in Egypt, Alhadeff had never seen her grandfather's cotton estates. Rather she simulated the experience, during research for her book, by visiting the cotton fields in rural Mississippi. She had wanted "to see what the commander [i.e., her grandfather, Silvio Pinto] had seen—fields of cotton, and with the sight of them, the notion of a living" (152). She appears ambivalent about the history she retraces, however. Referring to a 1940 publication of the Egyptian Chamber of Commerce entitled, *La Renaissance d'Egypte,* she observes:

> Making a living and making a fortune. The first is harder to do, a closer link between work and pay—because the essential piece in making a fortune in cotton is the cotton plant itself: there is no manufacturing one. But provided you have the soil, the climate, the water—Egypt and

> the Nile—as the *Renaissance of Egypt* put it, "This controlled, damned and disciplined river distributes its water along thousands of kilometers of canals . . ." (Alhadeff 153)

Thus Alhadeff considers the material conditions which contributed to her grandfather's ability to make both a living and a fortune from the trade in cotton. But she recognizes that the mere recipe of soil, water and climate, as asserted by the Egyptian COC, is a reductively simple account. She entertains another view, a familiar contention about the religious prohibition of usury:

> The commander [i.e., Pinto] had favorable circumstances: geography and climate. And? More favorable circumstances [she quotes]: "The Mohammedan code strictly forbids usury and pious Mohammedans followed the injunction to the letter of the law. In Egypt, moneylending passed into the hands of Copts, Jews and foreigners, thus in finance as in commerce, foreigners found themselves in a privileged position." (Alhadeff 153)

The Egyptian COC proposed that the Islamic prohibition of usury had engendered the primacy of enterprise conducted by Christians, Jews and foreigners, and consequently, the class power of Egyptian minority elites. Of course the notion is a fallacy that Western development was built upon the Muslim ban of usury. There had been generations of Ottoman commerce and finance in Egypt—that is, finance conducted by Muslims. By the middle eighteenth to early nineteenth century in Egypt, Rodenbeck notes, "practices such as the charging of interest, which traditionalists denounced as sinful usury, came to be widely accepted" (164). Thus, it is a mischaracterization to assert that Muslims abstained from profitable finance because they uniformly observed the traditional ban upon usury, while Christians and Jews picked up the slack, so to speak:

> From the beginning of the 19th century pressure ha[d] been brought to bear on traditional Islamic values by the colonial expansion of the European powers, and the financial institutions exported from the West. When the Ottoman Civil Code was promulgated in the 1870s there was no mention of loans at interest. This made it possible in 1888 to establish the Agricultural Bank, whose written constitution allowed it openly to lend and borrow money at interest.[1]

And earlier, a thirteenth century example of local business development initiated by the Mamluk rulers of Egypt sought to attract entrepreneurs from

Arabia and the Far East: "We extend this invitation to illustrious personages, great merchants desirous of profits, or small retailers . . . who inspir[e] charity by *borrowing* or who accomplish a good deed by *lending*" [italics added for emphasis].[2] As Braudel comments, "Against the weight of these [Muslim] merchant economies, what could religious scruples or reservations achieve?"[3] Technically, usury refers to the accrual of interest on a loan or the profit derived from currency exchange. In fact all three religions, Christianity, Judaism and Islam, prohibit usury. But how the prohibition has been implemented, and where and when it has been observed, is a different matter. Historically, usury and its prohibition have been variously and subjectively interpreted. It is sometimes construed as the charging of *exploitative* rates of interest, rather than the practice *per se* of charging interest. At times usury was seen as "moneylending" or loan itself—as in medieval Christian Europe. Most often, the religious strictures concerning "usury" were interpreted or circumvented to allow profitable interest and exchange rates. For example, moneylending and the accrual of interest were practiced by Christian traders in Europe, especially in the later Middle Ages, despite a Papal ban. European Christians simply looked for (and found) loopholes in the religious doctrine by which to conduct business. They were not singular among other peoples of faith in doing so. Nor was the Islamic prohibition universally binding or applied, in medieval or modern times.

At any rate the very notion of a religious ban upon usury, invoked by the Egyptian COC, seems to have been lifted from another "development narrative." It has often been claimed that Jewish bankers and financiers gained ascendancy in early modern Europe because of the prohibition of usury among Christians.[4] The claim derives in part from a distorted view upon the development of capitalism. The exploitative connotations of the term usury, and the association of "moneylending" and "moneychanging" with the Jews are replete with anti-Semitic overtones. Thus far from accounting for commercial development in any case, the notion of a "usury ban" attests to the fetishization of religious difference—regardless whether the "difference" is represented as Muslim, Jewish, or Christian. It is important to understand that essentialist, and in this case anti-Semitic, overtones attach to the notion of the "usury ban." Thus one also recognizes the discursive mobilization of a simulacral concept to "explain" commercial development in modern Egypt.

Alhadeff is, no doubt, familiar with the various contentions about usury and its prohibition. For that reason perhaps she appears to place narrative distance between her own observations and the claims made by the Egyptian Chamber of Commerce. Alhadeff doesn't so much counter the claims of the COC as provide a wealth of detail linking elite privileges to colonial rule and peripheral production. She describes "the notion of a living" underwritten by legal codifications. Her subtle observations and sheer attrition of detail attests to the centrality of global production in the formation of class society in modern Egypt. She therefore belies both the fetishistic notion about the Muslim "usury ban" as well as the reductively materialist claim that geography had simply favored the Egyptian elite. Her account has much significance, therefore, beyond its readerly and aesthetic prose and its engaging "Tales of a Mediterranean Family."

In the claims of the Egyptian Chamber of Commerce, circa 1940, one may see the outlines of modernization discourse. Importantly, the claims about favorable geography and, especially, the Muslim prohibition of usury, are not merely discursive attempts to explain elite privilege. Rather, the claims are also intended to rationalize the mass disenfranchisement of native Egyptian Muslims. The COC's claims about the usury ban echoes the modernization fallacy that cultural or religious "tradition" has inhibited the "progressive"—i.e., capitalist—development of local society. According to modernization fallacy, the native masses are alienated and impoverished by their own religious stricture—and not by Western colonialism or exploitative global production. Native society is "underdeveloped," according to discursive fallacy, because it is a "traditional" society which "clings" to old ideas and old ways. Conversely, the fallacy posits that elite society is "progressive;" elites embrace new ideas and new ways—i.e., those of the "West." Thus elites merely step into the commercial and entrepreneurial vacuum yielded by the native masses, according to such logic. Such logic is disingenuous, of course. But it typifies the rhetoric of modern development. Alhadeff provides testimony which can be seen to refute modernization fallacies about the leadership roles of elites in "local development." Her account intimates the degree to which the commerce and status of minority elites in Egypt were predicated upon not geography and essence but upon Western colonial agency. The minority elites, composed of various strata and background, occupied a hegemonic position in Egypt. Their lifestyles were a function of colonial hegemony and not, as modernization discourse would have it, the perquisite solely of inspired entrepreneurship.

While the lifestyles of Egyptian elites were based upon peripheral production, yet there was great variation among "elites" in terms of wealth and status, nationality and culture, occupation and profession, consumption and taste, and so on. When one refers to Egypt's "cosmopolitan community," one covers a lot of ground, perhaps indiscriminately so. It bears repeating that the "lifestyle" of a small grocer or shopkeeper would not approach that of a cotton planter or broker, nor could it be evaluated in identical terms, however much materially constructed through colonial privilege. Yet there was privilege inherent even in the petty bourgeois status of small businessmen. Businessmen of any scale who drew from Turkish, Levantine, or European nationality, as Berque and others have shown, enjoyed commercial and legal advantages over most natives, even those among their own social rank. The layers of status and privilege, however much removed from the top, are what constitute hegemony within peripheral society. And so one may understand that "elite" is a broad and somewhat diffuse category which has most meaning in relation to the majority of Egyptians who were excluded from colonial privileges.

The reputation for cosmopolitanism, however, appears to have been similarly shared or aspired to by Egyptian elites. The experiences of Egyptian elites, whether "native" or "ethnic" and of various religious backgrounds, are strikingly similar, as shown by many corroborating accounts. One concludes that cosmopolitan lifestyles in Egypt revolved around a constellation of "important" families, foreign schools, wealthy suburbs, and commercial attachments to colonial production. The "cosmopolitanism" of elites was lived or aspired to in much the same way, albeit varied by their respective social and ethnic strata. It may serve to define, then, what is meant by the "cosmopolitanism" of Egyptian elites. Typically, elite cosmopolitanism was characterized by the following criteria:

- multi-lingualism, especially the capacity for English, French or other European languages—Arabic was used less frequently and was usually spoken to servants;
- multicultural and transnational associations in business and leisure;
- religious tolerance or secularism;
- cultural/ideological ties to Europe and/or Turkey
- consumption of Western art, literature, film, sports, entertainment, food, clothing, etc.

Based on this criteria, one might be tempted to see the cosmopolitanism of Egyptian elites as a wholly cultural phenomenon—and at that, as a positive expression of "multiculturalism" as it is conceived of in the academy today, that is, as a progressive tolerance for and inclusion of "differences." Such cosmopolitanism would have ostensibly provided the best of many worlds to Egyptian elites of various backgrounds, whether native or ethnic minority, Christian, Muslim, Copt or Jew. But the conception of Egyptian elites as "happily multicultural" would be erroneous. Rather, one may examine

Egyptian cosmopolitanism in both its cultural and material aspects and perhaps synthesize a better view.

The criteria listed above, which typify Egyptian cosmopolitanism, appear as aesthetic effects. These aesthetics primarily existed by and for and within the elite class, according to strata. They appear as the attributes of elite class power. "Cosmopolitan aesthetics" represented the camaraderie of multi-ethnic elites who shared material power. Cosmopolitanism did not, conversely, characterize the experience of the Egyptian *fellahin* (peasants) as it did the *pashas* and *beys* (i.e., notables). The "aesthetics" which derived from elite privileges and status were indeed relative to the repression of mass society. Furthermore, the "Westernization" of Egyptian elites, however "cosmopolitan," was a marker of their own colonial oppression, regardless of their contingent class privileges. Minority elites identified with the West, in large part, because that identification was upheld by the colonial system. Homi K. Bhabha has made a similar observation in his discussion of what he calls the "mimicry" phenomenon among colonial elites.[5] Thus it can be argued that Egyptian "cosmopolitanism" pertained partly because the indigenous identity of Egyptian minorities, whether "native" or "ethnic," was devalued and/or repressed. Identification with the West was certainly encouraged among elites, but other kinds of identification or self definition were likely discouraged with varying degrees of material or social reprisal. Looked at in this regard, then, cosmopolitanism was hardly a "progressive" force within Egyptian society. Locally, it was understood as the ostensible marker of elite social status and of the "foreign sympathies" held by ethnic minorities.

This is not to say that cosmopolitanism was *purely* an aesthetic effect of colonial materialism. It was indeed a cultural phenomenon as well. Material conditions do not simply determine human actions and predilections. People do choose how to act or not, how to identify or not, etc. But people tend to act in their own interests, typically—although again, they may sometimes choose not to act or else choose to act against their own interests. Yet material conditions—in this case a colonial matrix of proscriptions which favored local elites—do establish a context and criteria for actions, behaviors, etc., which may be engaged or not, in response to a set of given factors.

However, it was in the self interest of multi-ethnic elites to get along as a class because their status was confronted by the pressing problem of legitimacy. Their perceived legitimacy as an elite or ruling class was insecure. Mainly they were viewed by the larger native society as collaborationists in foreign rule. Elites were comprised largely, though not solely, of ethnic minorities, many of which held foreign citizenship. Religious minorities, i.e., Christians and Jews, held special legal status apart from Muslim society even if they were not *émigrés* or so-called "third nationals." Not all elites were *émigrés* or their descendants; there were native families, Muslims and Copts, among the Egyptian upper classes. But because of their class affiliation with non-native ethnic minorities, and with the Western powers, they were associated in the common view with a "foreign" elite. Thus the local perception of Egyptian elites was that of a mostly non-native ruling class. This was generally so despite whether individual elites personally identified as native or as ethnic minorities.

Most elites did not tend to identify with the broader native society, which was largely underclass, but with the foreign powers which maintained their own relative privileges. But here, too, there was insecurity as the legal status and the privileges of ethnic minorities shifted according to political developments in the metropolitan countries which dominated Egyptian life. Elite status was insecure both in regard to the broader native society and to the external powers beyond the local periphery. Cosmopolitanism therefore seems as much a strategy to consolidate class power as it was an organic cultural expression among socially "progressive" elites. Given these considerations, the position of elites appears as much tenuous as hegemonic. This observation, of course, necessitates further explication.

Because the status of minority elites in Egypt was contingent upon external forces, one sees they faced a problem of social and cultural legitimacy. The privileges of ethnic elites would have been regarded from a nativist perspective as an imposition, even after generations of naturalization. Thus there was a need for elites to invoke signs of legitimacy. Without the semblance of social legitimacy, the elite position of ethnic minorities in regard to the native majority was transparently colonialist and oppressive. In particular, the material hegemony of the tiny strata of landowners in an artificially-repressed, agrarian capitalism would have needed the augmentation of social and cultural legitimation. This would be the case especially as Egypt's agrarian capitalism largely benefited the ethnic elites and foreign colonial powers to the exclusion of most other Egyptians.

It seems that because the status of Egyptian elites was artificially engendered or maintained through external forces, elite society tended to focus outward, toward European and Turkish—i.e., "Westernized"—cultural aspirations. This would seem to be a natural inclination, given that so many elites were foreign nationals or their descendants. However, Westernization (or, Europeanization) can be recognized as an elite strategy to derive cultural and social legitimacy. Ethnic elites would have associated Europeanization with monarchal "legitimacy" and colonial power. But further, Europeanized signs would have been associated with the global, technological, and "modern" power represented by the West. Europeanization as a strategy to legitimize class power would have had significance for ethnic minorities within the context of a broader society whose culture they either did not share or else shared only marginally in certain respects. This strategy would have been most significant for minorities who held ruling class powers.

Elite strategies of associative legitimacy, however, seem mainly to have been directed within the upper classes. Among the highest strata—the rarefied "Atmosphere" referred to by Alhadeff—wealthy landowning families courted the Ottoman aristocracy in order to derive associative legitimacy for their ruling class powers. One sees a haute bourgeoisie—comprised of Levantine and European Christians and Jews, Turkish Muslims and Egyptian Copts—trying to ingratiate itself to the Ottoman aristocracy of Egypt as well as to metropolitan European nobles. Alhadeff wryly tells of the pretension of a family acquaintance who lists the phone numbers of the queens of Mediterranean countries under the letter "Q," for "queen," in her address book (37). Haute bourgeois elites would have sought to derive a measure of social legitimacy from monarchal sources for their own class position—a position which was, *de facto,* if not ruling class then, at the very least, owning class. But this was likely only half the story. The Ottoman aristocrats themselves were not that much more stable than other elites, in terms of social and cultural legitimacy. Thus the aristocracy would have also needed to secure legitimacy through associations with sources perceived to embody power and efficacy. The aristocracy associated with the local haute bourgeoisie, because of the latter's economic power, and with the foreign agents of Western colonial power.

The Ottomans, likewise an ethnic minority elite, had been losing efficacy throughout the course of generations. Thus association with planter families like the Alhadeffs may have lent to the aristocracy a material legitimacy derived through landed wealth. The point is that both the aristocracy and the haute bourgeoisie may have sought to derive legitimacy, rather erroneously, from each other. They would have done so precisely because their privileges in Egyptian society had been created through the agency of foreign colonial rule, first that of Ottoman Turkey, then that of Europe and Britain. Associations between the aristocracy and the haute bourgeoisie, along with the appropriation of land, would once have assisted the historical transformation of the Egyptian ruling class "from a mandarin-type bureaucracy into a class of latifundia-owners."[6] But the pursuit of social and cultural legitimacy underscores the insecure position, however much a hegemonic one, of Egyptian elites.

The haute bourgeoisie likely failed to recognize the material weakness of the aristocracy—which was itself camouflaged by derivative signs of imperial power—and what that weakness meant in regard to the broader society. Rather, elites perceived ostensible forms of political power in the veneer of Western, European, and "modernized" signs of the Ottoman aristocracy. Yet even these signs appear to have been assimilated by the aristocracy from abroad, from the commercial, financial and colonial agents of "central" authority who figured as global powers. Ultimately, there was a slippage between these presumed signs of power and the cultural legitimacy for which they were invoked but failed to represent. For this reason it is likely that Farouk, the last reigning king of Ottoman lineage, often made references to his Islamic heritage, even as he himself identified with and was identified with "modern" European culture and its interests in Egypt. Farouk's references to Islam, and those of other Muslim or Ottoman ruling class elites, can as well be viewed as a strategy to invoke cultural legitimacy for a hegemony basically underwritten by foreign imperialism.

For the aristocracy and other Muslim elites, Islam may have provided a point of reference for nativist legitimacy, but it was not necessarily a nationalist position. Most Muslim elites in Egypt were likely not to be considered "native;" many were ethnic Turks and Circassians, however assimilated through the generations. References to Islam and to Muslim culture were probably invoked as a measure of assimilation within the broader society. Appeals for legitimacy derived from Western sources, however, seem self referential within upperclass society. These gestures would have simply underscored the illegitimacy of imperialism in the nativist perspective. Therefore, gestures or strategies of associative legitimacy among the upper classes would ultimately fail. They did nothing to address the issue of national sovereignty within the context of colonial rule. Nor did they soften the materiality of class oppression.

Given the polarization of elites and native society, the association of the haute bourgeoisie with the Ottoman aristocracy would have been an erroneous tact to derive social legitimacy. Rather, it may have served to conflate the perception of both elite groups as a foreign ruling class in regard to the native majority. Ethnic elites, particularly non-Muslims and non-natives, were largely viewed in nativist terms as the emissaries of colonial rule. Thus, the rise of nativism in nationalist politics had various implications for elite families of greater or lesser strata. By the late 1950s, after the depose of King Farouk and the repossession of the Suez Canal, Egypt's cosmopolitan lifestyle was rapidly dissipating into a new "atmosphere," as Edward Said describes it:

> There was a new uncertainty: the placid place for foreigners was beginning to lose its durability . . . and what had been "our" environment became "theirs," "they" being Egyptians to whom politically we had

> paid less attention than our inert stage set. I recognized this in the poetry of Cavafy some years later—the same indifference, the world taken for granted as privileged foreigners like us pursued our concerns and worried about our businesses without much consideration for the vast majority of the population. (*Out of Place* 272)

The indifference, or perhaps solipsism, which Said finds in the poetry of the Alexandrian Constantine Cavafy (1863–1933), the son of Greek *émigrés,* probably characterized cosmopolitan society as a whole. Communal solipsism may perhaps explain why elite strategies were aimed and engaged within the upper classes, rather than aimed without, where the threat to elite status materialized among the lower classes. Elite strategies to derive legitimacy seem at last to have failed because elites themselves did not or would not recognize the polarity between their own class and strata and the native masses. Nor did they seem to recognize the potential of a mass movement for native independence, one independent also of the *Wafd* (Nationalist) Party leaders who daily grew more imbricated in the *status quo.* Instead "[t]he vocabulary of Arab nationalism, Nasserism, and Marxism was to come," writes Said, "while we still lived deep in the illusions of hedonism, British education, and luxurious culture. Cairo was never more cosmopolitan" (199–200).

To recognize the instability of Egyptian elites, as a class, may inform and perhaps revise one's understanding of their "cosmopolitan" lifestyles. Thus, elite cosmopolitanism may be seen as a strategy to invoke social and cultural legitimacy for material powers. Whether or not this "strategy" was deliberate, intentional, calculated or else organic and unconscious is not a point for argument. The associations of cosmopolitan elites with European and Turkish culture, with imperial/colonial power, and with Western "modernity," appear as the most obvious features of a strategy, whether consciously or unconsciously conceived, to legitimize elite class functions and powers. Within the context of colonial domination, however, the "Westernization" of cosmopolitan elites provided little semblance of a local or national legitimacy. Thus the strategy of associative legitimacy, outwardly marked by a social and cultural "cosmopolitanism," appears at last to be a solipsistic phenomenon. Elites of various strata appear preoccupied with their relative positions within their own social class, ethnic or religious group. Cosmopolitanism, as a strategy of associative legitimacy, largely ignored the larger segments of society, that is, the native under classes. Yet the problem of legitimacy in regard to local rule and elite power became more pressing with the rise of Egyptian nationalism in the twentieth century. Cosmopolitan elites' failed strategy to legitimize their status in the perception of the native masses reflects also their failure to regard the class struggle inherent in modern colonial Egypt.

5.2 THERE ARE NO CROCODILES IN CAIRO

Incorporation into modern global production shaped the character and direction of Egyptian society in many ways. The development of a "Westernized," cosmopolitan elite was a feature of Egypt's peripheral function in the world economic system. Thus it is important to understand how the material conditions of Egyptian elites derived from Western agency. The ethnic minorities which largely comprised Egypt's elite, e.g., Levantines, were themselves the subjects of Western domination. One may observe their tenuous power and instability within a colonial hegemony engendered by the West. The dispossession of the "cosmopolitan" elite, during the period in which Egypt broke away from British domination in the 1950s, can also be seen as an effect of "modernization." Egypt's cosmopolitan community, as a whole, bore the effects and the signs of a Western, modern—but more importantly, unequal—development. Within Egyptian society, ethnic minorities appeared as a catalyst for local discontent and as the mark of foreign control.

A significant part of the Egyptian nationalist program after 1952 entailed the destruction of the power of ethnic elites.[7] The Egyptian nationalist movement, having displaced the ethnic elite in the 1950s, has typically been viewed as anti-foreign and anti-Western. But one may also observe that the dispossession of ethnic elites was a reactive measure, if also reactionary, to the prevailing conditions of unequal development. The movement for Egyptian independence arose as much from the exploitative conditions of modern development as from the need for legitimate sovereignty; indeed the two motivations were related. This observation does not dismiss nor minimize the injustices of expulsion, confiscation of property, intimidation, arrest, detention, and other harassment suffered by Egyptian minorities by the end of the 1950s. Rather, it provides insight into the very problematic nature of "modernization," the fallacy about "trickle-down" benefits, and the inherently unjust social formations which result from peripheral economic development.

One considers that Egypt's cosmopolitan community was considered a harbinger of modern development for its time. As a character in Lawrence Durrell's *Alexandria Quartet* observes, "The brains of Egypt . . . is its foreign community."[8] Even today, many accounts portray Egyptian "cosmopolitanism" in the first half of the twentieth century as a kind of lost age of commercial bustle and multicultural glamour. Yet the idea that "foreign" or indigenous ethnic minorities had developed Egypt is a misrepresentation typical of "modernization" logic. The "modern" developments engaged in by Egyptian minority elites hardly impacted the country outside of Cairo and Alexandria. The production of cotton, the construction and operation of the Suez Canal, the establishment of opera houses, foreign schools and *fin-de-siècle* apartment houses were considered to be hallmarks of "modern" Egypt. But such development projects were never intended for mainstream society. Modernization simply allowed elites to remain cut off from local society. Their remove from the masses was an aspect of elite privilege—but it also factored heavily into their downfall as a class.

Unequal development had largely created the privileged conditions of Egypt's modern elites. Thus it also set up the conditions for their fall when actual independence occurred in the 1950s. The previous section analyzed elite "cosmopolitanism" as a strategy to legitimize and consolidate material class power prior to 1952. Elites likely invoked such strategies because their external support from the foreign colonial powers necessitated a local semblance of legitimacy. The association of ethnic elites with one another, however, was not likely to have been a very effective response to the push of Egyptian nationalism as the latter assumed a more openly nativist tenor. "Cosmopolitanism," then, marked the tenuous position of elite power in Egypt. But it may also have covered over another weakness inherent within the hegemony of elite society. Despite the façade of mutual tolerance among ethnic elites, sectarian lines cut deeply across national, cultural, religious, and political affiliations. Cosmopolitanism, as a strategy, may have aimed to assuage or cover over the ruptures of sectarianism among elites as much as it aimed to consolidate class power *vis-à-vis* the masses. Again, to analyze Egyptian cosmopolitanism as a material strategy does not negate the organic nature of cultural affiliation and identification. One simply recognizes its material, as well as cultural, significance.

The complicated relationships of the Egyptian minorities, both within elite circles as well as in regard to mass society, obtained below the surface of their cosmopolitan fellowship. For all their privileges, elites were cut off from the broader society, plagued by sectarianism and internecine struggles, and subject to the laws and proscriptions of the foreign consuls. Thus elite strategies of cosmopolitan association appear as the marker of class instability. One may find nuances of trouble among the multi-ethnic elite as recorded in the memoir of Gini Alhadeff, *The Sun at Midday.* Alhadeff portrays the culture and social *milieu* of Egyptian elites by recounting anecdotes and interviews with relatives, as well as her own memories and research. The passage below is an excerpt from Alhadeff's interview with her paternal aunt, Sarah. At the time of the interview, Sarah was an *émigré* residing in Italy. Her generation's *milieu* was that of Farouk's, the young king whose father had grown up in Italy and whose grandfather had built the Cairo Opera House for the first production of Giuseppe Verdi's *Aïda:*

> La Scala came to Alexandria and La Comédie-Française, wonderful concerts, film premières where people got all dressed up. The Egyptian high-society ladies were all Turkish. King Farouk was white—Ottoman. All the princesses were beautiful. The women in Alex [Alexandria] were excessively beautiful. The Swiss saw only one another, but the Greeks, the Italians, the French, the Jews, when there were parties they were all there together. There was no anti-Semitism then. There was no sectarianism. There were many dinners in Alex, with many guests and lovely tables. People asked me in America whether there were crocodiles in Cairo and I was tempted to leave them in their ignorance, but I couldn't, I told them, "No, that's higher up the Nile." People imagine that Egypt was a savage country . . . (68)

Sarah's account reflects the highly Europeanized sensibility of Egyptian elites, their inter-ethnic associations, and, as she attests, their religious tolerance. These attributes characterize the cosmopolitan lifestyle as previously defined. Here also one sees the proximity of the Egyptian haute bourgeoisie to the Ottoman royal court. King Farouk's taste for a European "high life" was, of course, well known.[9] Elites of lesser strata likely cut less glamorous profiles. But they mixed at sporting and country clubs, beach resorts and fashionable cafes, all of which catered to eclectic Western tastes. Landowning families like the Alhadeffs identified with the Ottoman and European aristocracies and with the British. The Alhadeffs had even embraced early fascist incorporations of class power, before the advent of the anti-Semitic laws. They were assimilated Europeans as was typical of many ethnic minorities in Egypt. The author Alhadeff remarks that she herself mainly identifies as an Italian, and only discovered late in life that she is also a Sephardic Jew. Identification with Europe appears to have been simply an organic orientation for many ethnic elites, whatever their class strata. Indeed the Alhadeffs, as described by the author, seem to have identified most strongly within their social class, across the host of ethnic and religious identities which comprised it. However, the association of elites with imperial power in the guise of European culture and Western modernity also appears to mark a strategy of associative legitimacy for upperclass status.

In light of the family's long-standing identification with Europe and "modernity," one sees Sarah's consternation at the image of Cairo perceived by Americans as a backwater town besieged by crocodiles. The ungainly image recalls the "primitive East" fallacy of modernization discourse—and Sarah would have one know that Cairo is nothing short of civilized. She points the Americans away from Cairo to the Upper (Southern) Nile, the provincial Egypt of native peasants or *fellahin.* For her the latter is crocodile country—certainly not the Cairo of cosmopolitan elites. Her testimony intimates some anxiety over the Americans' confusion of her city with the outlying country of Egyptian natives. Yet her conception of Cairo is actually just as erroneous as that of the Americans who dismay her. Sarah sees a European city as the capital of Egypt. But that Cairo, conceptually and literally, was easily eclipsed in evidence of native society of all classes, urban and rural. Interestingly, the place name commonly used by Egyptians, *Misr,* is a nativist term which refers both to Cairo the capital and Egypt the nation.

The crocodile image associated with Cairo is seen by Sarah and her American friends as a sign of something "savage." The crocodile intrudes upon European or Western urbanity, modernity, "civilization,"—in short, it intrudes upon the self conception of cosmopolitan elites. "People imagine Egypt was a savage country" (68), Sarah recounts with injury. But the crocodile construed as a sign of savagery seems thoroughly Western and somewhat ironic. For the crocodile is also a local image which has held nativist associations both with Cairo and Egypt since antiquity; it figures in representations of the oldest settlements of the Nile River civilization. Sarah's gesture distances cosmopolitan Egypt from native Egypt by displacing the crocodile image onto the *fellahin.* Ironically, this is appropriate for it locates the nativist sign with those who are "essentially" native. Of course, what constitutes "native" is necessarily unstable criteria; for example, the Copts are often said to be the only "real" descendants of the ancient Egyptians. But the *fellahin* were generally perceived as "native," likely through their association with the land. The symbolic association with the land is an important (autochthonous) signifier for nativist identity, as was discussed in the previous chapter. Significantly, Sarah's rejection of the crocodile image distances Europeanized elites such as herself from an essential sign of local legitimacy. The Egyptians signified by the Nilotic crocodile, for the most part, comprised the disenfranchised native masses. She therefore underscores not only the cultural polarity between ethnic elites and natives but also the problem of legitimacy for elite power vis-à-vis the masses. Far from rendering "legitimacy," the Europeanization or Westernization of elites likely served to alienate them further from mainstream Egyptian society.

Egyptian elites of various ethnicities and religious identities would have enjoyed the camaraderie of leisured society as they did the solidarity of material class power. But the absence of sectarianism to which Alhadeff's

Aunt Sarah attests is not at all representative of Egyptian political life under Farouk. Rather, the period witnessed a complex and polemical set of political struggles both within the government and from without it.[10] There had long been a nationalist movement in Egypt, culminating in an uprising in 1919 and the formation of the *Wafd,* the nationalist party. By Farouk's reign, the *Wafd* was well established in the parliament. The party had opposition, however, from both the right and the left. Monarchists, socialists, and Islamists, particularly the more radical Muslim Brotherhood, represented contending factions of ideology and influence. These divergent factions viewed Egyptian independence and the role of Egyptian elites variously—for it must be noted that political factions, including the *Wafd,* were mainly led by landowners, notables, commercial and other elites. Egyptian nationalism was thus largely "anti-foreign" in tenor, more than class-based. In this regard, one sees that ethnic minorities among the elites were more likely to receive the brunt of anti-foreign sentiment. The erosion of ethnic minority power was one of the first effects of Egyptian nationalism after the deposition of Farouk.

The absence of anti-Semitism to which Sarah attests was probably not all that representative, either, of elite society under Farouk. Actually, the young Egyptian king came to power in 1936 and reigned as fascism and its anti-Semitic program were waxing in Europe.[11] German nationalism and its expression in fascist ideology were among the European discourses which were assimilated by many Egyptian intellectuals.[12] Fascist organizations were established in Egyptian elite circles in the 1930s and '40s. During the Second World War, Jewish civilians were requisitioned into forced labor camps in nearby Tunisia, then under Vichy control.[13] Thus one can recognize that anti-Semitism was a part of the Egyptian elite scene as much as any other European tendency. Nor was the tendency strictly a European one. Michael Laskier attributes Egyptian anti-Semitism before independence to several criteria:

> During the 1930s Egypt underwent the influence of Fascist and Nazi ideas, the impact of anti-Jewish notions promoted by Palestinian Arab political exiles, the interests of Egyptian nationalists in the Palestine Question and their support for the Arab struggle there against the Jews and the British, and growing anti-British sentiment which was also directed at Britain's supporters. All these trends eventually affected the Jewish community. (1)

As Laskier points out, anti-Semitic and anti-Zionist sentiment figured along with the anti-colonial rhetoric of Egyptians and Arabs, that is, it figured both in native society as well as among Arab émigrés.

Yet it is also notable that Palestinians and other Levantine Arabs would have been the targets of anti-foreign sentiments along with Jews and Europeans. Edward Said writes, for example, about his own experience as the target of nativist resentment in colonial Egypt:

> By the end of the forties we were no longer just Shawam [Levantines] but *khawagat,* the designated and respectful title for foreigners which, as used by Muslim Egyptians, has always carried a tinge of hostility . . . I resented the implication that I was somehow a foreigner, even though deep down I knew that to them I was, despite being an Arab. (*Out of Place* 195)

Said's account attests that minority elites of various ethnicities were subject to the anti-foreign tenor of anti-colonial rhetoric. However, whereas anti-foreign sentiments among Egyptians may have pertained toward ethnic elites generally, anti-Jewish attitudes were not always concerned solely with foreign or colonial power. Anti-Semitic racism would likely have been shared by many among the other groups, e.g., Levantine, Turkish, European and native, as well as across class, ethnic and religious lines. Here again one estimates that multi-ethnic solidarity and religious tolerance among cosmopolitan elites was a more "plastic" phenomenon than it appeared. Christians, Muslims or Jews of any ethnicity, Arabs of any religious identity or nationality—or any configuration of elites—may have aligned across cultural divisions against the other, depending upon their material motivations.

The sectarianism of elites and, conversely, their alignment across lines of ethnicity and nationality, can be observed in an anecdote told by Said in his memoir, *Out of Place.* In the anecdote, Said's relatives, Palestinians from Jerusalem who had emigrated to Lebanon, invoke their identity as Christians in a way in which the author finds disturbingly strident. Said notes that there were "early signs of . . . hostility toward Islam" among his mother's family, well before the civil conflicts between Lebanese Christians and Muslims might have precipitated them. His relatives' hostility toward Islam, he notes, first began "to emerge as unquestioning enthusiasm for Christianity, unusual even within Jerusalem's pious confines" (169). At family gatherings in Lebanon, he writes, "I found myself counted as a Christian, though . . . I must confess I am unable to feel any identification at all with Christianity as threatened by Islam" (169). The Saids were Christians, but like other Egyptian elites, religion was not a defining feature of their lifestyle or self conception. Thus he found the views of his mother's family distressing:

> [W]hen Eva and Lily, my mother's first cousins, who were close friends and former classmates of hers, seemed slightly skeptical of the Arabs collectively and Arabism as a creed I was nonplussed because their language, culture, and education, their love of music, their closeness to family tradition, their way of doing things struck me as much more unequivocally Arab than ours. Later I thought this aggressively Christian ideology was very paradoxical and difficult to accept, so little did I, or anyone in my immediate family, have any sense of primarily *religious* hostility toward Muslims. (169)

Young Edward's disaffection for Christian chauvinism was perhaps characteristic of his cosmopolitan Cairo upbringing. He is puzzled by the negative attitude of his aunts toward the "Arabs" and toward the growing discourse of Arab solidarity, i.e., "Arabism," because to him the two Lebanese ladies themselves strongly represent Arab identity. Yet the aunts' attitude suggests the marked politicization of the conceptions, "nativist" or otherwise, of Arab identity. The aunts apparently find a rupture between that identity and the "Christian" one. By the logic of that conception, what is essentially "Arab" must also be "Muslim" as well. In Lebanon at the time, the latter was likely a popular conception as the demographics of the Christian and Muslim populations were in dispute.[14] Interestingly, Arabism "as a creed" included many Christians in the formation of its ideology, such as George Antonius, the Lebanese author of *The Arab Awakening* (1938); the Syrian Michel Aflaq, the ideological founder of Ba'athism; and, the Palestinian militant George Habash, founder of the Arab Nationalist Movement in 1953, later the leader of the Popular Front for the Liberation of Palestine.[15] Arabism was not essentially anti-Christian but as a transnational, mass movement it threatened the position of Christian elites in Lebanon particularly and, as Said's aunts insinuate, those in Egypt as well. One ventures to say that Arabism posed not so much a risk to the religious identity of Levantine Christians as to their privileged status. The strident Christianity of Said's relatives was probably a gesture meant to establish them among other Lebanese as upperclass and to distinguish them from other Arab immigrants, principally other Palestinians whose increasing presence in Lebanon would become a flashpoint for political disputes. The Lebanese relatives would have sought to identify with the dominant (Christian) class locally as well as with other Christian elites where they were established, such as in Egypt. Christian solidarity among Levantine Arabs, and between them and other Christian groups, was likely to have been motivated at least in part as a response to the political and material challenges represented by the Arabist doctrine. Again, to emphasize the "strategic" aspect of Christian identification in this regard does not dismiss the organic nature of affiliations which would also have pertained among Levantine and other Christians. Merely it may be observed that sectarianism among Levantine Arabs was as much a part of the cosmopolitan lifestyle as was transcultural and trans-ethnic association.

Despite the cosmopolitan veneer, religious sectarianism in general and anti-Jewish sentiment in specific were current among the Egyptian elite. Anti-Semitism found expression in the Pan-Arab—i.e., "Arabist"—and Egyptian nationalist discourses as it did in German nationalist discourse. The establishment of separate tribunals for Jews, Christians, and Muslims also suggests that divisions based on religious identity ran deep throughout society.[16] These divisions are implied by the incidents of religious conversion recounted by Alhadeff and Andre Aciman, respectively, in their memoirs. Alhadeff's family had converted to Christianity, and in her own generation, to Roman Catholicism. One cousin, Pierre, became a priest. Catholicism appears to have been a feature of the Alhadeff's identification as Italian nationals. The author does not mention that the family experienced any pressure to convert. On the contrary, Pierre was a jet-setting priest who had *entre* to the circles of European notables and celebrities; such was his urbanity that she calls him, "Pastor to the Rich and Famous" (10). Yet one might assume that pressure, even discreet pressure, had been brought to bear upon the family to convert; after all, why would a secular family like the Alhadeffs need to convert in an "atmosphere" of tolerance? Given the long history of the religious oppression of the Sephardim, it is significant that conversion obtained after the Alhadeffs were established in Egypt and not earlier in the family's diasporic trajectory. Indeed, this gives some indication of the vagary or the "plasticity" of cosmopolitan elite tolerance. Comparatively, the Aciman family considered making a Christian conversion sometime after 1956, during the Nasser years. Aciman's account clearly illustrates that religious conversion was considered under duress, but was a choice which the family ultimately rejected.

What is remarkable about Christian conversion in the Aciman memoir is that it is an attempt to respond to Egyptian nationalism—rather than a response to Western religious suppression. This raises several speculations. First, one wonders what advantages were had, or were perceived to be had, by the Christian communities of Egypt in relation to the Jews. The Egyptian nationalist movement was essentially Muslim in character (not to be confused with Islamist) and not Christian, after all.[17] The movement's transformation under Nasser, at least officially, into Pan-Arab nationalism[18] might have provided ideologically for the inclusion of Christians, as well as Muslims of Arab descent. But this equanimity would hardly have benefited the Acimans, even if they had converted to Christianity. Nor were Christian Arabs, principally the Levantine *émigrés,* exempt from the nationalist programs which confiscated foreign assets and inhibited private commerce. Thus the Acimans stood to derive no appreciable advantage through Christian conversion. Rather, it seems the family considered conversion as an attempt to circumvent the anti-Semitism of the nationalist movement by assimilating with other, non-Jewish, minorities.

Anti-Semitic rhetoric increased throughout the period and after 1952 official policies were implemented which impacted the citizenship, residency and travel of Egyptian Jews, as well as nationalizing their property and assets. These developments occurred in pace with events seen by nationalists as key moments in the struggle for sovereignty, such as in 1948, when Egyptian soldiers were defeated in Palestine, in 1956 during the Suez War and later in 1967, the year of summary Arab defeat in the Six Day War with Israel. While the nationalist movement was generally anti-foreign and anti-European, Jews were especially subject to hostilities when Egypt's relations, or rather lack of, with Israel were also hostile. Thus one surmises from Aciman's account that Christians were able to retain somewhat more stability than Jews during the Nasser years, even as minority power was generally eroding away. This idea is supported by Laskier's study of the period, in which he analyzes the emigration statistics of Egyptian Jews.[19]

On the whole, whether the Christian minorities had relatively better stability or whether they were simply perceived as having somewhat more stability than the Egyptian Jews is probably a debatable point. The status of minorities depended upon a number of variables and their relative stability after 1952 likely varied among different families and elite circles even within the same minority group. Whether real or perceived, however, the better stability of Christians and the materiality of anti-Semitism in local and regional Arab politics would have provided the impetus for the Aciman's religious conversion. Yet in the end the Acimans chose not to convert, despite the behest of friends who had done so, and despite the harassment incurred by the family while they remained in Egypt. The Acimans, though quite cosmopolitan, held close to their own religious traditions. Their adherence to their faith appears to be the primary reason they rejected religious conversion as a material strategy to secure some stability in a politically difficult time. But one also infers that religious conversion, while it may have appeared as a possible strategy to secure or retain some stability, in fact would have accomplished little. One reason is that conversion would have carried most meaning only within the elite circles. That is, Christian conversion in this context was a phenomenon conceived and addressed within multi-ethnic elite society; it was a strategy directed, ultimately, at other elites. The conversion strategy might have influenced the nationalists who were counted among the elites, however this influence would have been more or less moot. Rich nationalists whose gradualism had mainly served the *status quo* under Farouk were not leading a movement which had grown more nativist and populist in tenor. However much (or little) the conversion strategy might have influenced the Acimans' standing among fellow elites, it would not have had much if any effect upon the forces which drove Egyptian nationalism. The dialectical tension between the small ruling class and the disenfranchised masses was a much larger force than the influence of a few highly positioned nationalists, who, anyway, had always shared power with the other minorities. It might be said that the tension between the two classes of Egyptian society, the "haves" and the "have-nots," drove the nationalist movement out of the hands of the *Wafd* Party and into the hands of the Free Officers of 1952. The latter statement necessarily reduces a complex set of conditions and forces which produced the Free Officers' Revolt; nor does one suggest that the Egyptian Revolution was a Marxian event. But the point is that the coup which overthrew Farouk signified a very different brand of nationalism than that which had been promulgated over the previous generation by the *Wafd.* It drew strength from a populist, nativist sentiment which made *Wafdist* politics rather irrelevant. After 1952, one's identity as a Christian or a Jew or a Muslim was likely less material an issue than whether one was perceived as "foreign" or "native," or whether or not one was viewed as a collaborator with foreign forces. Native elites, who had formerly benefited under the colonial system of minority rule, would now likely have seen a need to invoke the nativist or "anti-foreign" line. Thus religious conversion was not likely to further the Aciman's social stability where the mood was now nativist, both among the elite as well as in the broader society.

By analyzing Aciman's account, one might see that the conversion strategy was ultimately a class-bound concept posed against the more powerful movement of Egyptian society, i.e., the class struggle. In other words, Christian conversion was an attempt to assimilate deeper within an elite comprised of "Westernized" ethnic minorities at a time, however, when the very "Westerness" of elites was taken as a measure of their collaboration in the colonial hegemony. If in previous generations elites had sought to legitimize their status through association with the Western powers, this association was now more of a liability. The nationalist movement which emerged with the deposition of Farouk was more nativist and class conscious than that of the "gradual" or "bourgeois" nationalists who had earlier been dominant. Thus the situation of ethnic elites after 1952 was much more dire. The strategy engaged in by the Acimans, therefore, reflects this new situation. They sought to assimilate, rather than to "legitimate." That is, they do not appear to have been seeking to legitimize their social status as much as their residency in Egypt. "Third nationals" like the Acimans, holders of foreign passports, were routinely expulsed or forced to emigrate, and Jews were alternately expulsed or prohibited from leaving. Despite these conditions, the Acimans wanted to remain in Egypt because it was their home. Religious conversion appears to have been considered among scant few other options, if perhaps only to buy the family a little time to remain.

In *Out of Egypt,* Aciman tells how his family nearly underwent religious conversion during their last years in Egypt. He relates the conversion story in a textual sequence interwoven with other significant memories of his youth in Alexandria. Several key anecdotes—about his problems at school, the harassment and expulsion of friends and relatives by the Egyptian authorities, his private language studies, his kite fights with local boys—parallel, thread through and bracket the conversion story. A pervasive element of the interwoven anecdotes is the boy's struggle for autonomy with his domineering, if occasionally indulgent, father. The metonymic placement of the scenes or anecdotes in relation to one another reveals a conceptual relationship between them. The "interweaving" technique provides a deeper insight into the conversion account and into young Andre's own way of dealing with the family's troubles. Aciman's anecdotes are imbricated with meanings which seek to encompass the simultaneity of the various ethnic and religious identities of modern Egypt. Aciman's Egypt is at once Arab, Greek and European, Muslim, Jewish and Christian. The complexity of Egyptian ethnic identities is in conflict with the prevailing Arabist slant of Egyptian nationalism; young Andre experiences the latter as reductive and oppressive. He attempts to define himself against the political backdrop of postcolonial Egypt and against the strictures which his father has established for his education and upbringing. Andre's insistence upon the integrity of his multi-faceted experience, his refusal to relinquish any part of it, forms the central dynamic of his coming-of-age.

In youth, Aciman underwent some of his formative years at Victoria College. As in the Said memoir, "VC" appears as a watershed experience for the boy—Said's at the end of British domination, Aciman's at the wax of Nasserism. By their own accounts neither student did all that well with the curriculum, though apparently both gained much perspective upon postcolonial realities. Aciman's father was concerned that his son's poor academic progress would elicit political repercussions from the Nasser government. The school, formerly the repressive British "Victoria" College—still repressive but now renamed "Victory" College for the 1956 Suez War "victory"—had instituted a patently nationalist curriculum. Andre's father had enrolled him hoping to garner for his son some of the Anglophone prestige which the pricey boarding school once portended. The boy Andre resents having to fulfill what he suspects is his father's own idyll, however misdirected at the current institution, of a British education. Now the textbooks, teachers, and prevailing attitude at the school reflect the contemporary Arabist ideology, as well as anti-European and anti-Semitic hostilities. The boy is routinely subjected to these hostilities, as well as to corporal punishment meted out by ruler-and-cane-wielding pedagogues, the latter an old school tradition upheld by the new regime. Accordingly, Andre's studies languish. The father is insensitive to his son's predicament. But he fears that Andre's failure to learn Arabic and to reproduce the nationalist ideology, including its anti-Semitic overtones, could make the family appear as dissidents and as Jews unsympathetic to the Arabist cause. One of Andre's uncles had already been picked up by the police and forced to repatriate to France. The father's fears are not unfounded. But the boy feels the fate of his entire family weighted upon his ability or failure to recite the lines of a poem which he can only recall as a formula of unknown words. Under stress he loses the formula, and recalls only the offensive cartoon which accompanied the poem, a tattered and defeated Star of David. Andre is suspended from school because he cannot recite the poem, deemed a serious infraction because of its "patriotic" content. The elder Aciman is aware of the objectionable poem and of the son's routine mistreatment at school. But rather than complain he apologizes to the head mistress and leans on his son to fit in. He hires for Andre a private tutor whose lessons are based upon the text of the Koran, a traditional approach to studying Arabic. But as a hedge, an Italian tutor is also hired for alternate days; the boy will need one language or the other, depending on whether the family remains in Egypt or repatriates to Italy, where they hold citizenship. The Aciman's own languages are primarily Ladino and French.

Worried that government informers may use the boy's failure at school to make trouble for the family, the elder Aciman remarks, "Can't we try to be a bit more inconspicuous and be like everyone else for a change?" (255) A family friend, Ugo Montefeltro, responds that in order to elude repetitive harassment by the authorities, he and his wife have converted to Christianity. He recommends that the Acimans do the same and arranges a consultation with a Greek Orthodox priest, an old friend who understands such conversions. The pragmatic Father Papanastasiou had been a soldier, among other things, before becoming a priest. In his present capacity, he teaches the art of icon painting to Greek boys at the parish orphanage. Aciman's portrayal of the priest is likely a commentary about the prospective conversion. This is suggested by the very "duplicity" of the "ostensible" priest. Father Papanastasiou is no ascetic. Rather, he is a man of experience—*much* experience, he intimates—who still cares for the world. He tells Andre and his father that he is a "man first" and then a priest. His own "conversion," from a man of the world to a priest, seems to have been in name mostly—it has not been much of a change, really, for the same earthy man simply inhabits the garb of a priest. Father Papanastasiou's own "apparent" transformation thus suggests what religious conversion will amount to for the Acimans. It will be a pragmatic event, a change in appearance only, as if putting on another set of clothes.

This motif is also suggested by the cartons of shirts which the senior Aciman, a textile manufacturer, presents as a gift to the boys of the orphanage. The icons which the boys paint under the direction of the priest also bear the motif of surface appearance. The icons are the painted images of Christian saints, monolithic reproductions which mark the absence of the thing itself—the bone of contention for an old Byzantine battle. Julia Kristeva has referred to the religious icons as simulacra, a procession of signifiers emptied of "original" content.[20] Figuratively speaking, the Aciman's conversion to Christianity would produce such icons, too. That is, their Christianity would be a material, apparent gesture of a religious conversion which would not really occur. The superficiality, or surface appearance, of the conversion is what makes it seem tolerable; the Acimans would not actually relinquish their own religious identity.

There is subtextual significance in the repeated references to things Greek in the events recounted by the author. The references are textually linked to the idea of religious conversion, as during the visit with Father Papanastasiou, or linked to the issue of Egyptian residency. The Aciman family's moot desire to remain in Egypt is connoted in the title of the chapter, "The Lotus Eaters," which relates the conversion story. Like Homer's epic sailors who, intoxicated, refuse to leave port in the face of peril, the title suggests that the Acimans' attempt to stay in Nasserist Egypt, by means of religious conversion to Greek Orthodoxy, is something of a pipe dream. Classical and historical references to Greece throughout the chapter provide an elegant subtext to Aciman's narrative. But they also convey a sense of loss, both in regard to Jewish religious identity—which ostensibly might be exchanged for a "Greek" identity if the family chooses to convert to Christianity—as well as in regard to the family's loss of Egypt. For example Andre's father, pleased that his son has assimilated some classical culture, brags that the boy "knew the name of every Greek god and goddess—a revelation that brought no end of sorrow to both Aunt Elsa and Uncle Nessim when they found out that I knew all about Ares and Aphrodite but had never heard of Cain and Abel" (223). Disturbed, the uncle remarks, "What are we then, pagans?" (223) The fear of losing Jewish religious identity is conveyed in the uncle's sardonic question.

Andre's father had invoked the boy's success with classical culture in order to counter-balance Andre's failure with formal Arabic. To the discomfort of his relatives, Andre is quite adept at "kitchen Arabic," the vernacular and folk wit of the household servants who have taken the boy into their confidences. Andre's actual education, outside the rigidity of "VC," is an organic compilation of Egyptian influences, in whatever native and ethnic forms they entail. However the boy feels, as indeed does his family, ambivalent about the assimilation of any one "Egyptian" identity to the negation or the relinquishment of their own. This ambivalence characterizes their regard of religious conversion to Greek orthodoxy and, by extension, the narrative portrayal of things Greek. On the one hand association with and assimilation of some aspects of Greek culture might only reinforce the legitimacy of the Aciman family's incorporation, as Jews, in the national life and identity of Egypt. Both Greeks and Jews had long comprised important ethnic communities in Alexandria, well before the common era, let alone the modern age.[21] Symbolically, the association of Greeks and Jews portrayed by Aciman recalls this historical precedent to the issue of the family's residency in Egypt. The association of the two ethnic minorities underscores the legitimacy of both groups, at a time especially when their residency and assimilation within local society was under trenchant material contestation by popular Egyptian nationalism and the Pan-Arabist doctrine. The cosmopolitan association of Greeks and Jews described by Aciman obtains across otherwise sectarian religious lines in the common interest of both groups regarding the legitimacy of their inclusion in Egyptian national life and in local society. But the mutual association also entails the danger of religious subsumation for the Acimans in this particular context, i.e., in the context of religious conversion. So while cosmopolitan association on the one hand may appear beneficial or affirmative, on the other it represents too great a negotiation, the diminishment or the loss of identity.

At any rate the fate of the Egyptian ethnic minorities, whether Greek, Christian or Jewish, was itself far from secure at the time of Aciman's portrayal. This recognition is reflected in young Andre's observance of the silence which envelops the grounds of the Greek orphanage: "It was as quiet as it gets in the desert—the silence of the ancient Greek necropolis in Alexandria, or the clear, beach-day silence of early Sunday mornings in the city" (267). The ideas of sterility and the end of lineage are conveyed by the notions of silence and the desert, the orphanage and the necropolis, the Greek city of the dead, in Alexandria. The proposed conversion strategy to remain in Egypt is similarly rendered as futile, as the same sense of sterility falls upon the "early Sunday mornings in the city" (267), significantly the Christian day of worship. The conversion anecdote related in "The Lotus Eaters" features the association of the Acimans not only with fellow cosmopolitans, but also with the orphans of another local ethnic minority community. The imagery of the orphans appears as a subtle analogy of the dispossession of the Aciman family, and indeed, the dispossession of all the ethnic minorities deemed as "foreigners" under Nasserism. Thus there is a sense of loss implicit in the chapter which is expressed through cosmopolitan association as well as through the idea of religious conversion. As motif, the sense of loss, of sterility or futility, weaves through the series of interconnected scenes which frame the conversion anecdote in Aciman's narrative.

The conversion anecdote—specifically, the visit with Father Papanastasiou—is framed by a series of interconnected scenes in Aciman's memoir. The first scene portrays a kite fight between Andre's friends and their rivals, a group of Greek orphans from the school where the "pragmatic" priest teaches:

> The Greeks of Mandara had by far the best kites and always won. These were boys from a local Greek orphanage whose two giant kites, named the *Paralus* and the *Salaminia,* reigned over the skies each summer. As our kite bore toward them, the *Paralus* and the *Salaminia* would at first refuse to engage, hissing it away like lazy cobras, ordering it back with a graceful, peremptory swerve and nod of their heads. But once it got close, without warning, first one then the other came swooping down, tearing through it in two successive strikes without even getting tangled, until our stunned and helpless kite lurched awhile and then came plummeting down in a straight descent, crashing onto the sand as everyone scattered for fear of the blades [tied to the tail and head]. (247–248)

The rugged "Greek" kites embody the human skills in construction and strategy which produced them. The boy Andre admires these skills as well as the grace and power which the kites exhibit. He would like to exhibit some of these qualities himself in the battle which presently engages him: the attempt to learn Arabic and thus help the family to "fit in" better in Nasserist Egypt.

The latter is a doomed prospect, however, as everyone in the family more or less recognizes. Andre's Arabic studies and the Aciman family's prospective conversion to Christianity are two ways in which the family dimly hopes to "be a bit more inconspicuous" (255). But given the political climate, these attempts are about as likely to succeed as the little kite which takes on the mighty *Paralus* and *Salaminia*. The imagery of the kites is largely symbolic of this other battle. The kite imagery portrays the anxiety and tension which for Andre are centered upon learning Arabic. His father asserts that the outcome of Andres' studies will be seen as an indication of the family's loyalty to the government. If Andre fails, the family will appear disloyal. The perception of the family as loyal or disloyal will, in turn, determine their fate in Egypt. The father's assertions thus relegate a heavy burden of responsibility to the boy. Like the little kite which represents Andre's team, the boy undertakes a daunting task. He not only risks a failing grade or punishment, but the ruination of his entire family as a consequence! If Andre already had a mental block regarding Arabic studies, now he surely had a brick wall.

Aciman's narrative links the scene of the kite fight with the boy's study of Arabic. The initial portrayal of the kites, the clear and breezy sky at Mandara, where the Aciman family summers, occurs out-of-sight and out-of-sequence with the action of the boy. The imagery is envisioned by young Andre as he sits at his bedroom window, doing his Arabic homework. He remembers the battle from the previous summer and projects its image onto the current battle which he does not watch but can hear ensuing at the end of the beach. He copies out *suras,* or sections, of the Koran into his notebook, meanwhile listening to the other boys outside:

> In the back of my mind all through my scribal exercises were images of the *Salaminia* plunging from above as soon as it caught sight of our poor, unnamed victim and gashing it to pieces with its pointed rostrum. My mind would drift to other things as I kept copying, word after word. Then, all of a sudden, in the distance, I made out the victorious chant of the Greek orphans. The *Salaminia* had won again. (248)

Andre's Arabic studies and the family's prospective conversion are metanymically linked with the kite imagery through such interconnecting scenes. These linkages provide a subtext or commentary upon the family's struggles. Both language study and religious conversion are related to one another as strategies of assimilation. But Andre does not learn Arabic as much as he learns to mimic it; he memorizes whole passages of the Koran without any comprehension of the content. Like the prospective conversion to Christianity, his Arabic study is only an outward appearance which does not correspond to an "inner" reality. Assimilation would have much the same effect. The kites symbolize the overall effects of assimilation. The Acimans' strategies to "fit in" and to "be a bit more inconspicuous" are represented, ultimately, as symbolic acts of victimage and self-negation. The assimilation strategies would reject the Acimans' identity as Jews and Europeans in favor of an ostensible identity as Christians and "Arabists." The symbolic destruction or loss of the self is reflected in the little kite's fate as it plummets, torn, to the sand.

This symbolism is also reflected in Andre's discovery of the *Paralus* and the *Salaminia* in a workshed in Mandara, off season. Now stripped of their sails, the two kites reveal the secret of their peerless victories—bamboo spikes which extend from the frame and gut their rivals. The big kites had represented the power which assimilation would ostensibly have conferred to the family in the struggle to stay aloft in Egypt. Yet Andre finds now that he knows their secret, they have lost their mystique. The big kites have only appeared to be unassailable, just as religious conversion or the recital of Arabic text are only ostensible gestures which mean little in the end. In reality, the "Greek" kites are as vulnerable to fate as to whichever way the wind blows; that is, they are just as vulnerable as Andre feels himself and his family to be. The kites represent just how vulnerable are the Greeks or any other ethnic minority under Nasserism. On the ground, the *Paralus* and the *Salaminia* are quite powerless:

> The kites looked totally stripped, like unfinished rowboats, vulnerable to my searching gaze. The builders had discarded last year's cellophane cover sheets and were about to glue new ones. I moved closer to feel the ribs, but with caution, remembering that bamboo cuts worse than glass. Only then did I discover the ramming spikes that could tear other kites to pieces . . . All I would have had to do was take out my pen knife and cut the bamboo. We would rule the skies that summer. For a moment, I felt like a Phoenician spy sneaking into an empty Greek shipyard, determined to wreak as much damage to the enemy as possible, only to lose his nerve upon beholding the *Paralus* and the *Salaminia,* the pride of the Athenian fleet, sitting majestically on opposite docks awaiting minor repairs. (268–269)

Andre does not maim the kites, not even for the prospect of his side's victory next summer. He does not wish to dispel the illusion of invincibility which the *Paralus* and the *Salaminia* represent, even as he knows it is an illusion.

He leaves the "secret" and the honor of the kites intact. Andre's act of quarter for the fallen "Greek" heroes, the *Paralus* and *Salaminia,* affirms their integrity, regardless of their presumed power or vulnerability. This act symbolically undoes the negation of self implied in the renting of the little kite. Andre gains victory at the moment of the big kites' weakness. But Andre's victory preserves, rather than destroys. He rejects the battle and creates new terms for victory. In doing so, he wins something larger than the battle.

Andre's actions symbolically reject the assimilation strategy and represent the recovery of self identity. This is mirrored by his father's own rejection of the religious conversion. Andre's discovery of the kites occurs at the orphanage school meanwhile as his father and Senior Ugo discuss the technicalities of religious conversion with Father Papanastasiou. Just as Andre recognizes the impotence of the big kites, his father also decides against the conversion. Later, he tells Andre, "Don't worry, I don't think we'll be doing anything with our Greek priest. I couldn't stand facing him every week [in church]" (269). Even his expression, "to face him," underscores the ostensible, outward nature of the conversion, and by extension, assimilation as an appearance, in this context. Apparently both father and son have concluded simultaneously that assimilation just isn't worth the compromise it entails. The simultaneity of these events, told as interwoven scenes, provides the other bracket, or "book end," for the conversion story. After this, the idea of conversion is dropped from family discussion and Aciman does not return to it in his narrative.

The Acimans left Egypt in 1965 and settled in Italy. The author has elsewhere commented that his family was expulsed by "a modern Egyptian Pharoah named Gamel Abdel Nasser" (*False Papers* 108). Alhadeff, whose family also repatriated to Italy during the period of Egyptian nationalization, is less categorical than Aciman:

> Nasser takes most of the blame in the family for the bankruptcy of Pinto cotton—though there was mismanagement on the part of the family, and profligate spending. To what degree my grandmother knew who was responsible for what is unclear, but officially she designated Nasser the culprit. (156)

Alhadeff points out that most of the family business was lost over time due to her grandfather's mismanagement and as collateral for his personal debt, rather than through Egyptian nationalization. Company assets were therefore likely appropriated by business associates or by foreign stockholders. The point of comparing the two accounts, Aciman's and Alhadeff's, is to emphasize that the dispossession of Egyptian minorities cannot simply be reduced to the singularity of one political actor or "pharaoh," i.e., Gamal Abdel Nasser. Nasser was soon recognized as the organizer of the officer's coup which deposed the monarchy and its supporters, and he was the architect of Egyptian nationalization and land reform in the 1950s and early '60s. Yet there was a larger driving force than Nasser in the events of the Egyptian Revolution. Aciman's view is entirely sympathetic, however, given his family's predicament. But the polemic which drove the family and other ethnic minority elites from Egypt must also be understood in the context of decolonization.

If one takes a materialist look at Egyptian society in the last century, then the social evolutions which came with the deposition of colonial rule may be viewed in light of the economic legacy of peripheral production. This view is much more comprehensive than that which has typically been observed by "mainstream" opinion in the West. Rather, many critics have posited that Nasser's "charismatic leadership"[22] or else his "communist subversion"[23] were the motivating factors of Egyptian reforms. As is the case with the Cuban Revolution of 1956, proponents of so-called development typically ignore the abject conditions of agrarian capitalism, the monocultural production shackled to foreign profiteers, and the unfair empowerment of *comprador* elites—all factors which made a populist revolution necessary in both nations. "Modernizers" instead point to the icon of a revolutionary leader such as Fidel Castro or Nasser, and claim that the sheer, "charasmatic" will of an individual person had ushered in an—economically—apocalyptic age. The development narratives about Egypt and Cuba regarding the period in which both struggled to reform their peripheral economies and recover their sovereignty are steeped in capitalist fallacies about "freedom" and "injustice." But a more honest account will recognize the problems posed by unequal development and the lack of sovereignty which characterize the peripheral societies of so-called post-colonial nations.

The problems of peripheral society were evident in the "modern" Egypt "developed" by the West. The cosmopolitan community had largely incurred the advantages of unequal, colonial development to the broader disenfranchisement of the native masses. The roles of ethnic elites in managing the monocultural, client economy of Egypt and in supporting a para-feudal, peripheral social formation were quite visible and imminent within local society. When the Egyptian nationalist movement departed from the position of bourgeois gradualism—which had for at least a generation upheld the *status quo*—and grew more radical and populist, then the disenfranchisement of the native masses and, conversely, the privileged positions of ethnic minority elites, became a catalyst for political violence and societal reform. Of course, not all ethnic elites or minorities fared equally, for better or for worse, during decolonization. Again, the Egyptian nationalist movement which bore the revolution of 1952 was largely "anti-foreign" in tenor because foreign interests had "colonized" the Egyptian economy and social formation under the rubric of "modernization" and "development" for generations. Unfortunately, Egyptian ethnic minorities which were identified as "foreign" or "Western" in the nationalist discourse—often despite being indigenous or having been residents for generations—appear to have incurred the brunt of native reactionaryism.

To consider the fate of the Aciman family and other Egyptian ethnic minorities in light of the decolonization of Egypt in no way dismisses the injustices of expulsion, confiscation of property, intimidation and other forms of official and unofficial harassment which they suffered. In particular, the anti-Semitic harassment of Egyptian Jews through the 1950s and '60s should not be reduced as a purely materialist consequence of decolonization, especially given the promulgation of anti-Jewish notions by a variety of self-interested discourses which obtained among Muslims and Christians across otherwise sectarian lines of class, ethnicity and nationality within modern Egyptian society. Rather, it is important to recognize that the conditions of ethnic minorities within peripheral society are often constructed and manipulated by the agenda of foreign colonial powers. Unlike the families of Aciman, Said and Alhadeff which were all materially affected by the upheavals of the revolution, rather the real beneficiaries of unequal development in Egypt, "those who pulled the strings: the Liverpool import firms, the British, French and Belgian Banks,"[24] etc., did not experience expulsion and exile, dispossession and the disruption of their lives. It is an insight provided by the case of the Egyptian cosmopolitan elite, though not a universal paradigm, that unequal development will eventually provoke unequal "justice." One may thus regard the tenuous power of local elites who are themselves the subjects of colonial domination. Their eventual dispossession can be seen as a result of the unequal "development" which proponents of multi-national capitalism call, "modernization."

5.3 REVOLUTION FOR BREAKFAST

The various strategies engaged by Egyptian elites to retain or secure their social class positions seem, at last, to have failed because elites themselves did not or would not recognize the polarizing force of societal disparity. The disparity between elites and the masses, and generally between the cosmopolitan and native communities, assumed increasing significance for the Egyptian independence movement throughout the modern age. The significance of unequal development accrued to the independence movement especially as it became apparent that the *Wafd* (Nationalist Party) was unable or unwilling to substantially address the economic and cultural divisions which cleaved modern Egyptian society. Class struggle thus appears central to the movement for independence which culminated in the Free Officers' Revolt of 1952. It seems that the material reality of unequal development was more forceful in the end than the promises of "modernization" or its esteemed signs of Western power. Indeed, the "Westernization" pursued by Egyptian elites merely exacerbated the polarization of the broader society.

The privileged "world taken for granted" described by Edward Said[25] was characterized by the indifference of elites toward mass native society. Their indifference seems to reflect a kind of social alienation which, while indicative of privilege, also presaged the fall of the cosmopolitan community and of the political establishment. For example, elite social alienation is reflected in the difficulty which Silvio Pinto, the decorated Commander of Cotton, experienced in accepting, if not in recognizing, the erosion of his social status during Egyptian independence in the 1950s:

> The commander didn't believe he could lose Alexandria. He must have kept the knowledge of Egypt's need for independence segregated in an area of his brain. There is evidence that he possessed that knowledge: he was a friend of Nahhās Pasha [Mustafa al-Nahhas], head of the Wafd, the Egyptian Nationalist party, which paved the way for Nasser . . . He must have known what the Wafd would bring, he couldn't have been for it and not known: an end to Western domination. He seems to have been uncomfortably splayed between the world of many-housed pashas and that of impecunious nationalists. Nahhās himself occasionally lapsed into living the life he managed to corrode at its roots before retiring from political life in 1952. "He was fond of me," the commander reminisced, "because one year, while I was municipal governor, I uncovered a political plot to oust the only two Egyptian advisers who were members of the Wafd and I resigned, together with some of my European colleagues." Nahhās Pasha knew of this. Any support of the Wafd was in opposition to [King] Farouk. So the commander knew, but he stayed, hoping perhaps for some special immunity from the general course of history in deference to his congeniality. He stayed long enough to see Nasser come to power,

> and still he stayed, waiting to run through every last cotton cent. (Alhadeff 156–158)

It is not clear whether Pinto means there were only two native Egyptian advisors—elsewhere he refers to Muslim Egyptians as "Egyptian Egyptians"[26]—or if there were only two *Wafdists* in the local government. But the European representation in the municipality referred to above, probably Alexandria, reflects the administrative powers of the cosmopolitan community. Commercial elites such as Pinto and his "European colleagues" were likely to have been proportionately over represented. The lack in native representation would have loomed large, despite Pinto's well-intended solidarity with individual nationalists among his social rank and despite the presence of *Wafdists* in national government.

The inter-ethnic use of the Turkish titles, *pasha* and *bey,* among elites suggests the class distinction of *Wafd* nationalists such as Nahhas Pasha. These nationalists were not necessarily nativists; nor did they necessarily represent the interests of most natives. As discussed earlier, the *Wafd* appears to have evolved into a party that mainly reflected bourgeois nationalist interests. These interests may well have been perceived as better served by a *status quo* balance of power than by an actual independence which would have destabilized commercial class power. For example in 1942, King Farouk made Nahhas prime minister at the insistence of the British ambassador, Sir Miles Lampson, who felt that the leader of the established nationalist party was amicably pro-British.[27] Alhadeff wonders at her grandfather's apparently strange detachment from the implications of Egyptian nationalism. But Pinto may actually have had little to fear from the *Wafd,* whose leading members stood to lose as much as he did from actual independence. Of course there may have been subtle or not so subtle shifts of political sympathies among nationalist elites. But there was still the very visible, if ostensible, presence of Western modern power signified by the aristocracy and its foreign "advisors," if not also by the British military occupation of the Suez Canal Zone. It was ultimately this power—the semblance of Western "modernity" with which Egyptian elites saw themselves allied—that the Commander cannot accept has been undone.

The movement which eventually achieved real independence in Egypt was more populist and nativist in sentiment than *Wafd*-style nationalism. The difference between the currents of Egyptian nationalism, i.e., between the popular and the established, was probably misunderstood by the political establishment as well as by cosmopolitan elites such as Alhadeff's grandfather. The political establishment may have misinterpreted the role of *Wafd* leadership as one which also led or controlled the popular movement for independence, as well as the party machinery, during the critical period prior to the deposition of Farouk. This is suggested in Alhadeff's remark that the *Wafd* Party had "paved the way for Nasser." In fact, Nasser's coup preempted *Wafdist* politics and soon after taking power the new leaders dissolved the *Wafd* and the other political parties. Rather than paving the way for the revolt, it appears that the *Wafd* Party was incidental or irrelevant to the popular movement for independence by the late 1940s and early '50s. An indication of this was the presence of the *fedayeen,* the guerrilla fighters in the Canal Zone, who operated semi-autonomously of government control. Although one may not see the military coup of 1952 as synonymous with the Egyptian popular will, still it was identified more strongly with the nativist sentiment of mass society than was the compromised agenda of the *Wafd* during the same period.

The misconception that *Wafdist,* ruling-class "pashas" were steering the Egyptian popular will is portrayed by Lawrence Durrell in his novel *Mountolive.* The work, partly an espionage mystery and partly an alleged treatise on "desire," is one work in the author's "quartet" or series about the Egyptian cosmopolitan elite set around the time of the Second World War. In the story, an edgy attaché (really a spy) describes to the (fictional) British Ambassador David Mountolive what he believes to be the role of upperclass Egyptian nationalists—such as those which comprised the *Wafd*—in rousing up "anti-foreign" sentiments:

> Have I explained that one of the major characteristics of Egyptian nationalism is the gradually growing envy and hate of the "foreigners"—the half-million or so of non-Moslems here? And that the moment full Egyptian sovereignty [*sic*] was declared the Moslems started in to bully and expropriate them? The brains of Egypt, as you know, is its foreign community. The capital which flowed into the land while it was safe under our suzerainty is now at the mercy of these paunchy pashas. The Armenians, Greeks, Copts, Jews—they are all feeling the sharpening edge of this hate; many are wisely leaving, but most cannot. These huge capital investments in cotton, etc., cannot be abandoned overnight. The foreign communities are living from prayer to prayer and from bribe to bribe. They are trying to save their industries, their lifework from the gradual encroachment of the pashas. We have literally thrown them to the lions! (107)

In his correspondence with Ambassador Mountolive, the attaché Ludwig Pursewarden claims that "envy and hate" have motivated anti-foreign sentiment among Egyptian Muslims. The "paunchy pashas" to whom he refers are undoubtedly *Wafdists.* He sees the established nationalist leaders as the locus of Egyptian xenophobia. He reduces the Egyptian desire for sovereignty, national self-determination and for actual economic development, to a simple formula: the envy and hatred of natives for successful foreigners. Doubtless he fails to recognize anything like an indigenous mainstream society and the currents of its sentiments and will. If he sees mainstream society at all, it is likely the image of an undifferentiated mob which follows mindlessly the dictates of official leaders who are recognized, if not always tolerated, by the West. Pursewarden's portrayal of the ethnic minorities is likewise distorted. He sees them as "living from prayer to prayer and from bribe to bribe;" this is clearly an Orientalist stereotype which fetishizes religiousity and corruption.

It may seem too easy too criticize the perspective of Durrell's character which, after all, represents the blind spots and structural antipathy of British colonial administration toward native society. But one should not take Pursewarden's view as synonymous with Durrell's own regard. Rather the portrayal reflects Durrell's criticism of British colonial antipathy toward the local community. Yet colonial antipathy is not the prerogative solely of Britain's late empire. Pursewarden's views are typical of the West's disregard in general for the political and material realities of postcolonial nations. His views have disturbing resonance currently, for example, in the so-called "war on terror" in the Middle East. One is reminded of the claim, made by the U.S. Administration and the mainstream media, that anti-Western and anti-American sentiments among Arabs and Muslims are stirred not by U.S. foreign policy but by "madrasas" where students are "taught to hate" and by the broadcasts of *Al Jazeera,* the Arabic news organization familiar to Westerners. According to pundits of the "war on terror," Islamist militancy is motivated not by the political and economic interventions of the West, but by the "envy and hatred" of Muslims for "our Western lifestyle" and "freedom." Thus Pursewarden's perspective is far from being simply the timebound viewpoint of a minion of the British Raj annexed in Egypt. Rather the attaché provides insight into the imperial narratives which are easily reified and mobilized in the West's current adventure in the Middle East, i.e., the "war on terror." To further compare, one notes that the current U.S. political establishment seems to misunderstand Muslim resistance to Western intervention in the Mideast just as much as the British and local establishment in late colonial Egypt misunderstood the native popular movement for sovereign independence.

A central problem with the viewpoint of Ambassador Mountolive's attaché regards the political autonomy granted by Britain to Egypt in 1922.

Contemporary and subsequent observers in the West have typically viewed the qualified autonomy of 1922 as the establishment of formal independence in Egypt. The attaché refers to the event as "the moment full Egyptian sovereignty was declared" (107). However full sovereignty was not the case at all, given the oppressive strategic, political and economic ties which persisted between Egypt and Britain. Britain retained key controls, including that of the Suez Canal and the protection of foreign interests. The autonomy of 1922 was an important gradual move toward Egyptian independence; it was a significant victory for the nationalist movement represented by Saad Zaghlul, the popular leader who had founded the *Wafd.* But as the party drifted deeper into political gradualism and the maintenance of its own power in the Egyptian Parliament, full sovereignty must have appeared its lesser objective, especially to the party's native popular base. Thus far from steering the Egyptian popular will, the *Wafdist* leaders were likely more subject and reactive to the organic mass movement for independence which threatened to displace the established nationalist party. Yet if the texts of Alhadeff and Durrell are reflective of contemporary views, the idea persisted among the cosmopolitan and political elites that a coterie of "paunchy pashas" were running the show.

Furthermore it appears that the established *Wafd* leadership, though comprised of "Egyptian Egyptians," as Pinto adroitly described them, was similarly removed from the material motivations of popular nationalism as were the ethnic elites. Indeed, the *Wafd* Party's estrangement from the popular Egyptian nationalist movement is portrayed in *Autumn Quail* (1962:1985), Naguib Mahfouz's novel about the Egyptian Revolution. The protagonist of the novel, Isa al-Dabbagh, is a *Wafdist* who has attained power and status in the Egyptian government dominated by his party and by, of course, the Egyptian monarchy. On the morning of the twenty-third of July, 1952, Isa is at breakfast when he hears the radio address of the Free Officers who have assumed control of the government. Like a man who has just been woken from a dream—which is the implication of the breakfast scene—Isa is astonished by the *coup d'etat:* "He reeled, like someone coming out of darkness into brilliant light" (36). While he is happy to learn that the corrupt King Farouk has been deposed, still he is uncertain about what the events will mean for his own party, the *Wafd.* Isa recognizes that the movement for Egyptian independence is a thing apart from the nationalist establishment represented by the *Wafd.* He fears that what perhaps has been obvious for long—that the *Wafd* leadership is incidental to the independence movement—will now become policy. Though he welcomes some of the outward effects of independence, such as the deposition of Farouk, Isa's own interests are not invested in the fruition of the aspirations upon which the nationalist party is based:

> Here was the tyrant himself [i.e., Farouk] being dealt a blow of steel: it should match the brutality of his own tyranny and should be final—let him burn, in the contemplation of his own crimes. Just look at the consequences of your errors and stupidity! But where would this movement stop? What would be the Party's role in it? At one moment Isa would feel intoxicated by a sense of hope; at others he would be overcome by a feeling much like the whimpering uneasiness dogs show immediately before an earthquake. (36–37)

Isa would naturally welcome the removal of the Egyptian king for more than a few reasons. Farouk was unpopular with his subjects, profligate with the royal coffers, excessive in his vices, negligent in matters of state and ruthless with his opponents. In a structural sense, the nationalist party was opposed to the monarchy because of the latter's collaboration with colonial agents in order to preserve power. But moreover, the *Wafd* and the monarchy represented the two most powerful factions in government; they were political rivals for governing power as well as opposed on plainly ideological grounds. Thus the king's removal gives Isa much satisfaction; however it also gives him pause—for if Farouk falls, who will follow? His question—where will this movement stop?—recognizes a political reality. Farouk may be a catalyst for charges of corruption and collaboration, but who in the *status quo* government is above such charges to a greater or lesser degree? Isa's emphatic ambivalence, his dime-turn from intoxicated hope to whimpering dog-like unease, is portrayed with just a bit of irony and dry humor. Isa, like many of his colleagues, has been taking bribes and granting favors for years in pursuit of the personal gain which lay in maintaining the political *status quo.* Isa's fears indeed come to pass, and he finds a fate not dissimilar, if substantially lesser by degree, to that of Farouk.

One may see that it was not only the ethnic minorities or the cosmopolitan community which suffered a fall in the wake of the 1952 revolution but also many nationalists as well. If the cosmopolitan elite and the political establishment were alienated from mainstream society, even *Wafdists*—who were after all a significant part of the political establishment—seem not that much more in touch with ordinary Egyptians during the reign of Farouk. In *Autumn Quail,* Isa's fall from grace results from the alienation and irrelevance of the *Wafd* Party regarding the popular nationalist movement as a whole. Similarly, Isa represents the political establishment's obstruction of the militant nationalism enacted by the *fedayeen,* and later, by the Free Officers. The story parallels key events in the Egyptian Revolution, beginning with the Cairo fire of January 1952, presumably a spontaneous act of public outrage over the massacre of Egyptian police by British soldiers in the Canal Zone. The Cairo fire is generally regarded as a primary event in the revolution, followed a few months later by the military coup. These events, together with the political reforms and purges, the nationalization of the Suez Canal and the resolution of the 1956 Suez conflict, constitute the general outlines of the revolution. The story of *Autumn Quail* takes place over this period.

As the novel begins, Isa returns to a burning Cairo from the Canal Zone. He has witnessed the massacre of the Egyptian police and intends to file a report with the government—a typically ineffectual kind of "official" action meant to serve the *status quo.* Isa makes his way through the riotous city to the home of his friend, Shukri Pasha Abd al-Halim. The pasha is a once-powerful official in the *Wafd*-dominated parliament whose career is now waning. The two men discuss the fire from a position of detachment and impotence. They wonder who is behind it and what the conspiracy may portend for their party and for their own careers. Some of the dialogue nearly replicates the conjecture of Durrell's attaché about the incendiary motivations of Egyptian resistance:

> "Maybe it was just reckless anger," [Isa] suggested tentatively.
>
> The Pasha showed his teeth as he smiled. "It was anger all right!" he replied. "But beyond that anger there was envy. Anger may be genuinely reckless, but envy always follows a distinct plan of action."
>
> "How can this happen when we're in power?"
>
> The Pasha gave a dry and abrupt laugh. "Today's like an overcast night. Wait till we find out where the head and feet are."
>
> Isa breathed in sharply and then sighed so hard that the fringe of the velvet tablecloth rustled. "What about the parties?" he muttered.
>
> "They're too weak to organize anything at all!" the Pasha replied, both corners of his mouth curving down as a sign of contempt.
>
> "Who then?" asked Isa with a clear look of doubt in his eyes. (18)

Throughout the scene, narrative reference is made to suggestive details such as the furnishings of Shukri Pasha's study and to his mouth. The opulent furnishings, such as a crystal chandelier, period furniture and, as in the text quoted above, the velvet tablecloth, portray the trappings of a self indulgent, "paunchy pasha." Additionally, the repeated references to the pasha's teeth and mouth portray him as predatory and consuming, no doubt two political qualities which have accounted for his success in the past. The scene overall is intended to criticize the two men, and through them the *Wafd* nationalist leaders, as complacent, opportunistic and corrupt. Isa and

Shukri Pasha demonstrate that they are out-of-touch with ordinary Egyptians. Their assessment does seem accurate that anger or public outrage over the Canal massacre—and over the British occupation generally—had sparked the Cairo fire. However the pasha's remark, "beyond that anger there was envy," cynically regards a rival power. He suggests that some other Egyptian political group or entity has stirred or pushed the masses to violent protest. The pasha's suggestion, that a rival power controls the Cairo "mob," is very similar to the view of Ambassador's Mountolive's attaché, that the nationalist sentiment of mass society is a thing led or directed from without. It is clear to Isa and Shukri Pasha, however, that the militant nationalism signified by the Cairo fire is operating outside the official purview of their party.

Thus a quite different view of the *Wafd* Party's relationship to Egyptian independence is portrayed by Mahfouz than by Durrell or Alhadeff. This is probably because the latter two envisioned Egyptian nationalism as the provenance of the *Wafd* Party and Egyptian independence as synonymous with the qualified autonomy granted by Britain in 1922. Certainly these conceptions of modern Egyptian politics were accepted, at the time and subsequently, by many observers. Yet one gets another perspective if one sees how little the *Wafdist* agenda and "formal independence" had impacted the material conditions of mass society in "postcolonial" Egypt by the time of Farouk. This perspective is more readily pursued by Mahfouz. His body of work generally regards the material realities experienced by Egyptian natives of various social strata. But Mahfouz is known for his humanizing portrayals of the Egyptian poor and underclass.

In *Autumn Quail,* the protagonist Isa is a young *nouveau riche,* a senior civil servant who works for the government and lives in a fashionable Cairo suburb. After the revolution, he is called before the Purge Committee and sacked for corruption. Isa had risen in office through graft and bribery, and was poised for a promotion at the moment of his untimely fall. He sees his political network crumble with the new government and watches as former rivals are elevated to high posts. His engagement to a girl from a prestigious family is abruptly terminated and he is even forced to give up his villa. Dejected, Isa takes his severance pay, his pension, and the bank balance comprised of his years of bribe-taking, and rents a semi-furnished flat in the Greek quarter of Alexandria. There among "foreigners," isolated and brooding, Isa falls into a lifestyle of dissipation, drunkenness and self pity. He refuses respectable offers of work with private companies, remarking that he now lives the leisured life of a "notable." He takes up with a young prostitute, Riri, impregnates and abandons her. When it seems he cannot sink any lower, he cleans himself up as much as possible, sells off some of his property to a wealthy divorcee and marries her, seemingly as part of the bargain. During his fruitless marriage to Qadriyya, whose money now finances his "notable" lifestyle, Isa grows contemptuous of himself, his excesses, and the self preoccupation and shallow materialism of his wife. Once handsome, Isa has become fat, bloated and bored—the result of leisure, gluttony and alcohol—a "paunchy pasha," indeed. Self disgusted, he trims down; he begins to gamble, seemingly as a pastime to replace the gluttony which he has left off. But it is more than simply the exchange of one vice for another. Isa is ready to take a gamble. He risks losing both Qadriyya, who opposes his gambling, and her money, which bankrolls him. But Isa is more than willing to risk losing both.

The real gamble which Isa will take up is implied at the end of the story. He sits drunkenly on a bench in a Cairo square, at night, under the statue of Saad Zaghlul, his party's founder. There he is approached by a young revolutionary who he had once sent to prison on a trumped-up charge. The young man, now free, makes an offer to Isa—not for work in a company but in the revolution, helping to build Egypt's actual independence. Isa hesitates at first. But as he strains to clear his inebriated mind, he decides to accept the offer. Isa leaves the inert, fossilized icon of the old nationalist hero and follows after the living, free revolutionary. The final scene renders the motif from Isa's breakfast on July 23; i.e., the connotation of waking from a dream recurs as clearing one's mind of intoxication. The encounter between Isa and the young man takes place in the early morning, before dawn, a reference perhaps to how Isa felt upon hearing the Free Officers' radio address: "like someone coming out of darkness into brilliant light" (36). The motif of awakening, of coming into the light from darkness, of clearing one's mind of intoxication, suggests that Isa has shaken off the lethargy and self delusion of political unconsciousness and *Wafdist* "gradualism." He has awakened to the revolution.

Summarized thus, *Autumn Quail's* critique of the *Wafd* leadership may seem obvious, though the work reads more subtly than described above. Much of the narrative, for example, develops the internal contradictions of the protagonist. Isa has devoted his life to Egyptian nationalism, meanwhile subverting the cause in order to further party interests and his own career. Though the story means to criticize, it also humanizes the protagonist through the portrayal of his thoughts and motivations. Further, while the narration is replete with gentle irony and dry humor, it does not present Isa as an object of ridicule or opprobrium. Indeed, during the opening scene of the Cairo fire, demonstrators repeatedly chant the counterintuitive slogan, "Burn! Destroy! Long live the homeland!" (14) The chant conveys the irony of an urban riot which does damage to local society in the name of defending it against foreign occupation. In short, the novel is not propaganda for the Egyptian Revolution, as was suggested by the translator of the 1985 English edition.

Isa symbolizes the political corruption of his class and his party. The corruption finds metaphor in his relationships with the two women, Riri the prostitute and Qadriyya, his wife. In effect it is Isa who prostitutes himself, literally for money, in his loveless marriage to Qadriyya. She is depicted through his eyes as bovine and barren, though wealthy. A three-time divorcee, Qadriyya is not the woman Isa would have wanted for a wife; but in order to maintain his "notable" lifestyle, he feels she'll do. Qadriyya, the daughter of an influential police chief, signifies as does Isa the collaboration and profiteering of the native *nouveau riche* class of government functionaries. The motif of prostitution seems to criticize their class as political "prostitutes" who have sold out Egypt's sovereignty in exchange for personal gain.

Riri's portrayal, conversely, typifies the sympathetic regard of the urban poor and the underclass which characterizes much of Mahfouz' work. Significantly, Isa's refusal to recognize Riri in a diner, when she was poor and pregnant, seems to criticize the nationalist party's refusal, similarly, to acknowledge the human and political potential of the Egyptian under class. Indeed what separates Ibrahim and Abbas—Isa's friends who have successfully reinvented themselves with the revolution—from Samir and Isa who have been purged, is the lip service which the former give to the class struggle. Ibrahim, in particular, as a lawyer and journalist, appears to have mastered the language of the revolution. This is the language which Edward Said described as containing "the vocabulary of Arab nationalism, Nasserism and Marxism."[28] The new established discourse makes reference and address to the native masses. Thus Ibrahim does so as well, even if it is only a cynical act of self preservation. Once a *Wafdist* as his friends, he now writes newspaper articles which condemn his old party and support the new government. "Tell me what your feelings are," Isa asks him, "when you read your articles in the newspapers?" "I say we should keep up with the procession," Ibrahim replies (56–57). Ibrahim has hitched his wagon to the revolution. But there is the motif of prostitution in his actions.

Ironically it is Riri, the literal prostitute in the story, who represents something genuine, the aspirations of the common poor for dignity and livelihood. She achieves these things, it is suggested, coextensively with if not as a result of the revolution. Riri's rise in fortune parallels Isa's fall. After his change of heart, Isa seeks her out in Alexandria. He finds that Riri's life has greatly improved—no thanks to him—since he last saw her in the diner where he had refused to recognize her. She now has a respectable job, a husband and a beautiful young daughter. Isa is filled with yearning for what might have been his own family. Riri, however, once stung by his betrayal, rebuffs Isa's attempts to reconcile.

But if Riri represents the potential of the revolution, then it is significant that Isa has impregnated her. Their child, Nimat, born of political prostitution and the dissipation of *Wafdist* leadership, is yet something entirely new and pristine. Isa contemplates the child's beauty as he watches her play on an Alexandrine beach:

> There she was, the fruit of boredom on his part and fear on the part of her mother; and yet from these two reprehensible qualities, life had created an attractive being, overflowing with health and happiness. The hidden power's will had decreed, and all obstacles had collapsed in the face of the eternal, enigmatic awakening. This little girl was a sure sign of the idiocy of many fears, a token of nature showing us how it is possible to overcome corruption. Now, he thought, can't you imitate nature, just once? From your sorrows, losses and defeats, can't you make a victory, even if it's just a modest one? (139)

As Isa observes his daughter, he again has the feeling of an awakening. The motif of an awakening was portrayed in the breakfast scene in which Isa hears the Free Officers' radio address and in the final scene in which he follows the young revolutionary out of the dark public square and into the dawn. The recurring motif suggests Isa's awakening to the revolution and to his own role and responsibility regarding it. Further, his observation that the "will" of a "hidden power" had brought about an "eternal, enigmatic awakening" seems to acknowledge the organic, popular Egyptian nationalism which has motivated the events of the revolution. The "hidden power's will" is that of the masses which, though unforeseen by the nationalist party, has demolished obstacles of poverty and disenfranchisement to accomplish change. Nimat represents the birth of Egyptian independence and the hope for a new republic, free of corruption. Isa sees the girl as "a sure sign . . . it is possible to overcome corruption." Because Isa is her father, the metaphor of the child acknowledges the nationalist party's role in bringing about the independence achieved by the revolution. Indeed, to follow the metaphor, the *Wafd* had planted the seed of independence.

This interpretation is supported by Isa's change of heart. He decides to "make a victory" from his "sorrows, losses and defeats." He accepts the role offered him by the young revolutionary to help build the new republic. Isa chooses this role, rather than return to Qadriyya and their barren, benumbed life together. Indeed he had been sitting in the park because, after confronting Riri and Nimat, he felt he could never go home to Qadriyya, his wife of convenience. Isa's change of heart, his awakening, is the hopeful resolution of the story. It recognizes the contribution of the *Wafd* Party, which after all had set the course toward independence, even if it had fallen away or lost sight of its purpose. It also suggests the inclusion of the native bourgeoisie, if not as privileged elites but as fellow citizens, in the creation of the new republic. It is a hopeful ending to an ironic story.

Autumn Quail provides some perspective on the native elites of Egypt and their role in maintaining peripheral society and the political *status quo.* The portrayal of Isa, his friends and colleagues in the *Wafd,* exemplifies the "Egyptian Egyptians" with whom Silvio Pinto had associated in municipal government. Isa and his circle are nationalist, certainly; but while they may be "native" Egyptians, they are not necessarily nativist. Indeed, Isa's lifestyle both before and after his fall from office reflects the cosmopolitanism of his class. Thus far one has considered the Egyptian elite as ethnically and culturally heterogenous—that is, "cosmopolitan"—but as a group one which was basically "Westernized" or identified with "modern" European or Turkish forms. It may also be useful to consider an alternative view regarding Egyptian elites. Magda Baraka cautions that "[s]weeping generalizations about the cultural westernization of the Egyptian upper classes need, however, to be qualified" (153). Her view recognizes the presence of a culturally indigenous, native strata among the upper class. This strata was most notably represented by the *Wafd,* the nationalist party whose landowning members dominated Egyptian politics for most of the period between 1919 and 1952. Baraka cites the names of several important native families headed by urban and rural "notables," landowners and *beys* which she describes as having led "a thoroughly indigenous lifestyle." Her qualification is important in order to gain a perspective upon the complexity of forces shaping Egypt's push toward real independence. One sees that neither a coterie of "paunchy pashas" nor a "modern Egyptian Pharaoh" singularly initiated the developments which led to Egypt's sovereignty by 1956.

Yet Baraka's qualification about native elites, however compelling, must not obscure the more basic issues of elite class power. Regardless of whether the upperclass strata tended toward cultural Westernization or toward cultural (bourgeois) nationalism, their interests tended to dovetail in regard to the retention or consolidation of political power, private property and class privileges at the expense of the native masses. While a great many native elites may well have led a "thoroughly indigenous lifestyle," their advantages as members of an elite class derived from their capitulations to the *status quo* of Western colonial rule. Because of their collaboration with the Western agency of colonial domination, one may say that such native elites were quite "Westernized" in regard to the interests they served. Even nationalists could not ignore the terms of their own political power, which was sustained as much as it was kept in check by British authority. For this reason, established nationalists may have sought to qualify their concessions to foreign rule—and the preservation of their elite positions within society—as political expediency or as the gradual pursuit of sovereignty. One may thus recognize that nationalism was not a disinterested posture in regard to the possession and retention of class privileges. For example, the *Wafd* authored some important initiatives on behalf of the peasants and the lower classes, notably in education and land tenure, against the opposition of the monarchists and other conservatives. While any observer may view these initiatives as liberal advances, one may as easily view them as mere token concessions to the masses—without any real structural change in the *status quo*—in order to retain the populist base of *Wafdist* power. At any rate such concessions, either to the agents of foreign rule or to the Egyptian masses, did little to alleviate the great disparity between native elites and the native under classes, let alone serve the aim of national sovereignty.

The *Wafd* remained a catalyst of populist as well as bourgeois nationalism well after the 1919 uprising which gave birth to the party. However, it also became increasingly conciliatory to its opposition in order to retain political power. The nationalistic aspirations of the landowning *pashas* and *beys* represented by the *Wafd* were a thing removed from the interests of the petty bourgeoisie and the landless peasants from which the party drew its popular support. The Islamist political group, the Muslim Brotherhood, posed a more radical threat to the *status quo* and the government ordered it to dissolve in 1948, at a time when the organization comprised around a million members (Stillman 142).[29] The government ban was later removed. However, it is debatable whether or not the Brotherhood's political aims better represented the interests of native society than those of the *Wafd.*

Baraka's carefully detailed study of Egyptian elites, *The Egyptian Upper Class Between Revolutions 1919–1952,* takes in the generations after Saad Zaghlul's uprising until the Free Officers' Revolt. Her work includes oral history research and personal interviews with members of former leading families. Yet, as authentic and specific as this method appears, there is an atomized, solipsistic quality to the picture it represents. The economic and material power of the upper class appears minimized and diffuse, largely because of the methodology which Baraka employs. Her study cedes too much to her subjects' self-referential and internal comparisons with other elites and with relative strata of the same class. The atomized perspective of the subjects is more or less replicated in the study; thus it obscures a fuller recognition of the elite's hegemonic relations within Egyptian society. Granted, Baraka's study focuses specifically upon upperclass life as lived by elites—and not how it was experienced by the servants, serfs, employees and other class "inferiors" whose labor maintained that lifestyle. Yet Baraka could have broadened her view to situate elite privileges within a more representative context, i.e., one which sees the elite's hegemonic position *vis-à-vis* its colonial overseers in Britain and the West, as well as regards the Egyptian elite's own oppressed under classes. The comparison of elites with others of the same stripe, that is, within the same social class or strata, simply does not accurately represent class power or how it is maintained. Any study of class society which fails to look at the material disparities of the different classes within a given society renders the meaning of "class" moot. Social classes are, by definition, materialist categories which exist in relation to each other. To gut "class" of its material relationships to the other classes and "castes" within society simply renders the term as an opaque category characterized by arbitrary cultural phenomena. Baraka's study is overall a comprehensive social history, thoroughly researched and replete with specialized insights and details. But it does tend to ignore the hegemonic relationships of elites and to substitute "cultural" phenomena for materialism in the portrayal of elite lifestyles.

Further, while personal narratives such as the kind Baraka utilizes may provide a high degree of understanding and veracity to the task of historiography, they are necessarily limited to a single view. Even a number of different testimonies will generally reiterate the same viewpoint if drawn from the same sector and similar circumstance—in this case, the same class position, regardless of subtle differences in strata. While such methodology is critical to establish the veracity of specific events, etc., the method does not elicit a more faceted understanding of social phenomena. Typically the historiographer does not simply compile testimonies but tries to gain a broader perspective upon the subject through the comparison and interpretation of diverse and contradicting sources. Baraka conscientiously seeks to achieve veracity and understanding through her use of personal narratives; however, her deference to the self-referential narratives of elites might not get beyond their own biases. Elites of any society seldom recognize their class hegemony or its implications—though there have been notable exceptions. Generally the rich rarely see themselves as so; nor do they tend to engage the objectivity of self critique.

Naguib Mahfouz appears to make a similar point about the blind spot of elite self-preoccupation in one scene of *Autumn Quail.* Isa sits with his three friends at their favorite haunt, *El Bodega Café*. The men bemoan their fate under the revolutionary government, but two have found positions supporting it while Isa and one friend, Samir, have been purged—each with full salary for two years and a government pension. Preoccupied with his own fate, Isa dismisses a beggar who approaches him for a handout:

> "That's the real cause of our tragedy," he replied firmly, dismissing the beggar with a wave of his hand.
>
> "Sometimes," he continued, "it gives me great comfort to see myself as a Messiah carrying the sins of a community of sinners . . ."
>
> "We were the vanguard of a revolution," Samir Abd al-Baqi said, "and now we're the debris of one!" (56–57)

As with Shukri Pasha's house on the night of the Cairo fire, narrative details in the café scene convey substantial criticism of Isa's social class. (For example, the Spanish name of the café, *El Bodega,* means a little shop or store where goods are sold. The implication is, again, that Isa and his *Wafdist* friends are *compradors* who have "sold out" Egyptian sovereignty to the West, in order to maintain their self-indulgent lifestyles.) Though clearly not "pashas" but young *nouveau riche,* Isa and his friends commiserate over their "tragedy"—i.e., their displacement from power—meanwhile indulging in café life, liquor, tobacco and snacks. A poor shoe-cleaner who prevails upon the four men receives the same summary dismissal as the beggar. Isa claims to see himself as a martyr, "a Messiah carrying the sins of a community of sinners," but he does not see the poor who suffer all around him. Ironically, "Isa" is the Arabic variant of the name of Jesus.

Isa's comment about the cause of his tragedy was not actually directed at the beggar whom he dismissed, but rather replied to an earlier comment made by one of the friends. Yet ironically, Isa's gesture indicates the beggar as the cause of his and the others' fall from grace. His coincidental blame of the beggar is callous on the one hand because it would scapegoat someone poor and powerless. But on the other hand, Isa's gesture is ironically *apropos;* the Egyptian Revolution was predicated, at least ostensibly, upon the call to alleviate the chronic poverty of mass society as represented by the beggar. Isa's gesture thus indicates the beggar as the cause of his demise, yet he hardly even notices the man. His inability or unwillingness to recognize the impoverished condition of mass society is perhaps the real cause of his tragedy. Samir's comment, that the four *Wafdist* friends were once the vanguard of a revolution but are now the debris of one, seems to suggest this point.

One may see that "native" identity in the scene at *El Bodega* is a much less important signifier than class for Isa and his friends. All the men in the café may be natives, but the similarity means little in the face of the class divide. The young *nouveau riche Wafdists* share more in common with the cosmopolitan elites than with most other Egyptian natives. Isa would no doubt measure his own material and political power in relation to those of greater or lesser strata within his social class. He would not likely compare his lot with the poor, for he does not even see them.

If one accepts the blind spot of privilege as a material phenomenon, then, a reservation may be made regarding the subjective methodology applied by Baraka in her study of Egyptian elites. Again, while the study is impressively comprehensive, Baraka's deference to the personal testimonies of elites might actually undermine her own perspective upon her research. Her attempt to render an authentic, self-authorized representation of the Egyptian upper class is undertaken with sensitivity and care. Yet her portrayal of elites might be construed as lacking the necessary contextual analysis of colonial society. A less subjective approach would possibly account for elite hegemony and the conflict of interests between the upper and lower classes.

Given these considerations, Baraka's qualifications of differences in cultural outlook among the strata or among individuals of the upper class is less important an observation in and of itself. Rather, in my own view, it is important because it illustrates the effects of so-called "modern development" in the periphery of the world system. Egyptian society was substantially affected by its role as a producer in the world economy. The development of agrarian capitalism by external, i.e., colonial, forces in Egypt had solidified the custodial position of the old Ottoman elite. This elite retained its role even as its composition underwent fluxes of new blood, in terms of ethnicity and stratum, and of new ideas, some of which were in rapport with the West, some in reaction to it. Various ethnicities composed the elite, including natives and minorities, and reflected a kind of self-interested ecumenicism. Yet such "multiculturalism" had no kind of egalitarian bearing upon the peripheral social structures of the society at large. These structures remained in place, regardless of whether the elite positions within them were occupied by Turks, Europeans, natives, Christians, Jews, Muslims, liberals, conservatives, monarchists, or nationalists.

One can argue that individual differences in outlook or "lifestyle" within the spectrum of the upper class strata remain simply so, despite qualifications; the broader, material class interests are largely the same across strata. The subtleties of position among elites are generally inconsequential to the lower classes when the context of mass political disenfranchisement remains unaltered. As with the upper classes elsewhere in the world economic "periphery" during roughly the same period, the object of nationalism was often envisioned by *compradors* or elites as the independent power of their social class, but free now of colonial oversight. This kind of nationalism was materially at odds with the popular revolutionary nationalist movements which achieved independence in those countries. One may observe that in each broad movement, there were "many nationalisms," and that the vision of an independent nation and of one's own role within it varied according to class and material interests.

Chapter Six

The Radical Surgery of a Woman Doctor

Nawal El Saadawi

6.1 NILE SILT AND NATIVE EARTH

In many ways the unequal development of class society in modern Egypt can be seen to have produced nativist reaction to Western influence and to those strata which were identified with the West. The so-called "cosmopolitan" community appeared in local society as an imminent and visible aspect of Western colonialism. As well the maintenance, through Western development, of a largely native "second class" necessarily impacted upon nativist sentiment. The inequality between the modernized, "cosmopolitan" elites and the native masses, mainly the peasantry, was magnified by the contrast in their sheer numbers: "The astute members of the busy Stock Exchange, the personnel of firms and banks, the ruling class as a whole counted little, statistically, as against the prevailing mass of the peasantry . . . Society was a pyramid widening out from a powerful, exclusive group at the top, concerned with profit-making and modernity, to its ancient base, still in bondage to the Nile. But it was a step pyramid, like that of Sakkarah" (Berque 484). Berque's use of a metaphor, the pyramid at Sakkarah, graphically represents the hegemony of Egyptian society. It emphasizes the native identity of the largely disenfranchised. Yet it also suggests where the transformative power of Egyptian society actually lay—in the strength of numbers.

Popular Egyptian nativism reflected the class polarity of modern Egypt. Cosmopolitan elites were seen in the common view as "foreign" and illegitimate; "[p]opular animus was directed against the wealthy ruling class, foreigners, and the non-Muslim minorities that were closely associated with the foreigners in the popular mind" (Stillman 142). Conversely, the native masses and especially the rural peasantry came to represent Egyptian "authenticity" and national legitimacy. "[B]y the 1920s," observes Beth Baron, "the peasant had come to be prized as the soul of Egypt" (68). The conception of the peasantry as "authentically" native was not unique or novel to the Egyptian independence movement. Rather the point is that nativist sentiment and conceptions generally informed a moving current of Egyptian nationalism which existed apart from the *Wafd* Party. The nativist current was not steered or directed by *Wafd* leaders but likely derived organically from mainstream Egyptian society. Perhaps because the *Wafd* was perceived to have lost sight of its goal, nationalist legitimacy seemed more readily identified with the native masses. An initial claim of the Egyptian Revolution, for example, was that it had established the first native leader, the Free Officer Mohamed Neguib, to govern Egypt since the days of the ancient pharaohs. At least two other Free Officers, notably Gamal Abdel Nasser and Anwar Al Sadat, had only been able to attend military academy after the repeal of a law which prohibited natives from serving as officers. Previously, the officer class had drawn mostly upon ethnic Turkish elites (Dekmejian 20).

Egyptian nativism might be understood as a more diffuse and abstract phenomenon than the organized nationalist movement. The latter had its public leaders such as Ahmad Urabi, Mustafa Kamil, and Saad Zaghlul;[1] its parties—the *Watani* and the *Wafd;* and its platform, e.g., the drafting of a constitution, the development of public education, etc. These early nationalists did not exclude Egyptian ethnic minorities or non-Muslims from their vision of independence. Egyptian nationalism was envisioned by many early proponents as a secular movement based upon territorial integrity, rather than ethnic or cultural unity.[2] It might be difficult to define "nativist" organization or institutions in the same way. Yet there were pervasive signs of nativist sentiment among mainstream Egyptians. The signs of Egyptian nativism manifested in the broad, popular resistance to Western domination and, especially, to the British occupation. This resistance was apparent in everyday life. Rhetorically, it was extant in periodicals and common speech; in public protests; and in popular slogans. Its imagery informed popular photography and iconography. For example, Baron discusses how media photographs portraying the Egyptian masses significantly connoted group national identity: "The crowd . . . represented the passion, enthusiasm, and unity of the nation. Visually, pictures of the crowd—the individual as part of something larger—came closest to capturing the notion of the nation" (96). Materially, nativist sentiment manifested in anti-British riots, incidents and insurgencies. It was nowhere more material than in the guerrilla attacks of paramilitary *fedayin* upon the British soldiers in the Suez Canal Zone.

Perhaps what delineates the Egyptian nativism of the period is its "organic" nature, that is, its "autonomy" from the organized nationalist movement. According to R. Hrair Dekmejian, there existed a "pervasive vagueness" or ambivalence regarding Egyptian nationalism among what he calls a "key subelite group in the social structure." The alleged ambivalence reveals some essential differences between the nativist and the nationalist "movements" or predilections. Dekmejian describes the ambivalent "subelite" as an important group comprised of middle class and petty bourgeois professionals:

> Their conception of Egyptian nationalism not only lacked specific content beyond the achievement of complete independence from Britain, but also a concrete program to achieve this aim. Given the high degree of ambivalence at that level of society, one could infer that the attitude at lower levels was more ambivalent, perhaps bordering on indifference. (50)

While Dekmejian's insights about the ambivalence of "subelites" toward Egyptian nationalism may well hold, it is probably not true that native society harbored ambivalence or indifference about Egyptian sovereignty, or, actual independence from Britain. There is something thus to be said for semantics. The nationalistic conceptions held by the lesser strata—that is, the strata lesser than the elites who dominated national politics—may indeed have tended to focus specifically upon the withdrawal of the British troops and administration, as Dekmejian notes. Most Egyptians would likely have been ambivalent about or indifferent toward the gradualism of careerist politicians whose "nationalism" merely served to retain the *status quo* relations of colonial power and local hegemony. Yet this is an insight which Dekmejian does not make.

The meaning of "nationalism" to Egyptian natives probably varied according to their respective social strata. As Baraka observes: "The rank and file of the people . . . saw 'nationalism' not as the lofty and vague concept which the leadership was trying to promote but rather as an opportunity to alleviate the many real injustices they experienced in their daily lives. They perceived such injustices as a consequence of the occupation and wanted to remove them" (71). The semantic difference of national independence as understood by the lower classes is illustrated, for example, in Mahfouz' *Autumn Quail.* Isa, the fallen *Wafdist* official, questions Riri the prostitute about her feelings about Egyptian nationalism. The girl does not understand his meaning until he rephrases his question:

> Once it occurred to him to ask her what she knew about politics . . .
>
> Her eyes showed no sign of understanding.
>
> "What are your views on independence?" he continued.
>
> Her look did not change.
>
> "I mean the departure of the English," he said by way of explanation.

> "Oh!" she shouted, "Let them go if you want them to. But I've heard a lot about how good things were in their day. My mistress, the café proprietress, opened her café on their money!"
>
> For her, he thought, real independence meant being rid of the need for me and others like me. (81–82)

The passage is both ironic and astute. Riri appears completely void of an opinion about Egyptian independence, until Isa clarifies that he means "the departure of the English." That objective she understands very well; but even so, she seems indifferent. The girl says she has heard that the British provided some benefit to her madam. The madam was able to "sponsor" Riri, or rather, to facilitate her prostitution because of the "patronage" of British soldiers. This dubious "benefit" is actually withering exploitation from which the girl cannot extricate herself. One recalls that the prostitution motif in the story symbolizes the *Wafd* Party's "sell out" of the sovereign Egyptian nation. Isa's comment about what real independence means for Riri may thus be read as a political criticism of the *Wafd.* Real independence will come when the nation is free of opportuning "nationalists" who simply exploit the conditions of colonial bondage—just as the girl prostitute will only truly benefit when she is free of "patrons" and "sponsors" who simply exploit her abjection.

Isa and Riri are both Egyptian natives but are worlds apart in terms of social class and their material relationships to national politics. With or without the gradualism of *Wafd* leadership, Riri's abjection remains the same, as does that of the Egyptian under class. But the actual independence achieved by the Egyptian Revolution does raise Riri's fortune by the end of the story, just as it ends Isa's opportunistic career. Riri's stake in independence is different than Isa's stake in "nationalism." Thus the objective of independence understood by nationalists may have been quite different from that regarded by popular Egyptian "nativism." Nativism in this case might be understood as the regard of native society for a national independence which would have positive, material affect upon the mainstream, that is, an affect beyond the political aspirations of elites.

The degraded conditions of the native masses gave impetus and legitimacy to the Egyptian popular resistance, that is, to the independence movement which was irrespective of *Wafd* leadership. While establishment elites and the cosmopolitan community largely derived the benefits of political and economic life in Egypt, the native population mostly suffered poverty, illness, hunger and abjection. The abjection of the native populace, incidentally, is what Sartre called the "subhuman" conditions of colonial violence.[3] The condition of the native masses, many observed, was attributable to colonial rule.

Sartre and Laroui, for example, identified the underdevelopment of native society in North Africa as an apparatus, a tool, of Western colonialism.[4] The remedy to native abjection in Egypt would not have been envisioned by nativists as the private commercial investment or foreign aid of "modern development"—the hallmarks of Western colonialism. Such "modernization" had already been pursued by the successors of Muhammad Ali; it had resulted in Egypt's political and economic dependency and military occupation. "Modernization" would have been seen by nativists as having "developed" the abject conditions which the native masses unfairly bore in relation to the privileges of "modernized," *comprador* elites. The remedy seen by nativists thus would be the deposition of the political establishment and the collaborating elites, and with them, colonial rule. The deposition of the *status quo* offered an opportunity to realize the enfranchisement of the lesser Egyptian strata. The populist appeal of nativism was the legitimacy it voiced for the stake of mass native society in the national life of the country.

Various works that deal with the Egyptian revolutionary period associate legitimate national independence not with *Wafdist* politics but with the broader, largely disenfranchised native society. Indeed, the association holds the local Egyptian political elite as part of the problem of foreign domination. In *A Daughter Of Isis,* for example, Nawal El Saadawi portrays the nativist mood of Egyptian society in the days leading up to the revolution. Saadawi was a medical student in Cairo at the time. She had been deeply affected by the activism of her father, a schoolteacher who as a young man had joined the uprising in 1919 against the British. As a student, Nawal also joined and later led demonstrations against the king, the political establishment and the British. In the memoir of her early life, she recounts her father's influence upon her own activism. From her account, one gets the sense of the political establishment—i.e., the monarchy and its British "advisors," the parties and the wealthy elites—as a colonial apparatus which runs counter to the interests and the will of native society:

> [M]y father always followed what was happening in the country. He read government and opposition newspapers, always talked about the corruption of the king and the ruling class, about British colonial rule and the military occupation of Egypt. He used to say that the riches of our country went to the foreigners and to the handful of dishonest pashas who ruled the country. He called Egypt the country of the 2 per cent, meaning that 2 per cent of the population owned almost everything, leaving the rest of the population hungry, sick and ignorant. "It's a chronic triple misery and there's no solution to it without a change in the regime. People must wake up, must rebel, he would say. (260–261)

The elder Saadawi refers to the "foreigners and to the handful of dishonest pashas who ruled the country." His comments, interestingly, recall the motif of the "paunchy pashas" one encountered in the works of Durrell and Mahfouz. The "foreigners" to whom Saadawi's father refers are the British and, probably, the ethnic minority elites. His view contrasts these groups, collectively, with the abject native masses. Saadawi's representation of the "pashas" strongly identifies them with foreign rule. He sees the ruling class, native "pashas" as more than simply irrelevant to the Egyptian independence movement. The "handful of dishonest pashas," he observes, is counterproductive to the goal of independence and to the political and economic enfranchisement of mass native society. Durrell's portrayal, that ruling class pashas were leading the movement for native independence, rings false by comparison. The Egyptian independence envisioned by Saadawi is not the "gradualism" of *Wafd* nationalists but a clean break with the political establishment: "[T]here's no solution . . . without a change in the regime. People must wake up, must rebel." The use of the expression, "to wake up," and his invocation to rebel, indicate the more radical and nativist turn of popular sentiment by the reign of Farouk. Indeed, the motif of political "awakening" was used by Mahfouz to represent the Egyptian Revolution in *Autumn Quail.*

Importantly, in the view of Saadawi's father, Egypt's sovereign independence and actual economic development are linked prospects. He sees that there is no solution to the "chronic triple misery" of hunger, illness, and ignorance suffered by mass society without a summary "change in the regime" of *comprador* elites. He observes that the modern, Western colonial production supported by the local regime—i.e., the monarchy and the established political elites—has created the conditions of unequal development. These conditions characterize what the elder Saadawi calls, "the country of 2 per cent, meaning that 2 per cent of the population owned almost everything," while the masses lived in abject poverty. The author Saadawi recounts that in contrast with the landowning elite, "[t]he property of a poor peasant never exceeded three *feddans* [a feddan is about one acre]" (72). Saadawi's portrayal is essentially one of class struggle. The unequal development of a small sector of "peripheral" society to the abjection of the majority, one recalls, characterizes the world productive system, i.e., modern global capitalism. One sees that so-called "development" is clearly not the "solution" to Egyptian abjection but the very problem.

The elder Saadawi's assessment of the "country of 2 per cent" finds resonance in the recent biography of Nasser written by Said K. Aburish. In a passage which echoes the view of Saadawi, Aburish describes the conditions of Egyptian life which were observed by and which influenced the young

Nasser. The son of a petty clerk, Nasser spent part of his youth in the *said,* the rural south of Egyptian peasants. Aburish's description expands upon that of Saadawi and is worth reviewing for additional perspective upon the inherently unjust nature of pre-revolutionary society in Egypt:

> In the 1930s, the pashas, less than 2 percent of the population, owned more than 65 percent of the land and employed and exploited over four million peasants who tenanted for them. A tenant farmer usually lived off two acres of land and his small share of what they produced. He hardly had any rights, and when elections were held he was supposed to vote in accordance with what the pasha told him. Because banks would not deal with poor people, there was little social mobility, and very few ever overcame their peasant background. (8)

Given the perspective of Saadawi and Aburish, what becomes apparent is the essentially static nature of peasant abjection. As Aburish notes, there was little social mobility for the under classes. The stasis of the under classes was structural; their conditions were not only reproduced by poverty but, as well, by their exclusion from the rights of civil society enjoyed by the upper classes.

Again, one must evaluate such an observation in light of the claims of modernization. Claims about the benefits of Western development to local society had been made in Egypt at least since the days of Ismail. They were the same hollow claims with the same diminishing returns for the impoverished masses. Yet one may see clearly where the benefits of development accrued and where they fell short. The Egyptian peasants observed by Saadawi, and for that matter by Nasser, farmed the fields owned by others or served as domestics in the homes of the upper classes. A large segment of the Egyptian peasantry supplied serf labor to the estates and plantations owned by cotton and sugar "pashas" and other elites. The Pinto Cotton Company owned by Gini Alhadeff's grandfather, for example, would have depended upon the serf labor of Egyptian peasants. Even a petty bourgeois family like the Saadawis, who derived from the peasantry themselves only a generation earlier, retained a peasant servant in their modest, rented flat during Nawal's youth. Where the abjection of the native masses was imminent, so too were the privileges of the upper classes. The elder Saadawi's criticism of the "country of 2 per cent" thus regards the chronic class division of Egyptian society. The class divide obtained not only between elites and the under classes but also between the political establishment and the native masses. Importantly, Saadawi recognizes that the polarity of Egyptian society stems from colonial rule, and specifically from the Western unequal development which the local establishment maintains.

One has already considered how the "modernization" of Egypt by the West had developed the "parafeudal" conditions of the native peasantry. By the reign of Farouk, it would have been apparent to many that continued "development" had concretized the class division of local society and the conditions of excess or lack which pertained reciprocally to elites and to the under classes. The parafeudal conditions of local society characterized what Amin referred to as "agrarian capitalism," a mode distinguishable from classic feudalism mainly by its attachment to the world productive system. The markers of Egyptian agrarian capitalism are apparent in Nawal El Saadawi's observation that: "[s]peculation on the cotton market benefited the big landowners and the British, while speculation in land raised rents so that the landowners benefited all the time at the expense of the peasants who toiled to grow the crops" (72). While wealthy, landowning "notables" and their supporters in commerce and government grew richer through "development," the poor were driven deeper into poverty.

The poor peasants were not simply attached, "para-serf style," to the land; it bears recalling that their labor was also attached to the world productive system, i.e., to markets, consumers, investors and stockholders in the West which dominated Egypt's political economy. It was "[a]n economic system of which the primitive village was still the basic unit [yet] paradoxically, linked to cosmopolitan trade and the abstract speculations of capital."[5] Egyptian elites managed local production and, so doing, largely served the world system and its foreign beneficiaries. Meanwhile within local society, as Berque comments, "A fundamental inequality remained. The evolution which had enabled Egypt to play her part in international relations was due to the labours of her peasants. But the profits accumulated in the hands of an increasingly rootless bourgeoisie" (485). Development had mostly meant stasis for the disenfranchised masses, largely the peasantry. Neither development, nor for that matter nationalism, had affected much material change for the base of Egyptian society. The remedy to the poverty and disenfranchisement of the Egyptian masses, therefore, had to arise from within native society—rather than be imposed from without, rather than be another Western "development" scheme.

Ironically it was the "base" of Egyptian society, the peasant masses, which embodied the potential for social change. There was a quiet power inherent in the peasantry, which explicitly or implicitly lay at the center of all negotiations:

> It was in relation to a dense compact mass at the base that all changes took place, that the individual and the coterie, the reactionary member of a

> privileged class and the proletarian in revolt, the profiteer and the conspirator, the Muslim Brother, the intellectual, the mutinous officer, formed groups or broke away, assumed a personality or retreated into anonymity. That base was the peasant world. It had been a theme for eloquence for a long time; it had inspired stories, poems, sentimental arguments, electoral speeches. In fact it remained the great unknown. (Berque 616–617)

Berque notes that the peasants had long been invoked as the signifier of Egyptian native identity. Representations of the peasants figured into the rhetoric of various political actors. The image of the peasant, undoubtedly through association with the land and the Nile, was an essential and easily appropriated sign. Indeed, "[t]o think of Egypt is to think of her soil, that 'mother earth, *ummi' l-ard* which . . . even in the sturdy frames of her men we recognize [as] that same deep loam that feeds her luxuriant vegetation" (616). The imagery was powerfully evocative. However the reality of this potential—the actual, mass power of the peasantry—was yet a thing untapped. Berque refers to it as "the great unknown." The shadow cast by popular, organic Egyptian nativism was the threat of the class struggle. Egyptian nativism was thus an expression of the need for native enfranchisment, that is, the enfranchisement of the native masses and of mainstream, native society as a whole. Nativism can be seen to have evolved from a popular sentiment into a discourse and, after the 1952 *coup d'etat,* into an official policy.[6]

The criteria upon which any ethnic nativism is based is necessarily artificial or fetishized. One recognizes that any "native" or ethnic identity which establishes itself upon natality, bloodline, physiognomy, etc., is easily collapsed. Further, an agenda which pursues objectives on behalf, or in the name, of native society is necessarily subject to question and analysis. The agenda of nativism is not transparent; nor is it a thing apart from the special interests of those who invoke it. Thus its objectives and its methods bear examination. One may question whose benefit is mostly served by a "nativist" agenda.[7] Merely the identification as "native" does not suppose the equal status or similar interests of all who share native identity. One recalls the café scene in Mahfouz' *Autumn Quail* when the four nationalist friends brusquely dismiss the beggars who, nevertheless, are natives like themselves. The four nationalists may envision an Egypt governed someday by and for Egyptians, but the kind of empowered Egyptian natives they envision derive from elite circles. Indeed, Isa and his colleagues have benefited by keeping the native masses at bay from the instruments and institutions of national government. It is important, therefore, to recognize the clearly subjective and interpretive nature of what is alleged to be in the "native interest."

Yet however qualified, nativism can be understood as both an ideology and as an agenda, or set of material practices. One definition of nativism refers to "the rhetoric of decolonization which argues that colonialism needs to be replaced by the recovery and promotion of pre-colonial, indigenous ways."[8] On the face of it, however, such an argument or task would have been especially difficult to pursue in the case of Egypt. For which "precolonial past" in Egypt's millennia of foreign colonizations and influences would it suffice to recover? Even the pharaonic past, certainly a source of national pride, posed a problematic "recovery" for Egyptian nativism. This was so for many reasons, but in lieu of a long discussion, one obvious problem may be cited. Dynastic Egypt was, of course, pre-Islamic and most Egyptian natives identified culturally, as well as religiously, as Muslims:

> Regardless of its ancient glory, anchoring modern nationalism on the pharaonic period had a ring of unreality, especially to Muslim Egyptians. The weakness and ambiguity of its pharaonic foundations might have been overcome had it not been for the "foreignness" of its content; the adoption of a secular path was too abrupt a departure from the Islamic reality of Egyptian society. (Dekmejian 91–92)

An antique vision of native identity was not easily transposed upon Egyptian society, perhaps not even with the exception of the Coptic minority which claims continuity from ancient Egypt. Nor might the privileging of the distant past serve when the national mood looked ahead, rather, to the future.

Egypt like other postcolonial countries which had been underdeveloped, if overexploited, for generations, now saw in political independence the opportunity for actual structural and economic development. Most postcolonial nations actively pursued industrialization, new technologies and economic diversification immediately following independence. When independence leaders in the Third World set out to modernize conditions in the former colonies, they sought to address the determinant factors which had created underdevelopment, or rather, unequal development. The great achievement of the age of decolonization, the end of foreign occupation, was not enough; the peripheral conditions of local society yet persisted. Those conditions were maintained by the economy and social structures which had long accompanied the peripheral role in world production. The "modern development" pursued in the decolonized Third World centered not only upon industrialization and diversification, but also on reforming the "peripheral" relationship to the world system.[9] Thus the ideological leanings of nativism had to be negotiated with the will toward actual, modern, development. If Egyptian nativism depended upon "the recovery and promotion . . . of indigenous ways," it would have to be a qualified, interpretive representation of the "native."

Regardless of the inherent problems with the conception, however, "nativism" played a key role, at least ostensibly, in the decolonization of Egypt during the 1950s and '60s. But perhaps because the criteria which defines "nativeness" is necessarily abstract, subjective and unstable, the concepts of Egyptian nativism appear fluid and dynamic throughout the period. The fluidity of Egyptian nativism was likely suited to the necessity of political reinvention. The language of Egyptian independence had always hosted an array of political ideas, some of which seem complementary to Egyptian nativism, others which seem contradictory. It is interesting to consider nativism as one among several discourses which were utilized to express Egyptian independence from Western influence. Said had observed that Egyptian nativism possessed a "vocabulary" which drew from Arabism, Nasserism, and Marxism. Dekmejian actually quantifies the nationalist references, as opposed to the Arabist references, of the Nasser government in the content of official communications, such as radio broadcasts and political speeches:

> In the broadcasts, the general theme of Egyptian nationalism was characterized by specific references to "unity of the Nile Valley," "sons of the Nile Valley," "Egyptian people," "Egyptian territory," "Egypt will destroy," "glory and dignity of Egypt." In each case the emphasis focused exclusively on the Nile Valley in the Sudan and Egypt. In contrast, the themes denoting Arab nationalism were used in the context of a Pan-Arabist identification with the peoples of other Arab states. The themes included, "the Arab nation from the Atlantic Ocean to the Arab Gulf," "Arab Egypt," "Arab solidarity," "Arab people of Egypt." (93)

Laskier had identified the influence of German nationalism and fascist ideology upon the Egyptian independence movement of the mid twentieth century, while Laroui and Ajami note the same influences upon pan-Arabism. Bernard Lewis goes further to trace the various historical movements in political thought upon Egyptian nationalism, including an Arabism comprised of Western, Turkish, Levantine, Islamic, as well as nativist elements.[10] Lewis and Laskier both cite also the anti-Jewish and anti-Zionist components of Egyptian and pan-Arab nationalism. There is a point of making reference, however cursory, to the ideological "genealogy" of the movement for Egyptian independence; one recognizes the spectrum of thought upon which it drew. Whether one refers to "Nasserism," "Arabism," "nativism," "revolutionary nationalism," etc., to describe the discourse and practices of Egyptian nationalism depends upon the context one addresses or upon the particular aspect of this fluid political movement one chooses to emphasize. The intertextuality or collapsibility of discourses provided a language or vocabulary for a new set of circumstances and challenges: decolonization. The nativism of the period must be viewed, ultimately, in light of the struggle for national sovereignty.

The Egyptian Revolution initiated a series of political and economic reforms which might be called "nativist" because they were aimed at developing local, native society. Under the collaborative governments of the previous generations foreign business, foreign banks, foreign administration, foreign troops and foreign schools had been the marks of foreign domination. Thus after the deposition of the old establishment, it became a policy to replace the foreign with nativist markers. One encounters some of these markers in the memoirs of Alhadeff, Aciman, Said and Saadawi. For example, the troubles experienced by the Egyptian minorities, such as harassment and expulsion, confiscation of property, etc., were implemented during the period of Egyptian decolonization. The effects of a consciously nativist program may be seen in several anecdotes told by the memoirists: the loss of status suffered by Alhadeff's grandfather, Silvio Pinto, after the rise of Nasser; the prohibition and eventual nationalization by the government of the Said family business in Cairo and the Acimans' factory in Alexandria; the institutionalization of anti-Semitic rhetoric witnessed by Aciman as a schoolboy. These are historical details which portray how Egyptian nativism took shape during decolonization. One sees that the Egyptian minorities were unfairly targeted by these reforms. The larger historical events of the day were the withdrawal of British troops and the nationalization of the Suez Canal. Those events announced a nativism which defined Egyptian independence after 1952.

It is important to understand that there were many aspects to the nativist push for Egyptian independence, i.e., aspects which were momentous and minute, just and unjust, reactionary and repressive, as well as liberatory. All of these aspects defined a movement which was, at the end of the day, a response to colonial exploitation. This latter observation does not seek to smooth over or give spin to the apparent reduction, essentialism, and political self interest inherent in—any—ethnic nativism. The point, rather, is that Egyptian nativism evolved as a response to foreign intervention and domination. The rise of nativism in Egypt was a logical and predictable consequence of Western unequal development.

The hallmarks of a consciously "nativist" policy, implemented by the new government, were the land reform acts and the repossession (nationalization) of state resources and foreign assets. The break-up and redistribution of the big landed estates which began in 1952 were intended to respond to the central problems of colonial agrarianism. Parafeudalism, the abjection of the native masses, the oligarchical powers of wealthy, landowning elites, and the monocultural economy were problems which derived from the plantation system. The nationalization of foreign-owned property and capital aimed at developing a state economy which would not remain beholden or "peripheral" to the West. In short, land reform and nationalization sought to address the unequal development upon which Egyptian "peripheral" society was based.

"For Nasser, the land reform act gave the RCC [Revolutionary Command Council; i.e., the *coup* officers] identity and . . . transformed the events of July 23, 1952 from a coup to a revolution."[11] It was certainly a departure from the "gradualism" of pasha nationalists whose interests had mainly lay in maintaining colonial production. As a result of the new government's nativist policy, much of the old, status quo was indeed dismantled:

> [T]he land reform of 1952, which, abolishing the power of the latifundia-owners, gave the leading position in the country-side to the kulaks [landed peasants], and continued with the nationalizations of 1957 and then of 1961, which transferred to the state the ownership of undertakings belonging to Western capital and its partner, the Egyptian bourgeoisie. It had as corollary the gradual affirmation of a new ideology, that of Nasserism. (*Unequal Development* 313)

Amin describes how reforms in the ownership of land, assets, and capital shifted the locus of class power. Principally, land reform and nationalization disempowered the old elite in favor of the new government. Subsequently the policy has been characterized as either the outright "theft" perpetrated by a dictatorship or, conversely, as the "socialism" of a Soviet-styled government, depending upon the view of the observer.[12] Without deferring too much to those views, one may also call the policy "nativist" because no matter what else it was intended to achieve, it primarily aimed at developing native society and national government upon local—rather than foreign or global—terms.

Critics of Nasser's reforms do not often recognize that the commercial and class powers of Egyptian elites had been codified for generations by colonial administration. Nor do they recognize that the abjection of native society had likewise been codified by the same commercial, juridicial and political legislation which gave primacy to *comprador* elites. It may well be true that nationalization was an expedient way for the new government to consolidate power and to weaken the influence of political rivals among the old elite. But Egyptian land reform and nationalization were more than mere political expediency. The repossession of the Suez Canal, for example, was integral to building the Aswan

High Dam, a project to increase the arable land in Egypt by one third: "Clearly the canal was the focus of [Nasser's] attention as a source of income for building the dam and for underwriting Egypt's economic development, but also as a remedy for the historical damage done to the Egyptian people . . ."[13] One must recognize the structural nature of Egyptian peripheral dependency and its linkage to an exploitative world productive system. The recognition lends an appreciation of the predicament of decolonization. The deposition of foreign rule and the status quo political establishment could only have been necessary first steps toward sovereign independence. Military *coup d'etat* was not enough to remake Egyptian society; to stop there would have essentially replaced the collaborating aristocracy with a collaborating military elite not unlike the Mamluks, the soldier caste which ruled prior to Muhammad Ali. Without pressing the analogy too far, one notes that while Ali deposed the Mamluks to establish his own rule, he also envisioned the reform of Egyptian society. For the revolutionary government which deposed Farouk, there yet remained the old colonial problem of the peripheral economy and the parafeudal social formation it supported. Indeed it was largely an economic imperialism which had sustained parafeudal abjection in Egypt, long after the British Protectorate ended in 1922. The land reforms and nationalizations imposed by the new government therefore went several steps beyond the deposition of Farouk and the old establishment. The second-class conditions of the native majority necessitated massive social reforms. The new government had not only inherited these conditions—which had accrued over generations of "modern development"—but it had inherited as well the mandate for massive reform.

The materialism of land reform and nationalization was aimed at developing native Egyptian society and sovereignty. Of course there was an ideological component to this material development. Amin observes the role of ideology as a "corollary" to the Egyptian reforms pursued by the Nasser government. Anouar Abdel Malek also sees the relevance of an ideology which privileges "Egyptianess" in the process of decolonization. He identifies "the development of the national culture" as central to Egyptian independence. Further, he sees the actual development of Egyptian society coming about not through Western-style "modernization" but through a nativist program of political and material reforms. According to Malek, Egyptian sovereignty is essentially contraposed to Western-led development:

> [It is not] a question of "culturation [acculturation of Western forms]," "development," or "modernisation." The fundamental political objectives are political independence, the development of the national culture, nationalisation and planning. Moreover these are no more than

> instruments at the service of the great civilisational project, wherever they are posed; and it is that project itself which consigns the "Third World" parenthesis to the sideshow of history. (74)

The social reforms which Malek envisions are independent national government—as opposed to "autonomy;" a cultural nationalist program; the nationalization of resources which had been privatized under colonial administration; and, a planned economy which serves the nation state rather than foreign interests. Of course, this kind of "nativism" went by many names during the Nasserist period in which Malek wrote; it was often called by contemporary observers as, again, "revolutionary nationalism," or sometimes by the misnomer, "Arab socialism," or indeed, as "Nasserism," after the Nasser government which had initiated the reforms. The present description of these reforms as "nativist" is probably only useful to distinguish the populist tenor of Egyptian nationalism as a current apart from *Wafdist* nationalism after 1952.

The "pan-Arabism" which eventually became the official discourse of the Nasser government was yet again a current apart from Egyptian nativism. Malek's work, quoted here, actually draws from the pan-Arabist perspective of the age; thus one may get a sense of the intertextuality or collapsibility of the nativist, nationalist and Arabist discourses. Malek sees the remedy of the central problem which plagued postcolonial Egypt—the unequal relationship of the "periphery" and the "center"—in the total, nativist development of local society. It is this nativist, local development—rather than the Western-oriented kind—which will thereby "consign the Third World parenthesis to the sideshow of history," as he sees it. Malek's vision concurs with what has been called "Third Worldism,"[14] i.e., the proposed solidarity of the decolonized world in a geopolitical "bloc" independent of Western influence or domination. Again, without attempting too much to delineate the individual discourses of the period, one may yet observe their intertextuality. The discursive fluidity situates independent Egypt within the larger non-aligned movement of the Third World. Non-alignment was the response of postcolonial nations to the Cold War polemics of an "East" represented by the U.S.S.R., and the "West" represented by the U.S. and the NATO allies. Non-alignment produced a body of intertextual discourses which articulated the sovereignty of postcolonial nations and the intent of their collective influence upon the world stage.

The fluidity of discourse rose to meet the occasion of Egyptian decolonization. Amin notes that the reforms of the revolutionary government in Egypt "had as corollary" the acceptance of a new ideology, that of Nasserism. The ideology associated with Gamal Abdel Nasser is perhaps a case in point of postcolonial "intertextuality," because of its political evolution during the 1950s and '60s. Generally Nasserism is identified with the doctrine of internationalist, pan-Arabism (or, "Arabism") and with Nasser's attempts to expand Egyptian influence in the region. The evolution resulted in the union of Egypt and Syria in 1958 to create the United Arab Republic.[15] There were arguably many reasons for the Nasser government's pursuit of a pan-Arabist policy. One reason cited by both Lewis and Amin was the 1956 Suez War with Britain, France and Israel.[16] A pan-Arabist "bloc" was conceived by its proponents to counter Western and, especially, Israeli interests in the region.

It is neither cynical nor contradictory to observe that the attraction of pan-Arabism for Nasser was that it offered opportunities—which were never fully realized—for Egyptian regional primacy. "Arabism" also provided a rhetoric of international, Arab solidarity in the face of Western power. However, the invocation of the Arabist rhetoric by the Nasser government has generally been seen as motivated by Egyptian political self interest, rather than by transnational solidarity. Conversely, Nasserism as a whole drew criticism in the West, where it was regarded as pro-Soviet and communistic. Yet apart from some aid and support from the Soviet Union, the Nasser government could hardly be called communistic; Egyptian communists were vigorously repressed by the government and many were jailed as "counter-revolutionaries." It is therefore probably more accurate to view Nasserism as characterized by a nativist rather than a leftist leaning. It may have just so happened that the vocabulary of the international left, as that of Egyptian nativism, was easily applied to the oppressed conditions of the underclass, peasant masses.

To refer to Nasserism in the broad context of what may be called Egyptian "nativism," as I am doing at present, is perhaps an interpretation at best. Indeed it is somewhat difficult to pin a definition upon "Nasserism" as an ideology or a discourse, apart from acknowledging it as the rhetoric which promulgated the policies of the Nasser government. But Dekmejian identifies the following criteria:

> 1) belief in Egyptian nationalism and its concomitant values of national power, dignity, and prestige; 2) belief in social justice for [the Egyptian] people, whom [Nasser] regarded as the victims of centuries of political and economic exploitation; 3) commitment to rapid modernization; and 4) [Nasser's own] belief in a sense of personal mission to accomplish the above goals. (99)

The criteria identified by Dekmejian illustrates that Nasserism initially centered on an Egyptian nativist agenda. Certainly it may be viewed as such in relief to the apparent negligence of *Wafd* leaders to secure a meaningful political independence for mainstream Egyptian society. The Free Officers asserted a Six-Point Program for Egyptian independence in 1953 which appears nativist by comparison with the *Wafd.* Striking at the political establishment, the priority or "first principle" of the program was stated as "the liquidation of colonialism and the Egyptian traitors who supported it."[17] The other five points of the officers' program are similarly polemical, if also vague: to end "feudalism" and the domination of power by the wealthy, and to establish majority power through social equality, a powerful army, and free and fair elections. "However naïve," comments one observer, "the six-point program promised a structural change in Egypt and catapulted the officers to the center of Egyptian politics" (Aburish 37).

The Free Officers' Revolt was portrayed by the new government as a long-overdue, nativist moment. There seems little reason to doubt the popular acceptance of that portrayal at the time. General Neguib, the officers' figurehead, was seen as essentially native as were Nasser and the others who positioned themselves in opposition to the Western-oriented elites and the compromised political establishment. Nasser himself, after having publicly taken over from Neguib, consciously invoked Egyptian native identity in his demeanor, his manner, his speech, and ultimately in his political behavior. Aburish relates a telling anecdote about Nasser's instinctive political acumen and his nativist appeal. In 1954, an Islamist militant tried to assassinate the Egyptian leader as he gave a speech celebrating the signing of the British evacuation agreement. The assailant fired from near range but missed his target and Nasser, apparently with his considerable cool intact, seized the opportunity:

> Mayhem broke out, and the available audiotape of the incident has Nasser raising his voice above the din and authoritatively appealing to all "brothers and sisters" to stay calm. With a modicum of calm restored, Nasser, characteristically better at improvising than reading speeches, delivered one of his memorable lines. In his clear, distinctive, and attractive baritone voice he hooked into the veins of the audience and told them what they wanted to hear: "If Abdel Nasser dies then everyone of you is Abdel Nasser . . . Each of you is Gamal Abdel Nasser. Gamal Abdel Nasser is of you and from you and he is willing to sacrifice his life for the nation." The hall roared with approval. Transported by his own words, Nasser raised his hands beside his head in the typical *baladi* or native style peculiar to the Said [rural Southern Egypt], and shook them backward and forward in a gesture of triumph. The assassination attempt began backfiring and playing into Nasser's hands a mere few seconds after it took place. (53–54)

Nasser's identification as a native Egyptian was clearly part of his political "capital" and he knew to invoke it well. His nativism may be recognized as a strategy to claim political legitimacy for himself and his government. But simply because his invocation of native identity was conscious does not imply that it was cynical, false or merely "performed." Nor does his utility of nativism mean he was not "genuinely" native; for, if nothing else, he was certainly well accepted by most Egyptians as such. Indeed as the assassination attempt shows, his nativist sensibility appears genuine enough to be spontaneously reached for, and shared, in an unexpected moment of duress.

Perhaps the most significant element which identified Nasserism with Egyptian nativism was Nasser himself. He exemplified a native sensibility, especially in comparison with the Italophile court of Farouk and other Eurocentric and Turcocentric Egyptian elites. Nor did political power alter Nasser's indigenous demeanor:

> He continued to live in the same modest house in Manshia, though he built an additional room, and he never felt comfortable working in a palace. He still ate very Egyptian dishes such as white cheese, fava beans, falafel, *tumiya,* and *mulukhiya.* Even his manner of greeting others was down to earth, and he raised his hands in a typical *baladi* gesture when returning a salutation. (Aburish 90)

Interestingly, the simple lifestyle observed by Nasser was also shared by other revolutionary nationalist leaders of the period. Fidel Castro and Che Guevara were known to live without largesse or frills (with the occasional exception of a good Cuban cigar), seeking to establish their political legitimacy through identification with the peasant masses. Relatedly Mohammar Qaddafy, the Libyan leader, invokes tribal (rather than peasant) nativism when he meets with foreign heads of state and international journalists in a tent, a signifier of his Bedouin identity.[18] Nasser's *baladi* (country or rural) gestures were genuine to him, but they also served to signify the native identity and authenticity which he shared with the Egyptian masses. His gestures were quite symbolically "down to earth," deriving from the rural peasantry which farmed the Nile River Valley of Southern Egypt. The association with the land of the Nile, and with the peasants who for millennia had cultivated it, were an important part of Nasser's political power and his program. The peasantry represented an autochthonous native legitimacy which was far more potent than the formal nationalism of the *Wafd,* or indeed, more potent than the revolutionary nationalism of the Free Officers. Nasser apparently summoned the notion of autochthony through his very identification with the native peasantry. It was the essential sign of his enormous appeal.

The perception of Nasser as "genuinely" native is related by Nawal El Saadawi, for example, in *Walking Through Fire.* She identifies him with the Nile, with the peasantry and with her own family, specifically with her father and grandmother who were themselves peasants. Saadawi's triple invocation of native identity establishes continuity between Nasser and native society, and she suggests that he has evolved from the same struggle for social justice—that he bears "the same load" or burden—as that of native society:

> I met Gamal Abd Al-Nasser face to face for the first time in 1962 . . . His skin was brown, the colour of fresh silt brought down by the Nile. He was tall, very tall, with a slight stoop to his shoulders like my grandmother and my father, walked slightly bent, taking long strides. Was he carrying the same load they had carried throughout their lives? They had never bowed under it. He too looked as though he could carry it with the same dignity . . . (55)

Saadawi's description of Nasser is remarkable for its connotation of familial intimacy. But further, it nearly replicates her own mirror image, which she portrays as essentially native and peasant. In her earlier memoir, *A Daughter Of Isis,* Saadawi refers to her own "brown complexion with a tint of indigo in its depths like those of the peasants in the Al-Saadawi family" (21). As a young girl, Nawal's mirror was a source of nativist pride: "I was proud of my dark skin. It was a beautiful brown, the color of silt brought down to my land by the waters of the Nile" (7). Her description of the Nile silt is nearly identical in both the portrayal of Nasser's looks and her own. Significantly, her description of Nasser develops these two motifs of native identity: the basically familial concept of the Egyptian peasantry and the conception of the Nile, that most ancient signifier of Egypt, reflected in one's own native face and body. Both portrayals, that of Nasser and that of Nawal's mirror image, are autochthonous representations of Egyptian identity. They are representations which convey a sense of legitimacy and authenticity associated with the landscape and its traditional caretakers.

Saadawi's portrayal of Nasser is a hopeful, early impression. She would later become disillusioned with the revolutionary government which had promised so much. Many of her friends and acquaintances were jailed as political dissidents, as was she during the government of Nasser's successor, Sadat, one of the original Free Officers. For that reason perhaps, much of Saadawi's representation of Egyptian nationhood appears to refute the agency of political parties and individual actors, or leaders, altogether. She tends to locate Egyptian legitimacy in the organic, mass identity of the Egyptian peasantry, especially, and in that of native society as a whole.

Moreover, Saadawi's experiences with Egyptian nativism rather parallel the wax and wane of certain arbitrary aspects which comprise the movement's necessarily fluid, abstract and wholly subjective conceptions of native identity. If the secularized notion of Egyptian identity was at one time dominant, that aspect may probably now be considered diminished, with more influence from Islamist conceptions. Saadawi herself has at times alternately enjoyed the official and professional imprimatur of the Egyptian government; been dismissed from her position; seen her books banned; been imprisoned; harassed; sued by a third party to have her marriage nullified; and has been validated in court by winning the lawsuit. She lived in exile from Egypt during the 1990s because she was put on a militant fundamentalist group's death list. It is worth mentioning that Saadawi's own conceptions of Egyptian nativism are consciously not Islamist, which is not to say un-Islamic.[19] Rather, she is critical of the appropriation of Islam by various protagonists and opportunists to develop their own self interests. She has also pointed out the (often) classist and sexist applications of Islamic text and law. Without departing further into a discussion of so-called Islamism, one hopes it will suffice to note that, again, what is often claimed to be in the "native interest" is not transparent, neutral or "unhedged."

Because "the native" is inherently an abstraction, an effort seems needed to attach the concept to some definite criteria. The effort, consciously or unconsciously made, to fix ideas about "the native" upon material phenomena can be observed throughout the revolutionary period in Egypt. This can be said in one breath, even as the next acknowledges the fluidity of discourses which prevailed at the time. Of course, an immediate and reductive way to define "the native" was through opposition to "the foreign." For this reason—though perhaps not for this reason alone—the ethnic minorities were targeted by the nativist policies of the Nasser government and by the rhetoric of Egyptian nativism in general. Further, one may see the attempt to develop a "cultural" nationalism in Egypt along nativist lines. Malek's call for the "establishment of a national culture" seeks an ideological basis to privilege the essentially local and indigenous. His initiative toward "national culture" really seeks to define "the native" as the basis for nationhood.

Autochthonous representations, that is, those which associate indigenous identity with the landscape in order to "authenticate" tenure or nationhood, were an important aspect of Egyptian nativism. As we have seen, references to the Nile, the Nile River Valley and to those who farmed it, recurred within official and informal discourse. The nativist association of the peasants with the land was, however, not merely ideological or contrived—just as the association was not singularly an Egyptian one. The association of the land with its tenants, with those who tilled its soil, seems organic enough a concept; although it was one easily appropriated by various interested parties. Yet the appropriation or simulation of the concept attests to its centrality in Egyptian national politics. Berque pointed out that the submerged power of the Egyptian "base" needed to be negotiated by all political protagonists. The sheer numbers of the peasant masses in relation to the smaller, upper classes cast the shadow of class struggle upon society at large. The image of the peasant as a sign of nativist legitimacy drew power from this strength in numbers. But also, the abjection of the peasants incarnated the very problem of the colonial oppression of the Egyptian nation.

The peasantry, through its association with the land and the "traditional" lifestyle, with the Nile and "indigenous" ways, represented the essential Egyptian character romanticized by the nativist movement. Nasser, no less "authentically" native for his political acuity, drew upon the reservoir of nativist associations to impart legitimacy and credibility to the revolutionary government. Mainstream Egyptian society did, in fact, welcome the new government as a legitimate semblance of native power, especially in relief to the generations of foreign collaborative rule. Saadawi's first impression of Nasser seems reflective of native society's view as a whole. Yet when she grew disillusioned with the government, particularly because of its repression of intellectuals and dissidents, her regard for established leaders—if it is even fair or accurate to presume she had any such regard—flagged.[20]

Saadawi seems to have returned more emphatically to a view which distinguishes "organic" from established sources of national identity and which privileges the peasants as a sign of Egyptian "authenticity." In fact she had never departed from such a view. Her regard for the peasantry may be observed even in her medical work. Early in her career, she chose an appointment at a rural clinic treating bilharzias, a blood disease symptomatic of the peasants who live along the Upper Nile. In her memoirs Saadawi often identifies with the peasantry and with the "peasant," paternal side of her family. Her work portrays the notion of peasant Egypt as the essence of the nation.

In general, the literary scholarship regarding Saadawi emphasizes her portrayals of Egyptian women's struggles for human rights and social justice.[21] But there is just as strong a tendency in her work to portray the struggles of the peasantry. Saadawi's portrayal of the class struggle seems to garner less attention, at least in the U.S., than her feminism; although the pursuit of human rights in either case of gender or social class finds resonance in the other. Figuratively, the peasants appear throughout her *oeuvre* as the locus of Egyptian identity and nationhood. Their "organic" legitimacy is cast in stark contrast to the apparent hypocrisy and corruption of the political and religious authorities which comprise the established order. Her novel *God Dies By The Nile,* for example, tells the story of peasants whose exploitation and oppression under various municipal and clerical leaders for generations has remained an unchanging, static condition of village life. Significantly the work, first published in Arabic in 1973, can be seen to make oblique references to the national government of Anwar Sadat, then still somewhat in the revolutionary period which ostensibly championed the rights of peasants. Indeed, the work is described as a political allegory which criticizes the established order. Revolution or no, peasant life in Kafr El Teen, the village of the story, persists under the same old tyranny of notables, constables, mayors, and sheiks.

Saadawi's portrayal of the peasants' struggle with the oppressive establishment is, however, far from didactic or categorical. If the conditions of peasant life in Kafr El Teen are brutal, so are these conditions reflected in the comportment and demeanor of much of the peasantry. A reader may be reminded of the peasants portrayed by Jerzy Kosinski in *The Painted Bird.* Indeed like Kosinski's, Saadawi's allegorical peasants either pursue or are the victims of nearly every transgression known to humankind. The peasants in *God Dies By The Nile* are drawn into predicaments involving adultery, theft, rape, incest, infanticide, false witness, prostitution, pederasty, necromancy, necrophilia, bestiality, pedophilia, blasphemy and murder. Saadawi writes of these predicaments with compositional deliberateness; they are not intended as lurid episodes but as figures upon which existential considerations about morality may be posed. The work criticizes the hypocrisy of self-ascribed keepers of public morality, represented in the story by the mayor and his cronies, the chief of the village guard, the notables and the local imam. Further the story refutes the "moral" authority, and the "authority" in general of the political and religious establishment. The established leaders and their self-serving order are ultimately reprobate in their exploitation and oppression of the peasants.

Most of the peasants in Kafr El Teen are field laborers who live hard lives of agricultural subsistence. Although some engage in about as much "wickedness" as the powerful notables, a reader may observe that the peasants' crimes are the consequence of an ongoing, historic cycle of abuse. Indeed the crimes and transgressions which Saadawi has woven into the plot are intended as symbolic, rather than literal, and connote certain political and social ideas about post-Revolutionary Egypt. For example a symbolic, startling episode in the story occurs when Kafrawi, a poor tenant farmer, interrupts his afternoon work to relieve himself sexually with a field ox, or water buffalo. Details in the narration establish a symbolic linkage between the female buffalo, the landscape, Kafrawi's mother, his daughter, and the essential, unchanging peasant condition. The buffalo, named Aziza, is at once a maternal and nativist signifier. She "suckles" Kafrawi and nourishes him with her milk; she speaks to him with her eyes in an intimate language that expresses the daily, unspoken crimes of serfdom which victimize her, Kafrawi and all the peasants. Kafrawi's coupling with the buffalo is a deliberately overdetermined, surreal representation of autochthony. The buffalo, as the peasant farmer, is traditionally associated with the land; like the Nile River Valley, she is an essential sign of Egyptian native identity.

Autothchonous imagery typically represents the land as parent or originator, as author; the term "motherland" or "fatherland" carries the connotation of autochthony. The offspring of autochthony is the indigene, the native. Kafrawi's coupling with the buffalo is an image which conflates all these associations: mother, land, issue, origin. His unnatural act could not be more "natural" or organic in symbolic, representational terms. It signifies the essential source, in Saadawi's view, of Egyptian national identity: the indigenous, the native. This organic legitimacy needs no political or religious establishment to sanction it. The autochthonous peasantry is more legitimately Egyptian than either the politicians or imams who claim authority over the nation. The organic legitimacy of the peasants stands in contrast with the powerful establishment figures in the story. The mayor and his cronies are portrayed as disingenuous swindlers and the perpetrators of crimes which put them beyond the pale of human community. Indeed, when the mayor is murdered by a blow to his head from a field hoe, it is the only just act to occur in the story.

God Dies By The Nile defies a literalist reading of the crimes which occur in the plot. That reading would most likely have seen the work condemned for offending the "public morals." The story attempts, rather, to render a more insistent "moral" authority inherent in the peasants' struggle for justice. The struggle for justice and for human rights is most apparently waged by the women who are the main protagonists of the story, Kafrawi's female relatives. The mayor's lust for Kafrawi's daughters spawns a series of outrageous crimes against the peasants; it is Zakeya, the girls' aunt, who puts an end to the outrages with a well placed blow of her hoe. Her individual act may not resolve the historic, generational oppression of the peasants; but Zakeya does effectively disrupt the cycle of abuse which has destroyed her family.

Moreover, Zakeya's upraised hoe casts a shadow over the Egyptian hegemony as a whole. It insinuates the predictable and indeed "natural" outcome of native abjection: the realized violence of the class struggle, now and then dormant, now and again expressed, but always potentially extant. Saadawi's regard of the centrality of the peasants to the Egyptian struggle for justice and independence is similar to Mahfouz' regard of the urban *lumpen proletariat.* Both views recognize the "base of the pyramid," in Berque's words, upon which the superstructure of Egyptian society was built. No claim of Egyptian nativism or nationalism, however legitimate or contrived, could afford to ignore this elemental foundation.

6.2 EGYPTIAN BODY POLITICS

An inherent problem with the popular nativism of the Egyptian revolutionary period, as with any nativism, was the instability of the concept, "native," itself. Because "the native" is based upon abstract, unstable criteria, one seeks concrete material upon which to base the concept. The conception of the native which derives in opposition to "the foreign" is necessarily weak, derivative, and ultimately, reactionary and negative. The conception of the peasant masses as the locus of essential Egyptian identity was a graphic representation and one generally accepted within Egyptian society at large. Yet the conception posed some problems even for those who embraced it. It did not reflect the self image of the professional classes, the petty bourgeoisie and ultimately, the new political elite which held power after 1952. Nor did stereotypical images of the peasantry, steeped in associations of agricultural, "traditional life," reflect the goals of independent Egypt to pursue autonomous technological and industrial development, i.e., the pursuit of "actual" development. Both conceptions about "native" Egyptian identity, that which is contraposed to "the foreign," and that which draws "essence" from the peasantry, were of limited use for those who sought to utilize them for whatever agenda.

In light of these problems, another sign or trope may be seen to evoke the "essence" of Egyptian identity. Conceptually, "the body" poses as the carnal representation of identity and existence, as a presumably "legitimate" expression of identity and reference to natural origin. The idea of the body as a material referent for ethnic, national, or native identity is not a uniquely Egyptian conception. Indeed references to the body as the *habeas corpus* of "authentic" identity may emerge in any society where there are contesting claims about the legitimacy of origin or tenure, about the possession of power or wealth, or, about ideological or representational power. References or appeals to "the body" can be seen to mark the anxiety over contesting claims to Egypt in many ways. The works of the four Egyptian memoirists, Nawal El Saadawi, Gini Alhadeff, Andre Aciman and Edward Said, all contain such references to the body in their accounts of modern Egyptian society in transition to republican independence.

The writing of Nawal El Saadawi exemplifies some of the conceptual issues of nativism. Egyptian nativism appears to be an orienting element of Saadawi's political consciousness. Yet she is a humanist whose own conception of nativism does not easily subsume or reconcile with the reactionary bigotry aimed at the Egyptian ethnic minorities, however much "foreign" or "unsympathetic" they were alleged to be. In her memoir Saadawi recognizes the Coptic Christians of Egypt, for example, and regards them to be as "essentially" Egyptian as Muslim natives. Her recognition of the Copts is significant because, as a minority group, they have often been the target of xenophobic hostility in Egypt. Saadawi's conception of "the native" also rejects Islamic essentialism. Feminists have long taken note of her criticism of Muslim practices that disregard the human rights and spirituality of women. It is worth mentioning again that her criticism is not aimed at Islam *per se* but at Islamists, i.e., broadly, those who interpret Koranic text and Islamic law in terms of their own personal or political agenda. Her criticism of "Islamism," then, is characteristic of her rejection of ideological dogma on the whole, whether religious or secular. Her writing generally exhibits a contempt for hypocrisy and for self interest which veils itself sanctimoniously in the rhetoric of the prevailing religious, political, or administrative establishment.

Saadawi uses the body as a metaphor of native identity in her writing, it seems, in an attempt to skirt the dogmatism of vested ideologies. She "legitimizes" claims to Egypt upon the "native body," which she conceives as both a political and material entity. However, it must be said that "the body" is no less of a reduction than any other concept which seeks to "authenticate" ethnic or national identity. The significance of the body metaphor in Saadawi's work is that it makes an appeal for social justice on behalf of native society. The body metaphor makes an appeal for justice which includes all classes of Egyptian natives, but particularly refers to the oppressed rural peasantry. As with the novels of Naguib Mahfouz, Saadawi's portrayals attempt to humanize and dignify the images of the underclasses. Her work asserts the conviction that the peasantry, in particular, must no longer be ignored by the established powers, but included in the reconstructed life of fully independent Egypt.

In much of her writing, Saadawi's conception of "the native" centers upon the peasant masses. But further, she locates Egyptian indigenous identity seemingly within the "peasant body" on the one hand, and on the other, within the physical body of the native rank and file of all classes. Perhaps her metaphorical references to the body are not surprising; Saadawi is also a physician as well as a writer. She spent the early period of her medical career treating bilharzias among the peasants of southern Egypt. This period, together with her medical studies, coincided with the late movement for independence and the early days of the Egyptian Revolution. Saadawi's portrayal of this period seems to conflate the two experiences, that of her early days as a doctor and that of the radical movement for independence. Her work expresses hope for a metaphorical "healing" of the dissipation visited upon Egypt by the age of colonialism. She hopes that independence will restore vibrancy and health to the chronically ailing body politic. Indeed, such hope recurs in her considerations of the particular national, economic and religious politics of the successive generations after independence. It appears to be the same hope as that conceived by the young medical student, who, on the morning of July 23, 1952, witnessed an extraordinary event. *In Walking Through Fire,* Saadawi tells of the moment when the Free Officers broadcast their declaration of the *coup d'etat,* a moment also portrayed in fiction by Mahfouz. As Isa the protagonist of *Autumn Quail* would have sat down to breakfast, young Nawal Saadawi attended a lecture about cancer given by a doctor who, she says, resembled Mohandas Gandhi, an odd detail recollected in the hindsight of historical significance. Because of the lecture, the students did not immediately hear the broadcast. But there were radios in the hospital wards and the patients and staff listened to the announcement, delivered by one of the officers, Anwar Sadat.[22] Saadawi was moved by what she witnessed next:

> Suddenly as we stood there the patients rushed out of the wards shouting, "Long live the revolution!" I could see their mouths wide open, their arms waving in the air, their tattered shirts fluttering around their bodies. It was as though the corpses from the dissecting hall had suddenly risen from the dead and were shouting, "Long live the revolution!" (51)

Among the sick who Saadawi saw transformed by the advent of independence were a young amputee who crawled out of his bed to join the celebrants; a feeble elder shouting vigorously at the top of his voice; a pregnant woman, in her third trimester, running on bare feet; a girl with a broken arm, "lifted high up above her head like a banner." As the patients spilled out into the yard, they were joined by the staff, doctors, nurses and students. Saadawi notes with somewhat surreal detachment engendered by the euphoria of the moment: "My body propelled itself into the crowd, moved by a will of its own. I began to shout with them, 'Long live the revolution!'(51)" Pall bearers leading a funeral procession set down the coffin holding the body of the deceased and the mourners joined the crowd celebrating in the hospital courtyard.

Saadawi's portrayal of the advent of independence renders it also as a restoration, a miraculous healing, even a resurrection of the dead. The sick who stream out of the hospital wards are poor village peasants afflicted with bilharzias. Saadawi describes them as having the lifeblood sucked out of them by the river worms which cause the condition. One does not have to reach far for the vernacular connotation of "blood sucking" to indicate the exploitation, politically or materially, which is visited upon one whose veins are so abused. The bilharzias-afflicted peasants represent the exploited Egyptian nation. As discussed in the previous section, images of the Nile and of the peasants who farm its valley possess autochthonous, nativist associations with Egypt. The image of the sick peasants employed by Saadawi suggests that corrupt local leaders, Farouk's collaborative government and British administrators all daily "suck the lifeblood" of the Egyptian people. Their bodily ailment, bilharzias, is a metaphor of the political corruption and weakness which afflict Egypt, induced through colonialism. Some of the more immediate exploitation of the peasants even comes as a condition of their medical attention at the teaching hospital. The sick villagers are subjects of study at the hospital where, Saadawi predicts, they will likely end their days as dissection corpses or else be carried out the door in a funeral procession such as the one which joins the dying and the living in the courtyard to celebrate independence.

The scene in the hospital courtyard has much nativist significance. The portrayal is replete with references to the Nile, the peasants, the physical body and the national one. One notes that there is a general, organic acceptance of the military *coup* as Egypt's deliverance from colonial oppression. The acceptance is inherent in the crowd's ready slogan, "Long live the revolution!" The peasants obviously see their own oppression bound up with that of the nation. One points out that their understanding belies Dekmejian's opinion that the under classes were probably indifferent about independence. Indeed in Saadawi's portrayal, it is the peasants and workers (the non-professional hospital staff) who inform the others about the *coup* and thus lead them into awareness about revolutionary independence. Furthermore Saadawi's reference to Mohandas Gandhi, the leader of Indian independence, in the guise of an Egyptian cancer doctor, portrays the moment of the *coup* as another liberation of the masses from British colonialism. The portrayal represents the potential to heal an ailing Egyptian body politic, rendered incarnate by the sick and exploited peasants.

Saadawi's concept of "the body" is a layered, dynamic concept with which she attempts to resolve native class divisions. She means to extend the nativist "legitimacy" of Egyptian peasants to that of the broader native society as a whole. This intention is apparent in the hospital scene. The peasants are joined by other segments of native society, represented by the hospital staff, the nurses, doctors and students. These other strata, workers, professionals and petty bourgeoisie, are portrayed as essentially native through the synecdochal imagery which presents them heel-to-toe with the peasants. Collectively, the group comprises a communal "body" which draws its native "essence" from the (imagined) physical bodies of the Egyptian peasantry, or, the peasant masses. One's own body seems merely an extension of the "communal" body, as Saadawi herself finds when her own form manifests its will and moves of its own accord among the crowd. The communal body portrayed by Saadawi thus seems to resolve a central problem for the petty bourgeoisie with a popular nativism based upon conceptions about the peasantry. The peasantry may not necessarily reflect back the self image of the professional class; but the latter may takes its place, synecdochally, alongside the (symbolic) locus of native identity, from which it derives native "essence."

One sees a similar handling of "essence" in Saadawi's other memoir, *A Daughter Of Isis.* The derivation of "essence" from the peasantry is portrayed in Saadawi's descriptions of her own body, for example. She describes the "peasant looks" which she says she has inherited from her father's side of the family. She refers to her "native complexion" as being the color of fresh silt brought down to her land by the waters of the Nile. This Nile silt is represented in her work as the very stuff of autochthony, of native identity. It seems that Saadawi finds the Egyptian peasantry and, indeed, the landscape with which it is associated, located within her own body. Her body thus figures as an extension of the "communal" body which she poses as the (symbolic) reference for Egyptian identity. In Saadawi's conception of Egyptian nativism, all classes of native society may refer to the communal body as the repository of authenticity, origin, and other autochthonous significations.

Saadawi's conceptions of Egyptian nativism are encountered at length in *A Daughter Of Isis.* Her nativism is secular, liberal and intended to include, if also to define, the whole of native society. A reader sees at once that she rejects Muslim or Islamic essentialism. For her, religious identity does not serve as a marker of either indigenous or "authentic" Egyptian identity. It is also clear that she rejects the authority invoked by established organizations and entities which claim to represent and to designate the common interests of mainstream society. Saadawi relates her early suspicions, conceived as a child, about vested interpretations of the Koran which serve patriarchal and hegemonic interests. As a college student, she remained aloof from the campus chapter of the Muslim Brotherhood and its subsidiary, the Muslim

Sisterhood, although the Islamist group, as Saadawi herself, was involved in the student movement for independence.

Saadawi is quite direct that she has always found much of the Muslim establishment to be oppressive toward Muslim women. Presumably for this reason the title of her memoir draws not upon Muslim imagery but instead claims a figurative bloodline to the ancient Egyptian goddess, Isis.[23] The invocation of Isis connotes a consciously nativist conception of Egyptian identity. The non-Islamic nature of the reference, though it derives from ancient religion (or myth), is intended to be understood as a secular invocation of Egyptian history. Saadawi claims figurative descent not from one of the female relatives of the prophet Mohammad, traditional points of reference for many Muslim women, but from a pre-Islamic, pagan deity which is associated with the earliest conceptions of the Egyptian nation. Saadawi's symbolic "daughterhood" also has deliberately feminist connotations. It connotes the idea of gender equality in the notion of nation; that is, it suggests that the nation belongs equally to women as to the men who are usually privileged by nationalist rhetoric and politics. Saadawi's reference to Isis as a point of nativist "origin" reflects her secularism as well as her feminism.

Saadawi's rejection of Muslim or Islamic essentialism should not be viewed, however, as a rejection of Islam itself, nor of the Muslim cultural identity of most Egyptians. This is an important qualification, given that the "sexism" often alleged by non-Muslims to be inherent in Islam (but apparently not in any other religion) is often held up in the West as the justification for many a vested agenda which is hostile to Muslims of both genders. Rather, Sadaawi's rejection of religious essentialism seems characteristic of her rejection of the categorical thought inherent in any claim to cultural or political authority. Although, her own attempts to "locate" or situate Egyptian native identity hold up no better, really, than any other essentialism. Still her metaphorical privileging of the peasants as the locus of native "essence" seems to aim for their increased, proportional share in the independent Egyptian republic. As does Mahfouz, Saadawi envisions a role also for the native petty bourgeoisie in the project of independent nation building. Ultimately, though her nativism is no less essentialist than any other, Saadawi's conceptions of "the native" are intended to have material application toward social justice. Thus her views must be considered in context of the anti-colonial movement of the day.

In the fall of 1951, Saadawi was a student in her second year at medical school. There was a great deal of civil unrest, characterized by a number of competing discourses which attempted to define the Egyptian body politic. Factional leanings included loyalism, conservatism, liberalism, socialism, secular nationalism, nativism, religious fundamentalism, etc. Student groups formed extensions, more or less, of the contemporary debates. Most debates centered upon the objectives of independence and the problem of corruption in local and national government. Popular protest was aimed at the monarchy, the collaborative government and the British presence. Public demonstrations were often violently repressed by King Farouk's special police. Many university students left to join the *fedayin,* the resistance fighters who were waging a guerilla war upon the British soldiers in the Suez Canal Zone. Saadawi took part in the activism, gave speeches in support of independence and of the *fedayin*—who she once attempted to join—and wrote for the student papers. Often she was the only young woman among thousands of male protestors at the student demonstrations. Later she was joined by other women.

Saadawi portrays her medical school days as a coming-of-age, both for herself and for independent Egypt. She sees the political conditions of the times reflected in her studies. In a deftly subtle sequence of prose, Saadawi likens the Egyptian body politic to a medical dissection corpse. Its death has been induced through local corruption and foreign occupation. What is left of this cadaverous body politic is now subject to the push and pull of political factions, each intent upon having a piece. But Saadawi envisions a radical solution which will cut through petty factionalism to the heart of the matter. The students put their scalpels to the corpse in practice for the surgery they will someday soon perform upon a living subject. Saadawi suggests that "the patient," though already seemingly too far gone, might be restored through the radical surgery of her generation of activists. Radical surgery, like a *coup d'etat* or else the armed struggle of the *fedayin,* may eradicate the degeneracy which afflicts the body politic. The general health of the body politic may be restored, but not without some acute pain and invasive methods. It is an extreme treatment for a chronic illness too long gone without remedy.

Through metaphor and a series of linked anecdotes, Saadawi portrays the defunct body politic dismembered by factionalism, reanimated through common struggle, and finally, reincarnated in the popular aspiration for an independent republic. Her portrayal draws upon pharaonic imagery and motifs to invoke representations of Egyptian "essence." That is, she portrays the independence movement of her generation as a nativist struggle through association with signs or tropes which derive from Egyptian antiquity. Saadawi's stories about her medical school days contain the structural elements of Egyptian myth. These elements impart political, as well as cultural, significations to the anecdotes she tells. The narration shifts among what are for Saadawi three key "aspects" of the Egyptian nation: peasant, people, and pharaoh. The three are all at once the same in her view.

The body metaphor developed by Saadawi employs two central motifs of pharaonic association. First, the motif of dismemberment and reconstitution, and secondly, that of death and resurrection, are prototypically Egyptian. Both motifs are found in the ancient myth about Osiris, the first Egyptian king from whom all pharaohs derived the authority to rule. Briefly, Osiris was ambushed by Set who locked him in a chest and put it afloat upon the Nile to drift out to sea. Isis found the chest with Osiris dead inside and impregnated herself with his body. She gave (re)birth to her husband in the person of Horus, their son, who is also Osiris reincarnated. While she was in labor, Set discovered the body of Osiris and dismembered it, dispersing its parts across the land. But Isis, in meta-reenactment of childbirth, gathered up the parts and reassembled them into a reconstituted Osiris. Meanwhile Horus grew up, killed Set, and became king. Osiris passed into the afterlife where he continues his reign in the underworld.

While there are no singularly definitive interpretations of any myth, Max Rodenbeck relates a materialist reading of Set and Osiris which seems to put a finger on the pulse. He comments that the battle of the two kings probably refers to the historic rivalries of different Nile Valley settlements (6). Joseph Campbell explains that the Osiris myth functions to assert communal or group identity by emphasizing the reconstitution of the god-king in the sum of his parts (*Transformations* 84). In Saadawi's allusion to the myth, one can see both of these meanings, that of a political struggle for Egypt and that which emphasizes Egyptian communal identity as the essence of legitimate rule. She ultimately resolves the political struggle by locating Egyptian authority in the "communal" body which is comprised of native society of all classes.

The series of linked anecdotes in Saadawi's memoir about the fall of 1951 reproduce the central elements of the Osiris myth: death, dismemberment, reconstitution, and resurrection. The elements are woven into her accounts of medical study and of the popular movement for independence. The literal events in the stories she tells about the school dissection hall have political and mythic resonances. The stories ultimately make a nativist claim for independence. Saadawi sees real political independence as the result of populist momentum, the will of the masses, rather than as the possession or provenance of party leaders, organized factions, or self-described "authorities."

Saadawi tells how rampant corruption throughout pre-independent society extended even into student life. Students who were favored by administrators because of nepotism or the political clout of their families were routinely exempt from tuition fees and exams. Saadawi was outraged when she found that some well-connected students attended classes free, while her own father endured hardship to pay her tuition. She demanded—and got—a fee waiver in honor of his participation in the 1919 uprising led by the patriot Saad Zaghlul. Nevertheless, unconnected students had to struggle through the course of study and pay the "fees" which were extorted for needed materials. An extensive system of "fees" regulated the students' pursuit of their goals. Medical texts and autopsy subjects were obtained by bribes paid to various agents. There was the hearse chaser who negotiated with the recently bereaved family; there was the hall moderator who could procure specialty parts for the right price. Saadawi was only able to purchase a few joints of the hand or foot or a skull. But luckily, she was the lab partner of a rich girl who had assembled an entire human skeleton.

The corruption which the students endure is symptomatic of the problems which plague Egypt as a whole. The condition of the body politic finds analogy in the necrotic tissues of the pickled subject for autopsy. Visceral representations of the political "dismemberment" of Egypt are found in the university dissection hall:

> Am Osman [the hall moderator] used to lock the huge chests with keys as though they contained the riches of the earth, then he would stand in front of them haughtily, as though he were Lord Radwan, the guardian angel of paradise. He smiled only when a rich student went up to him to buy a corpse from him. The price of these corpses was three pounds apiece. He used to steal them in connivance with the undertaker and usually paid him fifty *piastres* for three dead bodies. During the night he crept into cemeteries and collected the bones of the dead which he sold to the students by the piece. (264)

Am Osman's chest and the barter for its contents are described against the backdrop of political corruption and the independence struggle. The narration about anatomy and dissection relates to the political fragmentation of the day. The imagery suggests that modern Egyptian society is coming apart at the seams. But it also replicates elements of the ancient myth of Osiris. The chest which holds the corpses alludes to the sarcophagus in which the god-king's body was contained. The cadaver parts which the students buy piecemeal from the hall moderator suggests the dismemberment of Osiris. Campbell describes the Osiris myth as one which communicates a threshold experience; it signals a psychic or experiential transition (*Hero with a Thousand Faces* 90–93). The sarcophagus represents the literal threshold in the myth and the dismemberment and reconstitution of Osiris signals a transition to another kind of consciousness. Saadawi's dissection hall studies are such a transition because the young novices learn the secrets of life and death. They make a transition in consciousness from naiveté to medical wisdom. Am Osman, the hall monitor, is clearly a gatekeeper to a symbolic threshold as he alone holds its keys and must be ameliorated with a bribe (like the three-headed watchdog of another, well-traveled threshold). The chest Am Osman guards is like an underworld, a realm of the dead, because of its contents. The dissection hall replicates elements of the Osiris myth quite well. But the myth has deeper significance for Saadawi and her generation. They are at the threshold of the most important political experience they may have: the transition to independence and the rebirth of the nation as an independent republic.

The transition and rebirth of independent Egypt is described by Saadawi as a communal experience, witnessed by ordinary Egyptians who she describes in nativist terms. She tells of a huge, silent demonstration which occurred in Cairo in November, several months before the Free Officer's Revolt. The students left the university and were joined by children, housewives, workers, villagers, peasants, doctors, nurses, lawyers, judges, Coptic priests, Muslim clerics, sheiks, shopkeepers, street hawkers, itinerants, beggars, and a vast crowd of "native" Egyptians across the social strata:

> The demonstrators moved out through the door into the street without a sound like a huge crocodile moving over the ground. Rivers of people flowed out from the side-streets to join in one mighty river that poured into Ismaila Square, for there were demonstrations coming from everywhere forming a huge mass of people, one huge body advancing on innumerable feet and carrying innumerable heads. Waves of people rising and falling in an endless sea. Millions of breaths mingling to create the single breath of the crowd. An immense silence that echoed in the ears more powerful than the sound of thunder. (286–287)

The crowd draws in all strata of native society to represent a singular, communal identity composed of the sum of its parts; it is a huge mass possessing innumerable heads and feet. Saadawi describes it as a crocodile and as a mighty river, with many tributaries. The river and the crocodile are both essentialist, nativist images of the Nile Valley which derive from antiquity. The images date back to the earliest murals and hieroglyphics of the ancient kings. They are also the earliest representations of Egyptian nationhood. The use of Nilotic imagery to portray the crowd emphasizes the nativist tenor of the protest demonstration and the movement for independence.

One compares the native imagery of Saadawi's account with that related by Alhadeff. Her aunt, Sarah, took offense at the association of the crocodile with Cairo. Sarah found the association to be vulgar; the Cairo she knew was an urbane, European city. Yet native Egyptians have seen the matter differently. Modern Cairo occupies the sites of Egypt's first settlements as well as the first Muslim camp in Egypt. The location retains the legacy of the early Muslim as well as the pharaonic dynasties. The name *Al-Kahira,* meaning "the victorious," is a commemoration of the Muslim conquest. But the vernacular name for Cairo is *Misr,* which is also the name for Egypt. The city is commonly understood as a synecdoche for the nation. The association of the city and its river, its symbols and motifs, with the nation is a nativist conception. Alhadeff's aunt was uncomfortable with the nativist connotations of the crocodile image. But Saadawi embraces it, exactly for the same reason; the crocodile's representational "commonness" is a powerful endorsement of Egyptian nativism. The crocodile signifies the native composition of the protesting masses and their aspiration for national independence.

Saadawi describes the native masses as a powerful force, one identified with the natural world. They are figured not only as the Nile River but also as "an endless sea," and as "more powerful than the sound of thunder" (287). Such references to the natural world are the autochthonous symbols which typically represent claims of land tenure and native origin. Peasants, natives, animals and natural phenomena evocative of the land and its topography represent an "authenticity" or nativist "legitimacy." Saadawi confers these images upon the protestors. She bestows a sense of political authority upon the protest masses which is derived from the representation of their native, essential Egyptian identity. Her account thus portrays the legitimacy of the independence movement as a nativist movement, one which is built "from the ground up," rather than "from the top down," as with the old pasha nationalism of elites. Saadawi sees the legitimacy of independence in the organic "will" of the native masses rather than in the official imprimatur of the upper class *Wafdists.*

Among the many nativist signs, the portrayal of the silent protest also contains a significant element of the Osiris myth. The coming together of the protestors to form "one huge body" replicates the reconstitution and rebirth of the god-king from which the nation draws strength and direction. Importantly for Saadawi, this god-king is the masses, rather than an individual leader. Saadawi describes the masses as moving together with a singular silence and will. The image has narrative proximity to the cadaver which the medical students theoretically abandoned on the dissection table when they joined the protest. The dissection corpse is replaced in the narrative by the "body" composed of the living, breathing masses. A reincarnation occurs when the body politic is resuscitated by "millions of breaths mingling to create the single breath of the crowd" (287). The silence kept by the protestors, which might have signaled the stillness of death, instead expresses the common aim of the nation in independence. It is a *nahda,* a rebirth; in Arabic a term which holds nationalist overtones. Saadawi portrays the mobilization of the native masses in the rebirth of independent Egypt.

The body metaphor developed by Saadawi thus attempts to ameliorate an array of problems or issues with implementing the popular nativism of the day. Other writers use "the body" variously, but with similar intent to bring materiality to a terrain necessarily fraught with ideology and abstraction. And yet for all its presumed materiality, "the body" is an abstract concept which fails to provide *habeas corpus* for the claims that make reference to it. Rather than supplying the proof, "the body" seems to indicate an anxiety about origin, identity, and "authenticity." In fact by comparing the Egyptian memoirists, Saadawi, Alhadeff, Aciman and Said, it seems apparent that references to the body mark a sense of loss or of exile. The body seems an attempt to represent tangibly the thing which is lost—origin, basically, whether that origin is conceived as a homeland, a previous life, family connections, generational continuity, etc. "The body" signifies the displacement of the subject from one's origin. This sign of the body appears perhaps because, indeed, the material body seems to be all one ever truly "has." Its materiality presumably stands in for an absence or abstraction.

Saadawi's figurative use of the body in her memoirs reflects a sense of origin perhaps sharpened by her experience of exile, or asylum, in the U.S, where she wrote much of *A Daughter Of Isis.* She had left Egypt because of the climate of intimidation engendered by some Islamist militants and because of threats and harassment which she and her husband, the writer and activist Sherif Hetata, had received. Egypt's political climate especially in the late 1980s through the middle 1990s was characterized by the harassment and even the assassination of various public and cultural figures allegedly considered by extremists to be too "secular" or else too much "compromised" by "the West." Although Mahfouz survived an assassination attempt in 1994 by an Islamist militant, others were not as fortunate.[24] The assassination of Egyptian President Sadat in 1981 by a disgruntled army lieutenant, an Islamist, who acted reportedly in retaliation for the Camp David accord with Israel, had opened a contentious era.

The situation points out the inherently subjective agenda of those who invoke nativism as a political force. Saadawi, Hetata, Sadat and the Islamist militants may all be seen to invoke substantially different concepts of Egyptian nativism and to have held different views about what constitutes the interests of Egyptian society. Saadawi, a secularist, was arrested and imprisoned under the secular leader Sadat.[25] Similarly, Hetata, an activist for independence, had been imprisoned under the revolutionary government of Nasser. One can therefore understand the reserve with which Saadawi regards established politics and why she locates Egyptian sovereignty among the masses, rather than with administrations or individual leaders.

Much of Saadawi's memoir seems to arise from the trauma of her arrests and from her ostensible exile. She says that writing relieves some of this trauma. She describes the writing process as a recovery of what has been lost through imprisonment and exile. What has been lost, for Saadawi, appears as the concept of origin and its recovery is represented as the image of her mother's face:

> Since I started writing I have understood my crime. My crime has been to think, to feel. But writing for me is like breathing the air of life. I cannot stop. I wrote to bring back my mother's face, to describe it as it was. Sometimes her features were lost, as though I never had a mother, as though she never lived. (54)

There is a discursive link between the political harassment which Saadawi endured as a dissident and her desire to conjure the elusive image of her late mother. The isolation of exile recalls for her the death of her mother. The loss of origin is thus figured in both the natal and the native sense. The idea of the Egyptian "motherland," connoted by the reference to Isis in the title of the book, is represented in her mother's face. Mother and homeland, both points of origin by which she may know herself, are absent—and that absence poses a singular grief.

The Sun At Midday by Gini Alhadeff similarly treats the motif of origin. There is a sense of displacement conveyed in Alhadeff's memoir of family life. Like Saadawi, she makes reference to a lost maternal or natal signifier. The signifier represents the displacement of origin. The notion of "the body" marks this alienation. Alhadeff tries to negotiate a sense of origin not with a nation but with the familiarity of her own body:

> [T]his body does not date back to the expulsion of the Jews [from Spain] in 1492 . . . This body has been in its own places and bears the mark of those travels. There, it finally forgot what it learned *por boca de madre.* It is the only geography through which I see all others, my only witness and nothing but a vessel of what I still have no idea about. And yet who am I trying to fool? I look at a picture of myself and think what Mediterranean features I have after all. A long oval face, long dark hair,

> brown eyes, a long nose that opens out at the end of the bridge in the shape of a bicycle seat, as my father's does . . . I may have broken with my past but my body hasn't. (14–15)

Alhadeff's location of identity within her own body is similar to Saadawi's; both make reference to landscape or geography, parentage and history. Unlike Saadawi, however, Alhadeff does not really identify with the concept of a motherland, though perhaps with a mother tongue. Ladino is the Spanish dialect of Sephardic Jews which Alhadeff says she has learned *por boca de madre.* Alhadeff's portrayal of origin is one of diaspora rather than nativism. She does not claim to be "a daughter of Isis." She derives a regional identity, rather, in the distinguishing features of Mediterranean peoples, a physiognomy which is readily identifiable but as easily collapsed. Yet it is no more abstract than the "peasant body" from which Saadawi derives nativist "essence."

While ethnic countenance may (or may not) be something real, still the interpretations imposed upon physiognomy are abstract and discursive. To make recourse to physiognomy suggests an urgency or anxiety in the face of contesting claims about material issues, such as political power and land tenure, etc. The "Mediterranean" concept comes with a political and historical baggage as much as does the concept of nativism.[26] Conflicts over legitimacy and tenure were inherent in the postcolonial conditions which both Saadawi and Alhadeff witnessed in Egypt during their youth. Significantly, too, both authors write their memoirs about Egyptian life from an existential remove of time, space and historical circumstance. Neither Saadawi nor Alhadeff will ever return to the Egypt they perceive as an essence, though both may at some time return to the land of their birth. Alhadeff claims to have made an uneasy peace with the displacement of origin: "I am surrounded by my own place, the body, wherever I go . . . I live in this organism, the country I come with. In it I am at home and the foreign is not foreign, though sometimes . . . my body feels as though nothing could be more alien" (213). Yet her account reveals a deep ambivalence.

Alhadeff writes about identity as subtly as Saadawi in terms of narrative development. As with Saadawi, the linkage of anecdotes occurs to express themes which are buried or subtextual. *The Sun At Midday* is notable not only for its content but for its experimental structure. The work is comprised of family stories, historical documents and quoted texts, Alhadeff's own journal notes and accounts of events, travel writing, interviews, genealogy, "found object" lists, and various subjective impressions. The book also incorporates a substantial testimony about the Holocaust and the Rome ghetto, which

Alhadeff recounts verbatim from her Uncle Nessim, a survivor. The structure of the narrative weaves these elements together, sometimes thematically, sometimes seemingly at random. But there is an overall pattern or direction to the narrative which suggests an undoing, an unraveling, "the end of the line." The movement depends upon images which are discursively linked throughout the sequence of narration. "The body" in Alhadeff's narrative asserts, finally, a sense of loss or severed connection. The writing attempts to resolve this displacement by producing one or another material referent; but ultimately, these references simply mark that which they are invoked to dispel.

Alhadeff's memoir eventually turns from stories about ancestors and more immediate relatives to an account of the cemetery at Chatby. There the author finds the tomb of her mother's family and the gravestones of her paternal grandparents. The anecdote is one among a series of which moves the text as a whole to conclusion. The "body" images in the Chatby anecdote are the remains interred in dusty graves. Alhadeff comments that they seem forgotten by the world of the living. In other anecdotes she describes a photocopy of a family tree drawn in 1969 in Paris (reproduced at the back of the book); tells of her uncle Piero, a Milanese architect who she admires for his self-made freedom from domesticity; and gives a candid account of her termination of a pregnancy. The photocopied family tree is a meta-representation of the relationships for which Alhadeff accounts in narrative form. The "frame" of the meta-representation seems to concretize the family history in the "past tense," so to speak, to render it as something finished or fetishized, or perhaps, fossilized. This seems also to be the connotation of locating the grave markers at Chatby. There is no mention of successive generations of the family beyond that of her brothers, Giampiero and Giancarlo, and herself. It may be so for reasons of privacy or perhaps it is the limitations of the memoir genre.

Though she has chosen to be single, Alhadeff remarks that she is often disturbed to think of herself as unmarried and childless: "[there are] moments when I still feel it is a strange woman who doesn't have a child, and . . . that it is unnatural to be so by oneself, day after day" (214). She appears ambivalent about her decision to terminate her pregnancy. The ambivalence finds connotation in a seemingly irrelevant, if imagistic, observation of the countryside in Chianti: "Two clouds, one incandescent white, one stormy grey, side by side drawing the shape of a plump baby between them in sky blue, releasing a steady spray of silvery rain on the upraised needled arms of pines and the silvery-leafed olive trees" (11). The two different clouds suggest the two opposing choices regarding the "baby" which lies between them: to have or to not have it. The "needled" embrace of the pines suggests pain in regard to choice she has made; the image of upraised arms is the typical gesture of a child to her or his mother. The cloud-baby of Chianti is borne on the wind. Such imagery, as with the cemetery at Chatby, renders a sense of finality, a bodily sense of origin lost.

Alhadeff attempts to resolve the sense of alienation in the kinship of friends (and hangers-on) whom Piero, her uncle, has assembled together. Piero has many friends but is unhampered by the confines of family and domestic life. He freely pursues his interests in art, design, beauty, and adventure. Gini finds this an enviable life, but it also represents the best of both worlds: a bachelor, Piero is yet never alone; refusing to be "domesticated," Piero and his friends simply move from house to house, finding exotic rentals in the most glamorous locales. Indeed, it is a life to be envied. However for Gini, it brings together the two polarities of her desire: to be free and to be connected. There is a sense of an idealized "family" life with Piero and his friends which also suggests the notion of lineage, if not "the body," *per se.* Gini calls them "a family in the line of beauty" (200). However, as might be expected, it is "feast or famine" for the weight-conscious *fashionistas* who make up Piero's set. Spartan diets follow lavish banquets and the gang appears obsessed with slimness. These details summon the notion of the body to Alhadeff's account as well as notions of desire and longing, which are represented by hunger. Although she finds an aestheticized family life with Piero, it tends to replicate her own ambivalence.

Alhadeff's memoir ends a bit abruptly and with the sense of ambivalence which had been an undercurrent throughout the text. Ahead of schedule, she decides to end her visit to Egypt—her trip of recovery embarked upon as research for her memoir. Her reasons are coincidental—dust; fatigue; nausea; a remote incident of Islamist militance, overblown in importance by local television news. New Year's Eve draws close and she does not want to spend it alone, she says, as a foreigner in foreign country. Yet she is not a foreigner and she has friends she may see in Cairo and Alexandria. The reasons she states for leaving seem to rationalize a deeper, unarticulated sentiment. Alhadeff returns to Italy for the holiday but she merely watches "distant fireworks from a darkened room" and finds the "relief of swooning into bed early, falling asleep instantly" (226). The final events of the memoir, significantly, are the leave-taking from Egypt and, at the end of the journey, repose in a darkened room. The events seem to embody and to reify what the narrative has expressed, subtextually, all along: displacement from one's origin, one's self as the end of a line.

However much "covertly" or imagistically, Alhadeff expresses an unarticulated grief over the loss of origin. "Origin" is variously figured or portrayed in the text. But mainly Alhadeff locates her "origin" within the family. She appears to see her generation, if not herself, at the end of a long family history. The separation or exile from Egypt, like the body metaphors employed in her text, signals a familial severance about which Alhadeff harbors a certain grief. The reader may sense that her grief is an unprocessed one; perhaps it seems so because she attempts to aestheticize her experience rather than to theorize it.

The other memoirists, in contrast to Alhadeff, recount their experiences from a more theoretically grounded—i.e., postcolonial—framework. Saadawi, Aciman, and Said all seem self-consciously intent upon explicating the conceptual loss of origin which is at the center of their works. Saadawi compares her memoir writing to exploratory surgery: "My pen has been a scalpel which cuts through the outer skin, pushes the muscles aside, probes for the roots of things" (*Walking Through Fire* 293). If Alhadeff seeks to aestheticize her memoir, Saadawi takes an opposing tack: "Words should not seek to please, should not hide the wounds in our bodies, the shameful moments in our lives. Sometimes words shock us, give us pain, but they can provoke us to face ourselves, to question what we have accepted for thousands of years" (*Fire* 292). Saadawi's writing conveys a sense of mission; she wants to bring "healing" to the postcolonial condition of the nation and to the status of women, etc. Yet the nativist body metaphor in her memoir is as imagistic and literary as it is startling and visceral. Conversely, it is hard to imagine Said waxing poetical about Palestinian identity. His memoir often seems a bit impersonal; he is neither as candid as Alhadeff nor as "surgical" as Saadawi. Said's "self" in the memoir often seems incidental to the political landscape he portrays. If he recovers a sense of origin, it is through his meticulous rendering of the postcolonial landscape, rather than a literal one, from which his experience derives.

It is interesting to compare the four memoirists in certain respects, though admittedly it may not be entirely fair to do so. The lived experience of each person is something which can only be evaluated on its own terms. Yet a memoir is not a life but the portrayal of one. How the author chooses to construct the portrayal is fair game for speculation. In this case, one looks at how four contemporaries have chosen to understand and to render similar ground. The "birth" of independent Egypt in the 1950s and '60s more or less paralleled each memoirist's own coming-of-age. Their works address the issues of origin and identity which the political and personal upheavals of the day offered to the author. Each sets about this task more or less overtly. Aciman, for example, deliberately sets out to chronicle a "lost age." Understanding the subjective, literary terrain, he invokes Durrell's line about Alexandria as "the capital of memory" (*False Papers* 4). Aciman's memoir,

Out Of Egypt, ends with the leave-taking to which the narrative has driven; yet unlike Alhadeff's work, there is a sense of the story yet to come. Indeed, the continuing story is taken up in the sequel, *False Papers,* a collection of personal essays. Notably, the sequel is as much a critique of memory as it collects the further episodes of Aciman's exile. The work renders Aciman's Egypt as an artifact of memory handled and examined in the living moment.

False Papers is a self-conscious examination of memory. Toward that end Aciman, speaking as the memoirist, calls himself an "armchair archaeologist" (119). His fascination with memory is similar in purpose to that which he holds for an old, defunct subway station, described in the essay, "Underground." The object may be in ruins, but it lives again in the meaning which it holds for the observer:

> I wanted to see how inanimate objects refuse to forget or suggest that all cities—like people, like palimpsests, like the remains of a Roman temple hidden beneath an ancient church—do not simply have to watch themselves go but strive to remember, because in the wish to remember lies the wish to restore, to stay alive, to continue to be. (119–120)

The work of the memoirist, he suggests, like that of the archaeologist, reconstructs the past to give new meaning to the present. Interestingly, like an archaeologist pursuing his subject, Aciman reinscribes the "necropolis" metaphor with which he portrayed his family's impending exile from Egypt. In *Out of Egypt,* Aciman had cast his family's prospective religious conversion to Greek Orthodoxy against the image of the Greek necropolis in Alexandria. The imagery connoted the fall of the minority communities in the revolutionary Egypt of Aciman's youth. In *False Papers,* he tells about returning to Egypt as an adult to visit the Jewish cemetery, *Turb'al Yahud,* to look for his grandfather's grave. The account of the visit figures in the first essay, "Alexandria," and in the second from last in the collection, "Arbitrage;" the two accounts thus form a kind of bracket for the experiences related in between. The first version is quite similar to Alhadeff's account of the cemetery at Chatby. Aciman speaks directly of the cemetery visit and remarks upon the symbolic finality it poses regarding his family's life in Egypt. He suggests that the cemetery is like a "necropolis" in that it remains all which is left of Alexandria's once vibrant Jewish community. But in "Arbitrage" he retells the story of the visit through a prism of variously related memories and recent moments. He describes a story he wrote as a graduate student in which the protagonist returns to Egypt to find the grave of his grandfather. The story presaged the actual event which, as Aciman explains, uncannily replicated the fictive portrayal in nearly every detail.

In "Arbitrage," Aciman shifts the frame of his narration back and forth between the fictive account and the actual event, interspersing related memories of lost love, exile, musings about memory itself and about Egypt as metaphor, and commentary about Wordsworth's *Tintern Abbey.* The account turns out to be an examination of the writing process, specifically that of the memoir, as the recovery of loss. In this regard, he finds the process of recovery, if not the "recovered" object itself, much the same way as does Saadawi; i.e., in the act of writing. However, one feels sometimes that his imagined Egypt is, at last, one more version of an unfulfilled desire. This symbolic "lack" is variously figured as an unattainable pretty girl he once knew, or an idyllic seascape, or the perfect shade of blue, or a hidden fountain. Yet the pretty girl, the sea breeze, the sky blue and the motion of the fountain invigorate what might have been simple loss, simply remembered. Instead Aciman consciously utilizes metaphors and memories to reconstruct new meanings in his portrayals. Thus he salvages much from the Egypt of his exile and his work renders a sense of continuity rather than finality.

Similarly Said's memoir, *Out Of Place,* closes not with finality but with a sense of conditionality or fragile temporality. His portrayal derives from his practice of music, much as Saadawi's portrayals derive from medicine and Aciman's examination of memory refers metaphorically to archaeology. In such references one may see reflected the memoirist's attempt to theorize her or his experience. Said was trained as a classical pianist and continued to play music throughout his life. Not surprisingly then, he renders a description of his existence which seems like a modernistic musical composition or arrangement, with its notions of time, theme, and contrapuntality:

> I occasionally experience myself as a cluster of flowing currents. I prefer this to the idea of a solid self, the identity to which so many attach so much significance. These currents, like the themes of one's life . . . are always in motion, in time, in place, in the form of all kinds of strange combinations moving about, not necessarily forward, sometimes against each other, contrapuntally, yet without one central theme. (295)

Said suggests that his life is a series of lived moments, which are expressed then extinguished. The moments are like musical notes which have no permanence but to persist in following one after another in a score. The abstract yet provocative description portrays the narrative of his life as a musical air.

Said's memoir closes not on a final note but upon a lingering strain, suggestive of the "immortality" of classical music. Yet the sense of "composition" or "arrangement" is perhaps too much inherent in the memoir. Said appears utterly in control of every bit of matter he relates, a somewhat frustrating experience for the reader. While the work is a richly detailed portrait of the Levantine elite in Egypt, Said simply will not give away anything too sensitive, too vulnerable or "untheorized." It is as if by "theorizing," and thus "objectifying" he may remain in control of his memories and their meanings for the reader as well as for himself.

Said's memoir, for all its density of detail, is quite deliberately opaque in certain places. He makes only sketchy and rare references to his marriages and mature relationships. One wonders why he bothers to make such references at all, since he exposes nothing but a general outline of some figures or events which obviously held much emotional significance for him. Again, the consideration calls into question the limits of the memoir genre, regarding privacy and decorum, or simply regarding the focus and purpose of the subject. Said purports to chronicle a "lost age" of modern Egypt as intentionally as does Aciman. But Said's memoir, as a whole, seems less a personal exposition than an eyewitness account of Western colonialism from the vantage of one both privileged and oppressed by it.

Said would seem motivated at least in part to address the issue of Palestinian exile. Yet his memoir seems least of all to explore issues about Palestinian identity or materiality. Indeed, as he himself comments, Palestine remained the thing largely unspoken about in his immediate family throughout his youth:

> The remoteness of the Palestine I grew up in, my family's silence over its role, and then its long disappearance from our lives, my mother's own discomfort with the subject and later aggressive dislike of both Palestine and politics, my lack of contact with Palestinians during the eleven years of my American education: all this allowed me to live my early American life at a great distance from the Palestine of remote memory, unresolved sorrow, and uncomprehending anger. (140–141)

Of course one would see that this absence marks a presence; that is, the subject of Palestine was avoided precisely because of the emotional wounds which it threatened to expose. Not all of Said's family avoided the topic, however; some of his mother's relatives were activists and relief workers in the Palestinian exile community. But their work caused conflict at times within the family. Yet the little which Said has to say about Palestinian exile in the memoir is surely not because of personal reluctance. After all, it is the topic about which he devoted most of his career. Rather what seems to be somewhat of an omission in the memoir probably reflects the general silence of his immediate family about the issue. The relative silence in the memoir probably accurately portrays the literal silence about Palestine observed by his family in his youth.

Yet regardless of his silence, Palestinian displacement or dispossession plays a vastly significant role in the narrative which Said relates. For one thing, Palestinian exile had made necessary the family's tenure in Egypt. They settled in Cairo when the British mandate in Palestine was dissolved. Born in Jerusalem, Said held American citizenship through his father, who received it when he fought for the Allies in World War One. Palestinian exile was that which made the young Edward feel "out of place" in whatever context he found himself engaged. In Cairo, he was a Christian among Muslims, a Baptist among Christians of the Eastern Church, an Arab among Westerners, an American among British subjects, a Palestinian among Levantine *émigrés,* and perhaps, though he does not say it, an Egyptian among Palestinians. These are the contrapuntal elements which compose his experience.

Young Edward's experience of feeling "out of place" seems accompanied, at least metaphorically, by the experience of being "made to fit." The uncomfortable fit is represented in a long sequence which deals with various contraptions, exercises, routines, diets and "disciplines" intended to "correct" Edward's body. The remarkable thing is that there was apparently nothing "wrong" with his body. Rather, his parents seem overly critical of the normal developments of puberty. From boyhood to young manhood Edward endured therapeutic devices for his posture, including orthopedic shoes with metal arches, and for his back, "a white cotton and latex truss with straps across [the] chest and over the shoulders" (64). He was subjected to a series of exercises, one of which entailed holding a cane crooked under his arms for two hours at a time (64), and similar such poses. Other routines were devised for his abdomen and torso. He was enrolled in sports and gym classes which met several times a week, though he was too self conscious, he says, to ever really compete effectively. Other parts of his body were singled out for criticism, if not reform: his hair, face, hands, tongue, eyes, mouth, and chin. At about age eleven, he recalls, "I felt myself to be seriously unwilling to let myself be looked at, so conscious was I of innumerable physical defects, all of which I was convinced reflected my inner deformations" (55). The strictures put upon Edward's body were meted out by his parents and by trainers hired by them. Some of these "disciplines" would be considered today to border upon, if not actually constitute, child abuse. Amazingly, Said recounts that he feels no anger upon reflection as an adult regarding these experiences. He claims to understand his parents' erroneous attempts to "mold" his character by subjecting his body to such disciplines.

A disturbing thought to some degree, one gets the sense that such treatments were fairly common in society at the time, and not only or specifically in Egypt. Such "discipline" of the body appears as a condition of "modernity" among the middle classes of various nations. In colonial society, however, the restriction of the body's natural inclination, represented as "correction," has inherent overtones of political oppression. The references to the body in Said's memoir have such overtones. Trussed, humiliated, and often hit or slapped as a punitive "reminder," Edward lived a bodily oppression in his everyday life. The repression of his body seems to pose a metaphor of that which is daily repressed by the family in lieu of open contemplation: their status as colonial subjects and specifically their exile as Palestinians.

Here again, as discussed in a previous section, one sees the tenuous "privilege" of the Egyptian cosmopolitan elite. The Saids' particular predicament casts them as elites in Egypt, but their privileged status is conditional. It has been created through the imposition of British colonial administration both in Palestine and in Egypt. The mandate which has functioned to deprive them in one case has allowed them privilege in another, presumably for its own design and not for their best interest. If the Saids are to try to make a place for themselves, it seems they must make a "fit" into Egyptian class society as privileged foreigners, rather than as displaced refugees. The focus upon young Edward's posture seems to reflect an obsession with the family's "standing" in society.

Said speaks of Palestine's "intricate wrenching, tearing, sorrowful loss as exemplified in so many distorted lives, including [his own]" (142). The body metaphor in his narrative suggests the kind of pain which wrenches and distorts, like that of the exile he describes. The body emerges as a metaphor in his narrative to materialize an abstract, emotive pain which attaches to the loss of exile. The image portrays Palestinian exile in a personal way uncharacteristic for Said's other writing on the subject. Whether or not he consciously conceived the body as a metaphor for exile in his tightly composed memoir is an interesting speculation. Regardless his imagery imparts "materiality" not only to an unspoken family issue but also to the subject of Palestine, a subject which is yet attended in American popular imagination by generative layers of ideology and discursive abstractions.

One sees "the body" deployed similarly in Said's work as in other conceptions about nativism discussed here. The body metaphor emerges upon a discursive landscape contested by various claims to legitimacy, representation, tenure, etc. References to the body attempt to establish *habeas corpus* for subjective claims to authenticity. It also marks a displacement or figures a material presence where the subject finds a grievous absence. "The body" attempts to recover an integral loss. As we have seen, the loss thus signified in bodily or visceral terms may regard a homeland, a sense of continuity or connection, a "lost age," a mother's face, or other representations of origin. These claims to origin are based upon all which the subject may ever really call one's own—and sometimes not even that—the imagined material of one's own flesh and blood.

Conclusion

In his *Defense of Globalization,* Jagdish Bhagwati finds that postcolonial literary studies, and postmodern literary theory in general, have given rise to the current climate of protest to global development. Bhagwati may accord too much importance to university literature departments in this regard. Yet he brings up an interesting point. Postcolonial studies may indeed provide the intellectual muscle to dissemble the rhetoric of "development." The literary record of Western empire provides an understanding of the real stakes of "modernization" in much of the world. To study colonial literature largely implies that one seeks to understand how its themes and motifs recur in the present. But whether or not one sees the reification of old colonialism in the practices of globalization today is another matter. There is just as much a tendency among academicians to isolate the insights of literature as pertinent only to the period and place from which it derives. The kind of specificity which misses the larger point is an unfortunate misreading of any literature.

One has considered the discourse of development in the late age of Western empire in the East. With "Americanization" after World War Two, the Western interventions in North Africa and the Middle East have largely been conceptualized as "modernization," or presently, as "globalization." One may observe the development of a discourse, it seems, as much as a discourse of development. The insights provided by the history of Western intervention in the East, however, emphasize that discourse, rhetoric or narrative, go in hand with material practices. The function of rhetoric about Western empire's "civilizing mission" was to provide a discursive cloak for pursuits which exploited the resources of colonial nations and appropriated the profits for metropolitan interests. Rhetoric about the "modernizing mission" of contemporary global development appears to follow the paradigms and fallacies of colonial logic. Thus one must question the motives and aims of the material practices to which modernization discourse refers.

The U.S. "war on terror" is currently the most visible example of the "modernizing mission" in the East. The war is a vaguely and arbitrarily defined pursuit which on one hand purports to eliminate "terrorist" groups and their acts of "terror," and on the other, to "spread" or "install" freedom, democracy and development. It can be seen to have "developed" or at least to have mobilized a set of concepts and terms which coincide with an aggressive stance toward the Muslim world. Most of these concepts and terms are not new, in fact, but draw from a much older, historical model of Western antipathy toward the East. One thinks of George W. Bush's invocation of a U.S.-led "crusade" against Islamist militants. The president used the word "crusade" in remarks made in a televised appearance shortly after the September 11 attacks. In the broadcast, he participated in group prayer with the Christian evangelist Billy Graham and made statements which rather amounted to the old adage, "praise the Lord and pass the ammunition." While the media event seems typical of an administration which has openly challenged the Constitutional separation of Church and State, Bush's use of the word "crusade" is as indicative of a world-view as it is tactless.

Since the events of September 11, 2001, words such as *"jihad"* and "holy war," "evil" and "evildoer," etc., have entered public discourse about the "war on terror." Such terms are charged with implicit Christian fundamentalist associations and with historical religious prejudice. The world-view implied by these terms has been simulated in the discourse of media figures such as George Will and Tim Russert, as well as by more mainstream journalists such as Tom Brokaw and Peter Jennings. The use of loaded terms and concepts such as these is problematic in many ways. Foremost, the fundamentalist and racist world-view which they imply in no way deserves the imprimatur of network television news. It is disturbing to see such religious terms conflated with secular public discourse about the policies of state. But indeed, fundamentalist Christian rhetoric at the service of political expediency has characterized much of the Bush-Cheney Administration's public relations.

It is fair to say that since the events of September 11, the U.S. mainstream media has for the most part uncritically reproduced a reductive, if not also hostile, view of the Muslim "East." (This situation might have changed slightly in the last couple of years, likely due to an entrenched American opposition to the war in Iraq.) Yet the ubiquitous American flag pinned to the lapels of virtually all of the network anchors and news pundits in the first years of the "war on terror" did not announce the kind of unbiased reporting one would expect from the "free world" media. How may one situate such flag-draped anchors and pundits with the stereotypical images of Muslims and Arabs which are presented in newscasts about the "war on terror"? It seems that the mainstream media has mostly lent unequivocal support for the war, rather than objectivity or analysis.

The U.S. media portrayals of the "war on terror" have implications for how the Middle East is conceived in American popular imagination. For example since 9/11, media and popular discourse have been taken with the notion of the "Arab street." The notion was popularized by the political analysts Thomas Friedman and Fouad Ajami, both who are regarded as liberals or moderates in their views. "The Arab street" is meant to signify the general opinions of Arab and Muslim people in the Middle East. Yet the discursive term probably derives from the media images, long promulgated in the U.S., of large street protests and demonstrations in Middle Eastern capitals. Edward Said has pointed out in *Covering Islam* that American television news represents Arab and Muslim people as a collective, undifferentiated mass, one which is characterized by the (putative) emotional excess and unruliness of the street protest. The conceptual imagery conjured by the term, "the Arab street," is much the same. One may recall the media images of the Iranian Revolution in 1979, for example, when American flags and effigies of "Uncle Sam" (as Jimmy Carter) were burned by students in street protests. The Iranian protest images, and others like them, have strongly polemical connotations. The connotation of a polemic between East and West, if not also the U.S. and the Middle East, is implicit in the imagery. "The Arab street" simulates the notion of a polemic.

Television entertainment, especially since 9/11, has readily engaged the conceptual polemic of East and West. Network dramas such as "24" and "Alias," which are largely jingoistic police-state fantasies, portray "Islamist terrorism" as the nemesis of American good will and self determination. "24," in particular, gleefully portrays an aggressive American security "apparatus" which violates international laws and human rights to apprehend fictive *jihadi* warriors intent upon a nuclear Armageddon. But such mediated fantasies are not so different from the nightly news portrayals which precede them in prime time. Both reflect a deep lack of critical engagement in the public discourse with the most serious issues of our day. In the absence of serious analysis about the motives of so-called terrorists, the usual discursive fallacies abound regarding "hate," "jealousy," irrationality, and the need to smite "evildoers." The motives which are thus usually attributed to so-called Islamist terrorists are those said to arise from religious dogma or an essential hatred of Western modernity. The collective lack of critical engagement invites a jumble of conflated, Crusade-era misconceptions and superstitions to take root. The modern, American popular understanding of the Middle East may well resemble the simulations of the fourteenth century author, Sir

John Mandeville, whose *Travels* never went so far as his imagination. It is therefore important to replace simulated chimeras with materialist analysis about the Middle East.

The "war on terror" is alleged to (eventually) bring "development" and "democracy" to the East. Americans are to understand that such things as "development" and "democracy" are modern qualities which essentially never evolved among Arabs and Muslims, presumably for reasons of religion and cultural traditions—or else for simple, collective lack of imagination. Such a view upon the East is, of course, fallacious. But further, one must question what is meant by "democracy" as much as one interrogates the meaning of "development." For often what is called "democracy" or "freedom" in the discourse of modernization actually refers to neo-liberalism or so-called free market economics. Anti-globalization critics assert that neither one has much to do with freedom or democracy. There is something ironic about a Western "crusade" to impart "modernity" or to install or enforce "democracy" in the East. It seems an aim which could only be conceptualized in the total lack of historical understanding about the relationship between the East and the West. Thus it is necessary to recover the historical perspective which "modernization" discourse elides. The thread of that history is found in the narratives of Western empires, old and new, and their "missions" to colonize, "civilize" and "modernize."

Notes

NOTES TO CHAPTER ONE

1. Wolfgang Sachs, "Neo-Development," *The Case Against The Global Economy,* Jerry Mander and Edward Goldsmith, eds. (San Francisco: Sierra Club, 1996) 239.
2. Bauer, writing in 1971, pointed out that the definition of development applied to a given country or region is not so much a scientific observation as a matter of the beholder's view: "The placing of the line of division depends quite often on accident, or on personal preference, but primarily on political pressures . . . The arbitrary nature of the current distinction between developed and underdeveloped countries on the basis of per capita incomes is compounded by the fact that per capita income is itself a seriously inadequate index of development. This inadequacy is at times recognized. For instance, some of the oil states of the middle east, habitually and appropriately classified as underdeveloped, have per capita incomes which are among the highest in the world. In many, perhaps most contexts, it is permissible to use interchangeably the terms developed and rich on the one hand, and underdeveloped and poor on the other. But this practice, as the above example shows, is inappropriate in discussions on an allegedly wide and widening gap in incomes [between developed and developing countries] (53)."
3. The view that "corporate imperialism" is neo-colonial is not new. Many cultural critics consider "globalization" to be the new expression of an old order. Recent works include Michael Hardt and Antonio Negri, *Empire;* David Korten, *When Corporations Rule The World;* Rashid Khalidi, *Resurrecting Empire;* and the anthology by Mander and Goldsmith cited above. These follow the earlier works of Noam Chomsky, *World Orders Old And New; The Washington Connection;* and, *Profit Over People.*
4. *Postmodernism, Or, The Cultural Logic Of Late Capitalism.*
5. *The Arab Predicament* 70.

6. See Stephen Kinzer, *All The Shah's Men* (Hoboken: John Wiley and Sons, 2003).
7. Baida, "The United States and the Franco-Moroccan Conflict (1950–1956)," *The Atlantic Connection,* Jerome B. Bookin-Weiner and Mohamed El Mansour, eds. (Rabat: Edino, 1996) 183–196.
8. Azzedine Layachi, "Images and U.S.-Moroccan Relations," *The United States And North Africa* (NY: Praeger, 1990) 17–30. See also Les Janka and Mark Tessler, separately, in Bookin-Weiner and Mansour. The essays collected by the editors discuss in historical detail the relationship between Morocco and the U.S. which has obtained since the late 18th century.
9. Alternately transliterated as the *Mashraq* or *Mashriq,* the Arabic term for, essentially, the "East" corresponds generally to the Middle Eastern or Muslim countries east of Libya, i.e., Syria, Lebanon, Jordan, etc. The *Maghrib* or *Maghreb,* transliterated Arabic for, essentially, the "West," corresponds generally to the Middle Eastern or Muslim countries west of Egypt and is often used to refer specifically to the region otherwise known as French North Africa, i.e., Morocco, Algeria and Tunisia. The countries referred to by either term, *Mashraq* and *Maghrib,* may vary according to context.
10. Baida. See also, Richard Brace.
11. Robert S. Norris and William M. Arkin and William Burr, "Where They Were," *Bulletin Of The Atomic Scientists,* Vol. 55, No. 6 Nov./Dec. 1999, 26–35. The authors analyze the document, "History of the Custody and Deployment of Nuclear Weapons: July 1945 through September 1977," released by the U.S. Department of Defense under a Freedom Of Information Act request filed originally in 1985.
12. Brace 168. Layachi 16–17.
13. M'hammad Benaboud, "Problems of American Protection in Morocco," Bookin-Weiner and Mansour 79–94. Baida 195 n. 25.
14. The Baku-Tbilisi-Ceyhan oil pipeline, completed in 2005, runs from the Caspian seaport city through Azerbaijan, Georgia, and Turkey ("Giant Caspian oil pipeline opens," *BBC News 24,* May 25, 2005, http://news.bbc.co.uk/1/hi/business/4577497.stm.) Furthermore, since the time of the Afghan *mujihadeen* struggle with the Soviet Union in the 1980s, the California-based energy company Unocal had wanted to build an oil and gas pipeline network in Central Asia. Afghanistan's political instability had impeded this aim until the rise of Taliban rule. Taliban leaders met with Unocal representatives in Sugarland, Texas, to discuss plans for a transregional pipeline. International women's rights groups were among the first to expose and to criticize Unocal's associations with the Taliban. See the following online journal articles: Brook Shelby Biggs, "Pipe Dreams," *Mother Jones,* October 12, 2001, http://www.motherjones.com/web_exclusive/features/news/ pipedreams.html-34k; Bill Sardi, "Is There an Oil Pipeline Behind the War in Afghanistan?" *Lew Rockwell,* October 15, 2001, Word Of Mouth Agency, San Dimas, Ca., http://www.lewrockwell.

com/orig/sardi7.html; Jack Beatty, "Do the Right Thing: Think Globally, Act Ethically," *The Atlantic Online,* June 10, 1998, Politics and Prose, Atlantic Unbound, http://www.theatlantic.com/unbound/polipro/pp9806.htm-14k-.

15. Mander and Goldsmith 253.
16. Under the direction of Conneticut Senator Joseph Liberman and Lynn Cheney, wife of Vice President Dick Cheney, the conservative watchdog group American Council of Trustees and Alumni (ACTA) produced the 43-page report, "Defending Civilization: How Our Universities Are Failing America And What Can Be Done About It," in November 2001. The report recommends that a "unity of opinion" be established among American academicians in regard to the Bush Administration's "war on terror." Critics view the ACTA report as part of an attempt to stigmatize dissenters and to silence public debate. The report identifies more than 40 professors who are reported to be "unwilling to defend" America and who, rather, "give comfort to its adversaries" (Solomon). For a detailed discussion, see the following online articles: David Glenn, "The War on Campus," *The Nation Online,* November 15, 2001, http://www.thenation.com/ doc.mhtml?i=20011203&c=17s=glenn nation.com; Alisa Solomon, "Things We Lost in the Fire," *VillageVoice.com,* September 2002, http:/www.villagevoice.com/issues/0237/ solomon.php; Kristine MacNeil, "The War on Academic Freedom," *The Nation Online,* November 11, 2002, http://www.thenation.com/doc.mhtml?i=20021125&c=1&c=mcneil.
17. Ashcroft, Griffiths and Tiffin 36–37.
18. See for example, Wallerstein, "Africa in a Capitalist World," *The Essential Wallerstein* 39–65; for technical discussion, see Amin, *Unequal Development.*
19. See Korten, "The Failures of Bretton Woods," Mander and Goldsmith 20–30.
20. Richard Jackson, *The Non-Aligned, The U.N., And The Superpowers* 172.
21. Ashcroft, et al. ibid.
22. The Greater Middle East Reform Initiative was announced by Security Advisor Condaleezza Rice in August 2004. It has since been renamed as the Broader Middle East And North Africa Initiative to include more of the region. Robin Wright, "U.S. Struggles to Win Hearts, Minds in the Muslim World" *Washington Post,* 20 August 2004, A01. See also, Emad McKay, "Mideast Reform Stresses Economic Liberalism," *Inter Press Service.* <http://domino.ips.org/ips%5cengnsf/0/1DCF82C619294BE8C1256EA 7007 B2894/?OpenDocument>.
23. David Ignatius, "Think Strategy, Not Numbers," *Washington Post,* 26 August 2003.

NOTES TO CHAPTER TWO

1. Horne relates: "At the top, Algeria—since it had been annexed as an integral part of France—was governed through the French Ministry of the Interior" (32).

2. Sartre's essay was published in *Le Temps Moderns* a year before a significant military build-up. On February 6, 1956, the French premier Guy Mollet had authorized the increase of French forces in Algeria to 500,000 (Horne 151).
3. As Horne comments, "[T]o escape from a life that held little prospect on the land, as in the poorer countries of Latin America the Algerian peasantry gravitated increasingly towards the cities. Here they found that nearly half of all available jobs in industry were firmly occupied by the *pied noir* eleven per cent, while twenty-five per cent of the urban Muslims were unemployed. The results were that during the twelve years between 1936 and 1948, as an example, the population of Algiers soared by forty-two per cent and with it the mushrooming of wretched *bidonvilles* and the simmering of new kinds of urban discontent" (63).
4. For more detailed discussions of the gradualism of the Algerian independence movement before 1954, see variously Malley 45–47; Haddour, *Colonial Myths* 7–10; and, Stora 16–19.
5. The Tunisian policy of gradual autonomy, aimed eventually at full independence, is named after Habib Bourghiba, the native leader with whom it is associated. For more on Bourghibism, see Memmi's discussion, *Colonizer and the Colonized* 151.
6. Assimilation is variously discussed by Haddour, *Colonial Myths* 4–19; Stora 15–19; Malley 43–46; Horne 35–37; and, Halstead 46–63; these authors basically concur with the view which sees French colonial assimilation as disingenuous and exploitative.
7. See the discussion by various authors about gradualism and assimilation in the notes above.
8. Henissart 157–158; Fleming 12–13; Amin, *Maghreb in the Modern World* 70–79.
9. De Gaulle had spoken, if disingenuously, the potent words "I have understood you!" and "Long live French Algeria!" to cheering *pied noir* crowds on a tour of Algeria in 1958. The tour is recounted by Stora 72–73; Horne 300–303; and, Henissart 33.
10. Kittler 127.
11. Laroui, *History of the Maghrib* 333–334.
12. This discussion is admittedly a gloss; the superficial observances which I make here cannot, and are not intended to, convey the breadth of a movement which comprised various, particular strains of nationalist activism in the Maghrib, and various concepts and ideologies.
13. *Colonizer and the Colonized* 150–152.
14. *Colonizer and the Colonized* xxv.
15. *Wretched of the Earth* 39, 44.
16. "*Pieds noirs* (literally, 'blackfeet'): how are we to determine the exact origin of this term? Some say it may have been invented by the Arabs, surprised to see soldiers landing in 1830 with black boots upon their feet. Others

suggest it was the color of the feet of wine growers in Algeria, tramping grapes to make wine. Whatever the explanation, the French of Algeria did not encounter that characterization until they arrived in the metropolis—in 1962" (Stora 8).

17. The Greek term "autochthony" has been utilized in the structural, cross-cultural analysis of myths. Mircea Eliade uses the term in *The Sacred and the Profane* (1959), for example. The term and its application are also associated with Claude Levi-Strauss.
18. In the context of discussion, my use of the term "native" refers to the indigenous people of "Arabo-Berber" descent. Although the progeny of European settlers might also be seen as technically indigenous, having been born in Algeria, their existence as a class or caste was primarily based upon and held fast to European culture and society. Legally the settlers were citizens of France (see note below). The people of Arabo-Berber descent however, who were primarily Muslims, would have had to renounce Islam in order to derive French citizenship, a condition for which few natives opted (Horne 35).
19. Several authors (e.g., Stora, Henissart, Horne) point out that most European settlers in Algeria derived originally from places other than metropolitan France, such as Spain, Italy, Corsica, and Malta. But in 1889, French law imposed French citizenship upon all the descendants of European settlers who did not refuse it.
20. Haddour and Said interrogate the existential readings of Meursault's actions, respectively, by Sartre, Roland Barthes, and Julia Kristeva, and by Conor Cruise O'Brien; see discussions by Haddour, *Colonial Myths* 42–52 and Said, *Culture and Imperialism* 169–185. Kristeva sees Meursault's actions as a kind of psychic break in *Strangers to Ourselves* 24–29. Anthony Rizzuto follows the existentialist tradition by tracing Camus' attempt to create an indifferent "man-god" in the figure of *L'Etranger* (*Camus' Imperial Vision* 1–28). Comparatively, Susan Tarrow's Foucaulvian-style reading of *The Stranger* examines the relationships of social power inherent in language and Meursault's attempts to circumvent them (*Exile From the Kingdom* 66–90).
21. *The Penguin Dictionary of Literary Terms and Literary Theory* cites Barthes' 1970 work *S/Z* and defines the term "writerly" as designating a text which "makes demands on the reader . . . to work things out, look for and provide meaning . . . A writerly text tends to focus attention on how it is written, the mechanics of it, the particular use of language. A writerly text tends to be self conscious; it calls attention to itself as a work of art" (769–770).
22. *Colonial Myths* 51.
23. Maryemma Graham, "Introduction," *The Outsider* by Richard Wright; NY: Perennial 2003, xx. See also Arnold Rampersad, "Chronology," *Native Son* by Richard Wright 560–561.

NOTES TO CHAPTER THREE

1. Aronson comments on the men's different attitudes toward revolutionary violence in Algeria: "If Camus worried increasingly about the harm it did to its victims and its negative moral effects, Sartre focused on its positive political and psychological effects on those who chose to practice it, especially the victims of oppression, when all other paths became blocked. In this sense violence became central to both Sartre's and Camus' politics and outlook, the one viscerally embracing it, the other equally powerfully repelling it" (34).
2. Cuddon describes some of the key features of existentialism, noting that "In *L' Existentialisme est un humanisme* (1946) Sartre expressed the belief that man can emerge from his passive and indeterminate condition and, by an act of will, become *engagé;* whereupon he is committed (through *engagement*) to some action and part in social and political life" (*Penguin Dictionary of Literary Terms and Literary Theory* 317).
3. For example, in *Being and Nothingness* Sartre writes that "to act is to modify the *shape* of the world; it is to arrange means in view of an end; it is to produce an organized instrumental complex such that by a series of concatenations and connections the modification effected on one of the links modifies modifications throughout the whole series and finally produces an anticipated result . . . This does not mean, of course, that one must foresee all the consequences of his act" (559). In further regard to the consequences of one's actions, he observes: "Now at each moment we are thrust into the world and involved there. This means that we act before positing our possibilities and that these possibilities, which are disclosed as realized or in the process of being realized, refer to meanings which can only be put into questions by special acts" (75).
4. Some observers feel that too much has been made of the differences between Berbers and Arabs in the Maghrib, and that too little is recognized about the ways in which French administration exploited and exacerbated differences between those two communities. Amin observes: "[T]he thesis of 'racial hostility' between Arabs and Berbers, put forward by the historians and sociologists of the French colonial period, is somewhat superficial . . . The Berber-speaking country people never regarded Arabism as a hostile force, but rather as a cultural model. Traditional Arab ideology was to remain the dominant ideology of the Maghreb throughout the intervening centuries. Here as in the eastern Islamic world—the world of Arab, Turk, and Persian—it was to preserve the memory of the Muslim's nomadic ancestors, whose values were to remain a model for all, even the civilized townsmen" (*Maghreb in the Modern World* 91–92). See also Laroui's discussion of the European historiography of the "Arabization" of the Maghrib in *History of the Maghrib* 86–89.
5. Aronson 211.

6. Albert Waterson comments upon the portion of Marshall Plan money earmarked for Algeria: "With the advent in 1948 of Marshall Plan Aid, which made funds available for the three North African Territories, the investment programs of Morocco, Algeria and Tunisia were for the first time taken into account in framing French modernization and investment plans (7)." Camus' conceptualization of Algerian development can perhaps be seen in this context.
7. Technically, Algeria was a department of France; Morocco was a French protectorate.
8. See notes 2 and 3 above.
9. Giles 135–136.
10. Camus describes this uncle at length in his unfinished autobiographical novel, *The First Man.*
11. Amin, *Unequal Development* 240–241.
12. Brace mentions some facts about the aid and development relationship of France and newly independent Algeria. The relationship implies that all links had not been broken, despite Algeria's sovereignty. He recounts that by 1964, only two years after the end of the war, France had contributed about $600,000,000 in aid of various kinds to the new government. Also in that same year plans were well advanced to develop Algeria's natural gas reserves for export to Europe. The project, called CAMEL *(Compagnie Algérienne de Methane Liquide),* was a joint venture of French and American investors in which the Algerian state was to own 20 percent of the interests. *Morocco, Algeria Tunisia* 162–165. In a different vein, Stora comments upon the current Franco-Algerian relationship: "Yet, at the same time, the two countries are absolutely attached to each other (if only by the virtue of the presence of more than 1 million Algerians on French soil), and the mutual historical, social, and cultural links (once colonial, now of immigration) continue to cause tormenting problems" (237).
13. Morocco's autonomous governmental body, the *Makhzen,* was in effect under the rule of the French Resident General. In Tunisia, Habib Bourghiba and other nationalists had struggled disproportionately hard to negotiate a qualified autonomy with France (See note on Bourghibism, in previous chapter.) Both countries gained actual independence in 1956. The independence struggles in Morocco and Tunisia, while not bloodless, were far less violent and protracted than in Algeria, where the war lasted from 1954 until 1962.
14. Roberts cites the major party of the movement, the Islamic Salvation Front (FIS): "[I]n so far as the FIS did take a position on the issue of economic reform [commercial privatization; private enterprise], it explicitly and unequivocally supported it at the level of principle. It is certainly true that it did so without placing any real emphasis on this position, but its tacit support for the implementation of the government's reform programme in practice was unmistakable" *Battlefield Algeria* 83.
15. Djebar 221–226; Kittler 52.

16. Fleming notes that Abdelkader has often been hailed as the "father of Algerian nationalism." *Sword and Cross* 8n.
17. Laroui, *History of the Maghrib* 297–301; Malley 37–38; Entelis 39–40.
18. The significance of Abdelkader's resistance for the guerrilla war carried on by the FLN is recognized by the three author's cited in the preceding note; see also Haddour, *Colonial Myths* 121–122; and, Amin *Maghreb in the Modern World* 96.
19. See Entelis 85–101.
20. The discussion of Abdelkader's body as a simulacrum is, of course, indebted to Jean Baudrillard's conception of simulation as put forth in his work, *Simulation and Simulations.*
21. Djebar 222–223.
22. "The Prophet [Muhammad] said, 'Wear white clothes, because they are the cleanest and most agreeable; and bury your dead in white clothes'" (D.S. Roberts, *Islam* 109.)
23. Two accounts, in English, of the scene of Camus' 1956 speech in Algiers are very similar in detail to that portrayed by Djebar: Aronson 188–190 and Horne 124–127.
24. Stora 214.
25. Roberts, *Battlefield Algeria* 373.

NOTES TO CHAPTER FOUR

1. Amin, *Unequal Development.*
2. "Focus of Egypt Air crash probe moves to Cairo." *CNN.com.* November 22, 1999. http://www.cnn.com/US/9911/21/egyptair.02/
3. "Wings and a Prayer." *The Guardian.* Monday, May 8, 2000. http://www.guardian.co.uk/egyptair/article/Ø,,218460,00.html
4. The subsequent discussion of the material history of modern Egypt, the reign of the Muhammad Ali dynasty, and, in the following section, the formation of ethnic class society, derives from and synthesizes my various sources. I am indebted to Amin, *Unequal Development* 298–317; Hourani, 282–298; Baraka 15–60; Berque 84–102; Rodenbeck 118–147; Robinson 138–140; and Finkel.

NOTES TO CHAPTER FIVE

1. D.S. Roberts, *Islam* 157.
2. Braudel, *Wheels of Commerce* 558.
3. *Ibid.*
4. Braudel refers to and refutes the idea. *Wheels* 165–167.
5. *Location of Culture* 85–92.
6. Amin, *Unequal Development* 303.

7. Historical accounts of the destruction of the Egyptian ethnic minority communities after 1952 are given by Laskier; Rodenbeck 157–159; Dekmejian 82–84; and, Woodward 90–96; the memoirs of Alhadeff, Aciman, and Said also provide personal accounts. See also Joel Beinin, *The Dispersion of Egyptian Jewry: Culture, Politics, and the Formation of a Modern Diaspora;* Berkeley: Univ. of California Press, 1998; http://ark.cdlib.org/ark:/13030/ft2290045n/
8. *Mountolive* 107.
9. Farouk's unofficial exploits are related in *The Last Pharoah: Farouk of Egypt* by Hugh McLeave and, in a more sensationalistic style, by Michael Stern in *Farouk.*
10. Accounts of the political *milieu* and events of the period of Farouk's reign are found in Baraka 84–93; Aburish 29–40; Rodenbeck 148–157; Woodward 20–26; and, Dekmejian 17–22.
11. Conversely, Farouk himself was known to have Jewish friends.
12. Ajami, *Dream Palace* 224–225.
13. See Memmi, *Pillar of Salt,* and Stillman 435–436, 438.
14. See Fisk 66–70.
15. See Haim's discussion, "Introduction" 3–72. Many proponents of Arab nationalism, whether Christians or Muslims, envisioned a secular movement; others defined a specific role for Islam as a unifying feature among Arabs; see also Tareq Ismael 2–8. Antonius' book is considered an important early history of the Arab nationalist movement.
16. Berque describes the system of separate courts: "Three sorts of tribunal had existed in Egypt since 1875; the Mixed Courts, the Native Courts and the Courts of Religious Law, dealing with the personal status of Muslims. The latter were not interfered with for a long time, and then with the utmost precaution. The Mixed Courts, which controlled the all-important relations between foreigners and Egyptian nationals, had their own organization. As for the Native courts . . . [c]omposed of three judges, one of whom was a European, they remained in fact quite out of touch with the problems of the country" (159–160). Regarding this same system, Rodenbeck notes, "It was Nasser who abolished the Christian, Jewish, and Muslim religious tribunals that had governed family law until 1956" (176).
17. That is, it was overall reflective of Muslim culture, rather than Islamic clericalism or religious doctrine. The distinction is apparent especially in light of the current rise of Islamism today in Egypt and other countries. Egyptian nationalism at the time of Aciman's youth was somewhat fusing or feeding into the broader Arabist political doctrine, Pan-Arab nationalism, as Nasser himself turned at least officially in this direction. Even so, Egyptian nationalism retained its various distinct and local characteristics and symbols, including Pharaonic and other non-Muslim elements; however the Muslim elements were dominant.

18. Jacqueline Ismael, "Nasserism," *Arab Left* by Tareq Ismael 78–91.
19. Laskier, "Egyptian Jewry under the Nasser Regime, 1956–70." See also Beinin, *Dispersion of Egyptian Jewry,* cited in note above.
20. *"Stabat Mater," The Kristeva Reader* edited by Toril Moi (NY: Columbia UP, 1986) 160–186.
21. Jean-Marc Ran Oppenheim writes: "After the Exodus under Moses and Aaron, some Jews returned to live in Egypt in the Hellenistic period (third century B.C.E.). Jewish communities of various sizes existed in Egypt during Byzantine rule, the Arab conquest of 641 C.E., and the subsequent medieval Islamic dynasties." "Egypt and the Sudan." *Jews of the Middle East and North Africa in Modern Times.* Reeva Simon, et al., eds. 412.
22. See Dekmejian.
23. Aburish objectively refers to the notion in his biography of Nasser, 127.
24. Berque 290.
25. *Out of Place* 272.
26. Alhadeff 153.
27. Woodward 17; Aburish 18.
28. *Out of Place* 199.
29. Rodenbeck cites the membership of the Muslim Brotherhood in the late 1940s at about half a million (169). Fawaz A. Gerges states the membership higher: "By the end of the 1940s, the [Muslim] Brotherhood had developed a formidable political machine, and thought to have almost a million members" (24). *Journey of the Jihadist.* NY: Harcourt, 2006.

NOTES TO CHAPTER SIX

1. Urabi, an Egyptian army officer, led a nationalist revolt against the British in 1882. Kamil founded the *Watani* nationalist Party in 1907. Zaghlul led the revolt in 1919, provoked by Britian's refusal to allow an Egyptian delegation *(wafd)* to the Paris Peace Conference in order to pursue Egyptian autonomy. He founded the *Wafd* Party and subsequently became the Egyptian prime minister.
2. Separately, Baron (58–62) and Oppenheim (423) mention one of the early advocates of territorial nationalism, Yaqʿub Sanuʿa, an Egyptian Jewish journalist who satirized the Khedive Ismail in his weekly journal, using political cartoons to make his criticisms. Oppenheim also mentions prominent Egyptian Jews who joined the *Wafd,* adding that: "Through the 1920s and 1930s the discourse of Egyptian politics focused on independence from Britain and a concept of national identity that was essentially secular" (424).
3. Sartre, "Albert Memmi's *The Colonizer and the Colonized," Colonialism and Neocolonialism* 50.
4. Sartre, "Colonialism is a System," ibid 30–47; Laroui, *History of the Maghrib* 334.

5. Berque 46.
6. Oppenheim observes some of the policy: "Economic relations implemented in the late 1950s . . . increased the percentage of real Egyptians to be employed by all corporations. Indigenous Egyptians needed permits to seek employment 'with foreigners,' and the government introduced the use of a work card listing the employee's religion along with his name" (429). The term "real Egyptians," to which Oppenheim refers, points out the abstract, subjective criteria of nativist rhetoric. But beyond the obvious injustice done to the religious and ethnic Egyptian minorities deemed not to be indigenous, or wholly "real" in the nativist discourse, such economic reforms as he describes were likely to have been oppressive as well for much of native society.
7. Kwame Anthony Appiah considers this question in regard to postcolonial transition to national independence in subSaharan Africa and as regarded in the work of Malian author Yambo Ouologuem. He comments: "The national bourgeoisie that took on the baton of rationalization, industrialization, bureaucratization in the name of nationalism turned out to be a kleptocracy. Their enthusiasm for nativism was a rationalization of their urge to keep the national bourgeoisies of other nations—and particularly the powerful industrialized nations—out of their way" (121).
8. Ashcroft, Gareth and Tiffin, *Key Concepts in Post-Colonial Studies* (159).
9. For a contemporary discussion about decolonized development aims of the period, see Guevara, "On Underdevelopment," and, "On Development," respectively. Gerassi 89–91; 317–335.
10. "Pan-Arabism," *Babel to Dragomans* 156–179.
11. Aburish 45.
12. Nasser's reforms have been variously defined and/or qualified as "socialism," "Arab socialism," and "Islamic socialism." See discussions in Lewis, "Return to Cairo," ibid 249–250; and, Aburish 200–201. Bassam Tibbi refutes the concept of "Arab socialism" (Ajami, *Predicament* 35). Amin discusses that "state capitalism" is a more relevant term for the economic reforms pursued in the decolonizing world at the time (*Unequal Development* 345–347).
13. Aburish 105. Various authors point out that the Suez Canal was nationalized after the U.S. pulled out of negotiations to fund the dam project.
14. See Malley's summary of the three central themes of "Third Worldism": (the belief in) historical progress, popular will, and power (94–95).
15. The union with Syria was dissolved in 1961, though Egypt retained the name until after Nasser's death.
16. Amin, *Unequal Development* 314; Lewis, "Return to Cairo" 249.
17. Recounted in Aburish 36.
18. For example, European leaders including Tony Blair, Silvio Berlusconi, Gerhardt Schroeder, and Nicolas Sarkozy have all been lately treated to Qaddafy's tent. See David Blair, "Blair, Gaddafi and the BP Oil Deal." *Telegraph*

May 31, 2007. http://www.telegraph.co.uk/news/main.jhtml?xml=/news/2007/05/30/wblair130xml; Salah Sarrar, "Gaddafi clears tent for Sarkozy to sign deals." *The Age.* July 27, 2007. http://www.theage.com.au/news/world/gaddafi-clears-tent-for-sarkozy-to-sign-deals/2007/07/26/1185339166661.html; Scott MacLeod, "Why Gaddafi's Now a Good Guy." *Time.* May 16, 2006. http://www.time.com/time/world/article/0,8599,1194766,00.html; Vivienne Walt, "Meeting Muammar: Is Libya's Leader 'Finished'?" *Slate.* December 16, 2004. http://slate.com/id/2111135/.

19. Saadawi criticizes religious dogmatism and the misappropriation of Islamic principles; she does not criticize or reject the religion of Islam itself. As she has said: "I am not anti-Islamic. Islam is justice." (Remark made at a workshop given at the University of Michigan-Flint on March 30, 2007.)
20. In answer to a participant's question at the workshop cited above, Saadawi said that she became disappointed with Nasser because his reform agenda did not include efforts to improve gender equality for Egyptian women.
21. An insightful discussion of the feminist meanings of Saadawi's work is Fedwa Malti-Douglas' book, *Men, Women, and God(s): Nawal El Saadawi and Arab Feminist Poetics.* Berkeley: University of California Press, 1995. Or relatedly, much feminist scholarly attention focuses on Saadawi's activism against the practice of clitoridectomy; for example, see Julia V. Emberley 54–74.
22. Aburish recounts that Sadat read the revolutionary proclamation on the radio that July morning (40).
23. Regarding the title, Saadawi herself said that she wished to make a feminist reference to the intellectual nature of women: "I named my autobiography after her [Isis] because she is the goddess of knowledge." University of Michigan-Flint, March 30, 2007.
24. See Ajami, "In the Land of Egypt," *Dream Palace* 193–252.
25. It may be a misportrayal to emphasize the secularism of Sadat; his government introduced constitutional reforms of religious character. Perhaps he may be seen, as Ajami views him, as a figure who incorporated secular and religious influences in an attempt to appease various political factions.
26. The conceptualization of North Africa as "Mediterranean" is generally considered to be a colonial notion. "Mediterranean" contextualizes the region in relation to the Levant and Southern Europe. The view contraposes the Arab and Islamic conceptions of the region, the nativist conceptions, as well as those which relate the north to the larger African continent. The point is that the "Mediterranean" notion is a subjective one, if no less subjective than the other conceptualizations of the region. See Berque 637–640; Ajami, "Egypt as state, as Arab mirror," *Predicament* 124–139.

Bibliography

Abernethy, David B. *The Dynamics of Global Dominance.* New Haven: Yale UP, 2000.

Aburish, Said K. *Nasser: The Last Arab.* NY: St. Martin's Press, 2004.

Abdel-Malek, Anouar. *Civilizations and Social Theory.* Albany: SUNY Press, 1981.

Aciman, Andre. *False Papers: Essays on Exile and Memory.* NY: Picador, 2000.

———. *Out of Egypt.* NY: Riverhead Books 1996.

Ajami, Fouad. *The Dream Palace of the Arabs.* NY: Vintage Books, 1999.

———. *The Arab Predicament.* Cambridge, UK: Cambridge UP, 1999. Updated ed.

Alhadeff, Gini. *The Sun at Midday.* Hopewell, New Jersey: Ecco Press, 1998.

Ali, Tariq. *The Clash of Fundamentalisms: Crusades, Jihads and Modernity.* NY: Verso 2002.

Amin, Samir. *Unequal Development.* Brian Pearce, trans. Sussex, England: Harvester Press, 1976.

———. *The Maghreb in the Modern World.* Michael Perl, trans. Baltimore: Penguin, 1970.

———. *Spectres of Capitalism.* Shane Henry Mage, trans. NY: Monthly Review Press, 1998.

Appiah, Kwame Anthony. "The Postcolonial and the Postmodern." *The Post-Colonial Studies Reader.* Bill Ashcroft, Gareth Griffiths and Helen Tiffin, eds. NY: Routledge, 1999. 119–124.

Aronson, Ronald. *Camus and Sartre.* Chicago: University of Chicago Press, 2004.

Ashcroft, Bill and Gareth Griffiths and Helen Tiffin, eds. *The Post-Colonial Studies Reader.* NY: Routledge, 1999.

———. *Key Concepts in Postcolonial Studies.* NY: Routledge, 1998.

Baida, Jamaa. "The United States and the Franco-Moroccan Conflict (1950–1956)." *The Atlantic Connection.* Jerome B. Bookin-Weiner and Mohamed El Mansour, eds. Rabat: Edino, 1996. 183–196.

Banfield, Edward C. *The Moral Basis of a Backward Society.* NY: The Free Press, 1958.

Baraka, Magda *The Egyptian Upper Class Between Revolutions 1919–1952.* Reading, UK: Ithaca, 1998.

Baron, Beth. *Egypt as a Woman: Nationalism, Gender, and Politics.* Berkeley: University of California Press, 2007.

Bauer, P.T. *Dissent on Development.* Cambridge: Harvard UP, 1976. Revised ed.

Beinin, Joel. *The Dispersion of the Egyptian Jewry: Culture, Politics and the Formation of the Modern Diaspora.* Berkeley: University of California Press, 1998.

Benaboud, M'hammad. "Problems of American Protection in Morocco." *The Atlantic Connection.* Jerome B. Bookin-Weiner and Mohamed El Mansour, eds. Rabat: Edino, 1996. 79–93.

Benbassa, Esther and Aron Rodrigue. *Sephardi Jewry: A History of the Judeo-Spanish Community, Fourteenth-Twentieth Centuries.* Berkeley: University of California Press, 2000.

Berque, Jacques. *Egypt: Imperialism and Revolution.* Jean Stewart, trans. London: Faber and Faber, 1972.

Bhabha, Homi K. *The Location of Culture.* NY: Routledge, 1994.

Bhagwati, Jagdish. *In Defense of Globalization.* NY: Oxford UP, 2004.

Brace, Richard M. *Morocco, Algeria, Tunisia.* Englewood Cliffs: Prentice-Hall, 1964.

Braudel, Fernand. *Civilization and Capitalism Fifteenth-Eighteenth Century: The Wheels of Commerce.* Sian Reynolds, trans. Berkeley: University of California Press, 1992. Vol. 2.

———. *Civilization and Capitalism Fifteenth-Eighteenth Century: The Perspective of the World.* Sian Reynolds, trans. Berkeley: University of California Press, 1992. Vol. 3.

———. *The Mediterranean and the Mediterranean World in the Age of Phillip II.* Sian Reynolds, trans. Berkeley: University of California Press, 1995. Vol. 1 & 2.

———. *Afterthoughts on Material Civilization and Capitalism.* Patricia Ranum, trans. Baltimore: Johns Hopkins UP, 1981.

Bookin-Weiner, Jerome B. and Mohamed El Mansour, eds. *The Atlantic Connection: 200 Years of Moroccan-American Relations 1786–1986.* Rabat: Edino, 1996.

Bowles, Paul. *Without Stopping.* NY: G.P. Putnam's Sons, 1972.

———. *The Sheltering Sky.* NY: Ecco Press, 1998.

Castro, Fidel. "We represent the immense majority of humanity." Speech given to the United Nations Assembly. NY: Pathfinder, 1979.

Castañeda, Jorge G. *Compañero: The Life and Death of Che Guevara.* Marina Casteñeda, trans. NY: Alfred A. Knopf, 1997.

Campbell, Joseph. *The Hero with a Thousand Faces.* NY: Meridian Books, 1956.

———. *Transformations of Myth Through Time.* NY: Harper and Row, 1990.

Camus, Albert. *The Stranger.* Stuart Gilbert, trans. NY: Vintage, 1954.

———. *Exile and the Kingdom.* Justin O'Brien, trans. NY: Vintage, 1991.

———. *Resistance, Rebellion, and Death.* Justin O'Brien, trans. NY: Vintage, 1995.

———. *The First Man.* David Hapgood, trans. NY: Vintage Books, 1996.

Cesaire, Aime. *Discourse on Colonialism.* Joan Pinkham, trans. NY: Monthly Review, 2000.

Choukri, Mohamed. *For Bread Alone.* Paul Bowles, trans. London: Saqi Books 1993.

———. *Jean Genet in Tangier.* Paul Bowles, trans. Introduction by William Burroughs. NY: Ecco Press, 1990/1974.

Cragg, Kenneth. *The House of Islam.* Belmont, CA: Dickenson, 1969.

Cuddon, J.A. *The Penguin Dictionary of Literary Terms and Literary Theory.* London: Penguin, 1992. Third ed.

Dekmejian, R. Hrair. *Egypt Under Nasser.* Albany: SUNY Press, 1971.

Djebar, Assia. *Algerian White.* David Kelley and Marjolijn De Jager, trans. NY: Seven Stories Press, 2000.

Durrell, Lawrence. *Mountolive.* NY: E.P. Dutton and Co., 1959.

———. *Justine.* NY: Pocket Books, 1963.

———. *Balthazar.* NY: Dutton, 1961.

———. *Clea.* NY: Dutton, 1961

El Saadawi, Nawal. *A Daughter Of Isis.* Sherif Hetata, trans. London: Zed Books, 2000.

———. *Walking Through Fire.* Sherif Hetata, trans. London: Zed Books, 2002.

———. *God Dies by the Nile.* Sherif Hetata, trans. London: Zed Books, 2002.

———. "Unveiling: Interviewing Nawal el Saadawi." Saadawi with Ahmed Nassef. "Women's eNews." March 8, 2004. *Znet.* http://www.znet.org/content/print_article.cfm?itemID=5108§ionID=30.

———. "Women and Sex." Donna Lee Bowen, trans. *Everyday Life in the Muslim Middle East.* Donna Lee Bowen and Evelyn A. Early, eds. Bloomington: Indiana UP, 1993. 81–83.

Emberley, Julia V. *Thresholds of Difference: Feminist Critique, Native Women's Writings, Postcolonial Theory.* Toronto: University of Toronto Press, 1993.

Entelis, John P. *Comparative Politics of North Africa.* NY: Syracuse UP, 1980.

Fanon, Frantz. *The Wretched of the Earth.* Constance Farrington, trans. NY: Grove Press 1993.

———. *Black Skin, White Masks.* Charles Lam Markmann. NY: Grove Weidenfeld, 1991.

Finkel, Caroline. *Osman's Dream: The History of the Ottoman Empire.* NY: Basic Books, 2007.

Fisk, Robert. *Pity the Nation: The Abduction of Lebanon.* NY: Thunder's Mouth Press/Nation Books, 2002.

Fleming, Fergus. *The Sword and the Cross: Two Men and an Empire of Sand.* NY: Grove Press 2003.

Geertz, Clifford. *Islam Observed: Religious Development in Morocco and Indonesia.* Chicago: University of Chicago Press, 1971.

Genet, Jean. *Prisoner of Love.* Barbara Bray, trans. Introduction by Ahdaf Soueif. NY: New York Review of Books, 1993.

Gerassi, John, ed. *Venceremos! The Speeches and Writing of Che Guevara.* NY: Simon and Schuster, 1969.

Giles, Frank. *The Locust Years: The Story of the Fourth French Republic 1946–1958.* NY: Carroll & Graf Publishers, 1994.

Green, Michele. *The Dream at the End of the World: Paul Bowles and the Literary Renegades in Tangier.* NY: HarperPerennial, 1992.

Goldsmith, Edward. "Development as Colonialism." *The Case Against the Global Economy.* Jerry Mander and Edward Goldsmith, eds. San Francisco: Sierra Club Books, 1996. 253–266.

Guevara, Ernesto "Che." *Guerrilla Warfare.* Brian Loveman and Thomas M. Davies, Jr., eds. Lincoln: University of Nebraska Press, 1985.

———. "The Role of Foreign Aid in the Development of Cuba." Speech given at the Min-Far Theatre on March 9, 1961. Havana: Editorial En Marcha, 1962.

Haddour, Azzedine. *Colonial Myths: History and Narrative.* Manchester: Manchester UP, 2000.

Hahn, Peter L. *The United States, Great Britain, and Egypt 1945–1956.* Chapel Hill: University of North Carolina Press, 1995.

Haim, Sylvia G. *Arab Nationalism.* Berkeley: University of California Press, 1964.

Halstead, John P. *Rebirth of a Nation: The Origins and Rise of Moroccan Nationalism 1912–1944.* Cambridge: Harvard UP, 1969.

Hancock, Graham. *Lords of Poverty: The Power, Prestige, and Corruption of the International Aid Business.* NY: Atlantic Monthly Press, 1989.

Hardt, Michael and Antonio Negri. *Empire.* Cambridge: Harvard UP, 2001.

Hartmann, Frederick H. *The Relations of Nations.* NY: Macmillan, 1978.

Heartfield, James. "Algeria and the Defeat of French Humanism." *The "Death of the Subject" Explained.* Sheffield, UK: Sheffield Hallam UP, 2002. 111–128.

Hennisart, Paul. *Wolves in the City: The Death of French Algeria.* NY: Simon and Schuster, 1970.

Hoisington, Jr., William A. "The American Presence in Morocco During the Second World War." *The Atlantic Connection.* Jerome B. Bookin-Weiner and Mohamed El Mansour, eds. Rabat: Edino, 1996. 153–168.

Horne, Alistair. *A Savage War of Peace: Algeria 1954–1962.* NY: Viking Press, 1978.

Hourani, Albert. *A History of the Arab Peoples.* NY: Time-Warner Books, 1992.

Howe, Marvin. *Morocco: The Islamist Awakening and Other Challenges.* NY: Oxford UP, 2005.

Huntington, Samuel P. *The Clash of Civilizations and the Remaking of the World Order.* NY: Simon and Schuster, 1996: 2003.

Ismael, Tareq. *The Arab Left.* Syracuse: Syracuse UP, 1976.

Jackson, Richard L. *The Non-Aligned, the U.N., and the Superpowers.* NY: Praeger, 1983.

Janka, Les. "United States-Moroccan Military Relations After The Green March." *The Atlantic Connection.* Jerome B. Bookin-Weiner and Mohamed El Mansour, eds. Rabat: Edino, 1996. 197–206.

JanMohamed, Abdul R. "The Economy of Manichean Allegory." *The Post-Colonial Studies Reader.* Bill Ashcroft, Gareth Griffiths and Helen Tiffin, eds. NY: Routledge, 1999. 18–23.

Jones, Richard. "Egyptian Copts in Detroit: Ethnic Community and Long Distance Nationalism." *Arab Detroit: From Margin to Mainstream.* Nabeel Abraham and Andrew Shyrock, eds. Detroit: Wayne State UP. 219–240.

Kahin, George McTurnan. *The Asian-African Conference: Bandung, Indonesia, April 1955.* Ithaca: Cornell UP, 1956.

Kelley, Robin D.G. "A Poetics of Anticolonialism." *Discourse on Colonialism by Aime Cesaire.* Joan Pinkham, trans. NY: Monthly Review, 2000. 7–28.

Kenbib, Mohammed. "The American Impact on Moroccan Nationalism (1930–1947)." *The Atlantic Connection.* Jerome B. Bookin-Weiner and Mohamed El Mansour, eds. Rabat: Edino, 1996. 169–181.

Khalidi, Rashid. *Resurrecting Empire.* Boston: Beacon 2004.

Kinzer, Stephen. *All the Shah's Men: An American Coup and the Roots of Middle East Terror.* Hoboken: John Wiley and Sons, 2003.

Kittler, Glen. *Mediterranean Africa.* Camden, NJ: Thomas Nelson and Sons, 1969.

Kristeva, Julia. *Strangers To Ourselves.* Leon S. Roudiez, trans. NY: Columbia UP, 1991. 24–29.

———. "Stabat Mater." *The Kristeva Reader.* Toril Moi, ed. NY: Columbia UP, 1986. 160–186.

Korten, David C. *When Corporations Rule the World.* West Hartford: Kumarian Press, 1995.

———. "The Failure of Bretton Woods." *The Case Against the Global Economy.* Jerry Mander and Edward Goldsmith, eds. San Francisco: Sierra Club Books, 1996. 20–30.

Laroui, Abdallah. *The Crisis of the Arab Intellectual: Traditionalism or Historicism?* Diarmid Cammell, trans. Berkeley: University of California Press, 1976.

———. *The History of the Maghrib: An Interpretive Essay.* Ralph Manheim, trans. Princeton: Princeton UP, 1977.

Laskier, Michael M. "Egyptian Jewry Under the Nasser Regime 1956–70," *Historical Society of Jews From Egypt.* 1995 http://www.hsje.org/egyptian_jewry_under_the_ nasser_.htm

Lappe, Frances Moore and Joseph Collins and Peter Rosset with Luis Esparza. *World Hunger: Twelve Myths.* NY: Grove Press, 1998. Second ed.

Lawrence, T.E. *Seven Pillars of Wisdom.* NY: Anchor Books, 1991.

Layachi, Azzedine. *The United States and North Africa.* NY: Praeger, 1990.

Lerner, Daniel. *The Passing of Traditional Society: Modernizing the Middle East.* NY: The Free Press, 1958.

Lewis, Bernard. *From Babel to Dragomans:* Interpreting the Middle East. NY: Oxford UP, 2004.

———. *What Went Wrong: The Clash Between Islam and Modernity in the Middle East.* NY: Harper Collins/Perennial, 2003.

———. *The Crisis of Islam: Holy War and Unholy Terror.* NY: Random House/Modern Library, 2003.

Lockwood, Lee. "Interview with Fidel Castro, January 1967." *The Playboy Interview.* G. Barry Golson, ed. NY: Playboy Press, 1981. 235–260.

MacMillan, Margaret. "Setting the Middle East Alight." *Paris 1919: Six Months that Changed the World.* NY: Random House, 2002. 366–455

Mahfouz, Neguib. *Autumn Quail.* Roger Allen, trans. Revised by John Rodenbeck. Cairo: American University Press, 1988.

———. *Midaq Alley.* Trevor Le Gassick, trans. NY: Anchor Books, 1992.

Malley, Robert. *The Call from Algeria.* Berkeley: University of California Press, 1996.

Mamdani, Mahmood. *Good Muslim, Bad Muslim: America, the Cold War, and the Roots of Terrorism.* NY: Pantheon, 2004.

Mander, Jerry and Edward Goldsmith, eds. *The Case Against the Global Economy.* San Francisco: Sierra Club, 1996.

Memmi, Albert. *The Colonizer and the Colonized.* Howard Greenfield, trans. Boston, Beacon 1967.

———. *The Pillar of Salt.* Edouard Roditi, trans. Boston: Beacon Press, 1992.

Mernissi, Fatima. *Dreams of Trespass.* Cambridge, Mass: Perseus Books, 1995.

———. *Scheherazade Goes West.* NY: Washington Square Press, 2001.

Norris, Robert S. and William M. Arkin and William Burr. "Where They Were." *Bulletin of the Atomic Scientists.* Vol. 55, No. 6, Nov./Dec. 1999. 26–35.

O'Connor, V.C. Scott. *A Vision of Morocco: The Far West of Islam.* London: Thornton Butterworth/Keystone Library, 1933/1923.

Oppenheim, Jean-Marc Ran. "Egypt and the Sudan." *The Jews of the Middle East and North Africa in Modern Times.* Reeva Spector Simon et al., eds. NY: Columbia UP, 2003. 409–430.

Porch, Douglas. *The Conquest of the Sahara.* NY: Farrar, Straus and Giroux, 2005.

———. *The Conquest of Morocco.* NY: Farrar, Strauss and Giroux, 2005.

Prahalad, C.K. *The Fortune at the Bottom of the Pyramid.* Upper Saddle River, N.J.: Wharton School Publishing, 2005.

Rampersad, Arnold. "Introduction" and "Chronology." *Native Son* by Richard Wright. NY: Harper/Perennial, 1993. Restored text ed.

Reich, Robert. *The Work of Nations.* NY: Vintage, 1992.

Rist, Gilbert. *The History of Development: From Western Origins to Global Faith.* Patrick Camiller, trans. London: Zed Books, 2004.

Rizzuto, Anthony. *Camus' Imperial Vision.* Carbondale: Southern Illinois UP, 1981. 1–28.

Roberts, D.S. *Islam: A Concise Introduction.* NY: Harper and Row, 1981.

Roberts, Hugh. *The Battlefield Algeria 1988–2002: Studies in a Broken Polity.* NY: Verso, 2003.

Robinson, Francis. *Atlas of the Islamic World Since 1500.* Oxford: Phaedon, 1987.

Rodenbeck, Max. *Cairo: The City Victorius.* NY: Vintage 2000.

Said, Edward W. *Out of Place.* New York: Vintage, 2000.

———. *Covering Islam.* New York: Vintage, 1997.

———. *Culture And Imperialism.* NY: Alfred A. Knopf, 1993.

———. *Orientalism.* NY: Vintage, 1979.

Sartre, Jean-Paul. *Colonialism and Neocolonialism.* Azzedine Haddour, Steve Brewer and Terry McWilliams, trans. NY: Routledge 2001.

———. *Being and Nothingness.* Hazel E. Barnes, trans. NY: Washington Square Press/Pocket Books, 1966.

———. *Existenialism and Human Emotions.* Hazel E. Barnes and Bernard Frechtman, trans. NY: Wisdom Library, 1957.

Sachs, Wolfgang. "Neo-Development: 'Global Ecological Management.'" *The Case Against the Global Economy.* Jerry Mander and Edward Goldsmith, eds. San Francisco: Sierra Club Books, 1996. 239–252.

Simon, Reeva Spector and Michael Menachem Laskier and Sara Reguer, eds. *The Jews of the Middle East and North Africa in Modern Times.* NY: Columbia UP, 2003.

Stiglitz, Joseph E. *Globalization and Its Discontents.* NY: W.W. Norton and Co., 2003.

———. *Making Globalization Work.* NY: W.W. Norton and Co., 2006.

Stille, Alexander. "Resurrecting Alexandria: Can rebuilding the Great Library also redeem the city?" *The New Yorker.* May 8, 2000. 90–99.

Stillman, Norman A. *Jews of Arab Lands in Modern Times.* Philadelphia: The Jewish Publication Society, 2003.

Stora, Benjamin. *Algeria 1830–2000: A Short History.* Marie Todd, trans. Ithaca: Cornell UP, 2004.

Tarrow, Susan. *Exile from the Kingdom: A Political Rereading of Albert Camus.* Np: University of Alabama Press, 1985. 66–90.

Tazi, Abdelhadi. "An American Protectorate in Morocco?" *The Atlantic Connection.* Jerome B. Bookin-Weiner and Mohamed El Mansour, eds. Rabat: Edino, 1996. 71–77.

Tessler, Mark. "The Middle East, Morocco and the United States." *The Atlantic Connection.* Jerome B. Bookin-Weiner and Mohamed El Mansour, eds. Rabat: Edino, 1996. 207–214.

Theroux, Paul. *The Pillars of Hercules.* NY: Ballantine/Fawcett Columbine, 1995.

Trainer, Ted. *Developed to Death.* London: Green, 1989.

Wallerstein, Immanuel. *The Essential Wallerstein.* NY: The New Press, 2000.

———. *The Modern World System.* NY: Harcourt Brace/Academic Press, 1974.

Wattar, Tahir. *The Earthquake.* William Granara, trans. London: Saqi Books, 2000.

Waterson, Albert. *Planning in Morocco.* The Economic Development Institute of the International Bank for Reconstruction and Development. Baltimore: Johns Hopkins Press, 1962.

Waltz, Susan. *Human Rights and Reform: Changing the Face of North African Politics.* Berkeley: University of California Press, 1995.

Weaver, Mary Ann. "The Novelist and the Sheik: The Stabbing of Naguib Mahfouz." *The New Yorker.* January 30, 1995. 52–69.

White, Edmund. *Genet.* NY: Alfred A. Knopf, 1993.
Woodward, Peter. *Nasser.* NY: Longman, 1992.
Wright, Richard. *Native Son.* NY: Harper/Perennial, 1993. Restored text ed.
———. *The Color Curtain.* NY: World Publishing Co., 1956.

Index